THE KETO KIT

COOKBOOK

STEPHANIE PEDERSEN

STERLING
New York

STERLING
New York

An Imprint of Sterling Publishing Co., Inc.
1166 Avenue of the Americas
New York, NY 10036

This publication is a component of the *The Keto Kit*
(ISBN: 978-1-4549-3507-0) and is not to be sold separately.

ISBN 978-1-4549-3508-7

For information about custom editions, special sales, and premium
and corporate purchases, please contact Sterling Special Sales
at 800-805-5489 or specialsales@sterlingpublishing.com.

Manufactured in Canada

2 4 6 8 10 9 7 5 3 1

sterlingpublishing.com

Cover design by David Ter-Avanesyan

Image credits: Christopher Bain: 32, 35, 36, 43, 121, 163, 167, 183; Bill Milne: iv, 9, 10, 44, 47,
53, 56, 61, 66, 72, 74, 90, 95, 98, 106, 111, 115, 117, 128, 133, 137, 142, 153, 154, 161, 168,
175, 180; Shutterstock: © Brent Hofacker 97; StockFood: © Helena Krol 149

CONTENTS

Big Batch Chicken
Thighs, page 3

MAKE-AHEAD BASICS

THE PERFECT HARD-BOILED EGG

Makes 8 servings

You can use this method to make as many as you'd like, be it just one egg or a dozen. It works on eggs of any size.

8 eggs

1. Place the eggs in a 2-quart saucepan just large enough to contain them without touching each other. Cover them with cool water by 1 inch.

2. Slowly bring the water to a boil over medium heat. When the water has reached a boil, cover the pot and remove it from the heat.

3. For extra large eggs, let sit for 14–16 minutes, depending up on how hard you like the yolk. For large eggs, let sit 10–12 minutes. For medium eggs, let sit 6–8 minutes.

4. Transfer the eggs to a colander in the sink and let cold water run over them to stop the cooking process. You can even plunge the eggs into an ice bath, which some people say makes them easier to peel. Serve immediately or place in a container or egg carton in the refrigerator for up to 1 week.

PER SERVING: 78 calories, 0.6g net carbs, 0.6g total carbs, 0g fiber, 0.6g sugars, 5g fat, 6.3g protein

BIG BATCH CHICKEN THIGHS

Makes about 6 servings

If you're someone who likes convenience, batch-cooking is a lifesaver. Making a batch of these chicken thighs (pictured on page iv) not only ensures something healthy to eat but also gives you a building block for many of the recipes in this book. Go ahead and play with the seasonings if you'd like.

⅓ cup melted butter, coconut oil, macadamia nut oil, bacon fat, or avocado oil, plus additional for greasing the pan

3–8 garlic cloves, minced

3 tablespoons soy sauce or coconut aminos or 2–3 teaspoons salt

Black pepper or red pepper flakes, to taste

½–2 teaspoons fresh rosemary, chives, basil, parsley, thyme, oregano, or cilantro, chopped

3½ pounds boneless, skinless chicken thighs

1. Preheat the oven to 425°F.

2. Lightly grease a large baking pan with your fat of choice.

3. In a medium bowl, whisk together the butter, garlic, soy sauce, pepper, and rosemary.

4. Arrange the chicken in the baking pan. Pour the butter mixture over the chicken, coating the pieces thoroughly.

5. Bake the chicken for 25 minutes, then turn the chicken thighs, basting with the pan juices.

6. Return to the oven and bake for an additional 20 minutes or until the juices run clear.

7. Remove the pan from the oven and allow the chicken to cool before placing it in a covered container. Keep in the refrigerator for up to 5 days.

PER SERVING (3 thighs, made with butter and fresh rosemary): 392 calories, 1g net carbs, 1.1g total carbs, 0.1g fiber, 0.2g sugars, 23.7g fat, 45.3g protein

CHICKEN BONE BROTH

Makes about 3 quarts

This is a great beginner's bone broth recipe, one that will create a lovely chicken broth that can be used as an ingredient or enjoyed alone. To add great flavor depth to the broth, freeze leftover bones from T-bone steaks, pork shoulders, chicken wings, and such in an airtight container and use a variety of bones.

1 (4-pound) chicken, whole, or the carcasses of two or three chickens (parts or whole, such as from a rotisserie chicken)

1 medium onion, peeled and quartered

2 stalks celery, quartered

1 teaspoon whole black peppercorns

1–3 tablespoons salt (Start with 1 tablespoon and adjust with more as needed at the end of cooking.)

OPTIONAL: The green stalk from leeks or scallions (as many as you'd like—even just one—will make your broth more savory; just make sure they are clean), parsley stems, thyme sprigs left whole, fennel fronds, bay leaf

1. Place all ingredients in a large stockpot and cover with about 4 quarts of water, or until all ingredients are covered by about 1 inch.

2. Place the pot over high heat, cover with a lid, and cook until it comes to a rolling boil. Reduce the heat to a simmer and cook for 4 hours. If desired, skim off any fat that collects on the top during the cooking process.

3. After 4 hours, turn off the heat and allow the broth to cool in the pot for 90 minutes or more.

4. Carefully strain out the solids, using a strainer such as a spider or pour the broth into a colander set over a large bowl.

5. Decant the broth into a large container or into individual 1-cup serving containers.

6. Store the broth in the refrigerator for up to 3 days. If storing longer, freeze it.

PER SERVING (1 cup): 45 calories, 0g net carbs, 0g total carbs, 0g fiber, 0g sugars, 0.5g fat, 9g protein

· ·

How to Clean Leeks

If you've ever purchased fresh leeks, you know that dirt often hangs out between the sheathlike leaves. The best way to clean leeks is to chop them (unwashed), place the chopped leeks in a large bowl, and add cold water. Agitate the water with your hands, aggressively moving the chopped leaks around. Wait ten minutes, and all the dirt will have fallen to the bottom of the bowl. Gently lift out the cut leaks (being careful not to disturb the sediment at the bottom of the bowl) with a handheld strainer, slotted spoon, or spider. Transfer the leeks to a colander and let them drain until dry.

· ·

SLOW-COOKER COCONUT BEEF ROAST

Makes 4–6 servings

You can start this recipe in the morning and come home to a hot meal—or a meal component that can be used for sandwiches, bowls, tacos, and more.

---

4 cups beef broth (or Chicken Bone Broth, page 4)

2 large onions, chopped

7 garlic cloves, minced

2 cups sliced mushrooms

1 cup chopped red bell pepper

½ cup sliced celery

Salt and pepper, to taste

½ teaspoon sweet paprika

½ cup canned coconut milk

2 pound beef rump roast

---

1. Add the broth, onions, garlic, mushrooms, red pepper, celery, salt and pepper, paprika, and coconut milk to a slow cooker. Stir once.

2. Nestle the roast among the mixture.

3. Put the lid on the slow cooker and cook on low for 6–8 hours or on high for 4–6 hours.

PER SERVING (1 cup): 510 calories, 5g net carbs, 10g total carbs, 5g fiber, 4.4g sugars, 13g fat, 78.4g protein

TIP: Do not use "lite" coconut milk in this dish.

KETO MEATBALLS

Makes about 5 servings

These versatile meatballs are filled with good keto-friendly fats, such as coconut. For a more Asian-style flavor profile, substitute curry powder for the basil and oregano.

1 tablespoon bacon fat or extra-virgin olive oil

½ cup heavy cream or coconut cream

1 teaspoon salt

Black pepper, to taste

1 teaspoon dried basil

½ teaspoon dried oregano

1 pound ground beef, bison, pork, turkey, or chicken, or a combination

¼ cup unsweetened, shredded, dried coconut

2 or 3 garlic cloves, minced

¼ cup minced shallot, leek, or onion

OPTIONAL: 2 teaspoons seeded and minced fresh jalapeño or serrano chili or pickled pepperoncini pepper

1. Preheat the oven to 400°F.

2. In a large bowl, gently mix all the ingredients.

3. Divide the meat mixture into 10 equal portions, about ¼ cup each. Roll each portion into a ball.

4. Place the meatballs on a baking sheet lined with foil or parchment paper, or lightly greased with any type of oil, and place in the oven. Cook for 20 minutes or until browned and no longer pink in the middle.

5. Remove the baking sheet from the oven. Allow the meatballs to cool on the baking sheet. Once cool, store the meatballs in a sealed container in the refrigerator for up to 5 days.

PER SERVING (2 beef meatballs, made with extra-virgin olive oil and heavy cream): 659 calories, 3.5g net carbs, 5.4g total carbs, 1.6g fiber, 0g sugars, 56.6g fat, 32g protein

PULLED PORK

Makes about 12 (1-cup) servings

Pulled pork is not a small-size endeavor, but a slow cooker makes this dish much easier. Pulled pork freezes well and can stay in the freezer for up to three months. Feel free to play with the spices listed here—this recipe is flexible!

1 teaspoon onion powder

1 teaspoon garlic powder

2 teaspoons salt

½ teaspoon black pepper

½ teaspoon paprika

½ teaspoon ground allspice

½ teaspoon celery salt

⅛ teaspoon ground cloves

½ teaspoon mustard powder

¼ cup extra-virgin olive oil, avocado oil, or another oil

¼ cup apple cider vinegar

3 pound boneless pork shoulder or butt, sometimes called picnic roast

OPTIONAL: Keto Barbecue Sauce (page 30)

1. In a small bowl, whisk together all ingredients except the pork and barbecue sauce, if using.

2. Rub the spice mixture all over the pork. Place the pork roast, fat side up, in the slow cooker and cover.

3. Cook on high for 4–6 hours or until the meat is tender and falling apart.

4. Remove the roast to a large bowl and shred using two forks. Discard the melted fat and liquids in the slow cooker, or pour a few tablespoons into the shredded pork for a moister, fattier, pulled pork.

5. Serve as is, or with Keto Barbecue Sauce (page 30).

6. Store in a container in the refrigerator for up to 1 week.

PER SERVING (made with extra-virgin olive oil): 374 calories, 0.2g net carbs, 0.4g total carbs, 0.2g fiber, 0.2g sugars, 28.9g fat, 26.5g protein

FISH BAKED IN COCONUT MILK

Makes 4 servings

This is an incredibly versatile recipe. Use your favorite mild white fish, such as cod. This recipe also works well with salmon or tuna.

6 tablespoons liquid coconut oil, divided

4 teaspoons lemon juice

1 teaspoon salt, divided

2 pounds thick cod fillets or steaks

2 cups finely chopped onion

2 teaspoons minced garlic

2 teaspoons minced ginger

1 teaspoon minced green serrano or jalapeño chili pepper

1 cup chopped tomatoes (fresh or drained canned)

5 teaspoons ground coriander

1 teaspoon ground cumin

¼ teaspoon cayenne powder

¼ teaspoon ground black pepper

¼ teaspoon ground turmeric

1 teaspoon dried parsley

½ cup canned coconut milk

OPTIONAL: ¼ cup chopped chives, parsley, or cilantro for garnish

1. Lightly grease a baking dish with coconut oil. Make sure the dish is large enough to hold the fish in a single layer. Set aside.

2. In a small bowl, whisk together the lemon juice, 2 tablespoons of the coconut oil, and ½ teaspoon of the salt. Set aside.

3. Cut the fillets crosswise into 2-inch-wide strips. Pour the lemon juice mixture over the fish, making sure to coat it evenly. Cover the baking dish and refrigerate for 1 hour.

4. In the meantime, heat the remaining 4 tablespoons of coconut oil in a medium frying pan over medium-high heat. Add the onions and fry until the edges are browned.

5. Add the garlic, ginger, and chili pepper, and stir over medium heat for 2 minutes.

(continued)

6. Add the tomatoes, coriander, cumin, cayenne powder, black pepper, turmeric, parsley, and the remaining salt. Let the sauce simmer, stirring occasionally until the tomato breaks down into a chunky sauce, about 20–30 minutes.

7. Add the coconut milk and simmer about 5 minutes, until the sauce becomes thick. Cover and set aside.

8. Preheat the oven to 350°F. Remove the fish from the refrigerator. Uncover the baking dish and bake the fish for 10 minutes.

9. Remove the fish from the oven, pour the sauce over the fish, cover tightly with foil, and return to the oven for 15–20 minutes or until the fish is opaque.

10. Garnish, if desired, with chopped herbs such as chives.

PER SERVING: 802 calories, 4.7g net carbs, 6.3g total carbs, 1.6g fiber, 3g sugars, 13.1g fat, 15.5g protein

TIP: Many people do not make fish at home because they aren't sure how long to cook it. Here's an easy tip: Insert a fork into a piece of fish at a 45° angle at its thickest point. Pretend the fork is the hand on a clock and scoot it 5 minutes to the left or right, then try to pull up some of the fish. If it flakes beautifully, it is done. If it does not flake or looks translucent, it is undercooked (let it cook 5 minutes more and retest).

PERFECT GUACAMOLE

Makes 4 servings

This guacamole recipe is a classic—always delicious, always easy, and always healthy. Eat it as a snack with celery and jicama sticks or as a topping in the Keto Chicken Enchilada Bowl (page 152).

1 large ripe avocado, peeled and pitted

1 small jalapeño, stem and seeds removed, minced (add more or less, to taste)

¼ cup finely chopped red onion

½ tablespoon fresh lime juice

¼ cup fresh cilantro leaves, finely chopped

¼ teaspoon salt

Dash of cumin

1 Roma tomato, cored and chopped

1 tablespoon cilantro leaves, minced

1. Mash together avocado, jalapeño, onion, lime juice, cilantro, salt, and cumin with a fork until well mixed.

2. Gently stir in the tomatoes and cilantro.

3. Tightly cover the bowl with plastic wrap, ensuring the entire top layer of the guacamole touches the plastic. Refrigerate for up to 2 days before serving.

PER SERVING (½ cup): 128 calories, 3.5g net carbs, 9g total carbs, 5.5g fiber, 2.0g sugars, 10.2g fat, 2.7g protein

KETO HUMMUS

Makes about 4 cups

Hummus is a healthy, easy, portable dip, dressing, spread, and more, except that it is on the carb-heavy side. This version, which uses steamed cauliflower or raw zucchini (you choose) in place of chickpeas, is a great alternative.

4 cups steamed cauliflower florets or peeled and chopped raw zucchini

¾ cups tahini (sesame paste)

½ cup fresh lemon juice

¼ cup extra-virgin olive oil

4 cloves of garlic

Salt and pepper, to taste

1 tablespoon ground cumin

1. Combine all ingredients in a blender and puree until thick and smooth.

2. Taste and adjust seasonings to your preference.

3. Store for up to 1 week in a covered container in the refrigerator.

PER SERVING (¼ cup, made with cauliflower): 104 calories, 1.9g net carbs, 3.4g total carbs, 1.5g fiber, 0.7g sugars, 9.7g fat, 2.3g protein

TIP: Substitute leftover Cauliflower Rice (page 138) for the steamed cauliflower if that's what you have on hand.

Hummus Quick Changes

Hummus lends itself to an amazing array of flavor variations. Here are some of my favorites—simply make the recipe, and drop one of the following add-ins into the blender with the recipe's primary ingredients:

. . . .

Jalapeño

Add 4 or 5 pickled jalapeño slices, chopped—or an entire pickled jalapeño. I also like to toss in 1 tablespoon of chopped cilantro.

. . . .

Chipotle

Add half a chipotle chili canned in adobo sauce, as well as 1–2 teaspoons of the adobo sauce.

. . . .

Dill and Scallion

Toss in a tablespoon of fresh dill and 1 scallion, chopped (the white and some of the green portions).

. . . .

Wasabi

Replace the salt with soy sauce and add 1 teaspoon (or more, if you can handle it) of wasabi paste.

. . . .

KETO SALAD DRESSING

Makes about 1 pint

Everyone needs a good basic salad dressing. Enjoy this as is, or add the optional ingredients for additional flavor. You can also use a different type of vinegar or oil, if desired.

1⅓ cups extra-virgin olive oil

1 cup balsamic vinegar

1–2 teaspoons salt, to taste

OPTIONAL: 1–2 teaspoons Dijon or another type of mustard

OPTIONAL: ¼–½ teaspoon garlic or onion powder

OPTIONAL: ¼–½ teaspoon dried or powdered herbs or spices, such as basil, thyme, or oregano

1. Combine all the ingredients in a quart jar.

2. Screw on the lid and shake well.

3. Store in the refrigerator for up to 2 months. Shake before using.

PER SERVING (1 tablespoon, made with 1 teaspoon Dijon mustard): 64 calories, 1.3g net carbs, 1.3g total carbs, 0g fiber, 1.1g sugars, 6.7g fat, 0g protein

TIP: Mason jars are great for making and storing dressing.

HOMEMADE MAYO

Makes 1 cup

Store-bought mayos often include sweeteners and other unwanted additions. Homemade mayo is a cinch to whisk together and ensures a fresh and rich taste. Plus, you can personalize it with garlic or onion powder, as well as dried herbs.

1 large egg yolk, free-range or organic

1 teaspoon Dijon mustard (or Easy-Peasy Mustard (page 21)

¾ cup avocado oil or macadamia nut oil

1 tablespoon apple cider vinegar

1 tablespoon lemon juice

Salt and pepper, to taste

OPTIONAL: ¼–½ teaspoon garlic or onion powder

OPTIONAL: ¼–½ teaspoon dried herb of choice

1. Place the egg yolk and the Dijon mustard in the bowl of a food processor and process on low.

2. As the egg and mustard combine, remove the cover from the feed tube and slowly and steadily drizzle in the oil.

3. When the oil is incorporated, slowly drizzle in the vinegar and lemon juice.

4. Pulse in salt, pepper and any optional ingredients. Taste and adjust the seasonings.

5. Scrape into a jar or airtight container, cover, and store in the refrigerator for up to 3 weeks.

PER SERVING (1 tablespoon, made with avocado oil): 94 calories, 0.1g net carbs, 0.1g total carbs, 0g fiber, 0g sugars, 10.6g fat, 0.2g protein

TIP: Make sure all ingredients are at room temperature before you begin.

AVOCADO MAYO

Makes about 1½ cups

I don't love mayo—it's just too rich for my taste. But I adore this yummy, superfood version. If you don't like cilantro, swap in dill or parsley or another herb—even a small garlic clove. Or leave out the herbs altogether. If you don't have lime juice, lemon juice works well, too.

½ cup store-bought mayonnaise or Homemade Mayo (page 17)

1 avocado, peeled and pitted

¼ cup cilantro, chopped

2 teaspoons lime juice

Salt and pepper, to taste

1. Add the mayonnaise, avocado, cilantro, and lime juice to a food processor or blender and blend until smooth.

2. Add salt and pepper to taste.

PER SERVING (¼ cup, made with store-bought mayonnaise): 156 calories, 5g net carbs, 9g total carbs, 4g fiber, 1.9g sugars, 13.3g fat, 1.6g protein

SPICY FATILICIOUS SPREAD

Makes 1 cup

Spreads are an easy way to up your homemade food game. For keto eaters, a good spread is a fast, effective way to incorporate healthy fats. You can also use this as a dip (great with chicken chunks or radishes), a sauce for a piece of turkey or fish, or to bind a fast tuna or chicken salad.

½ cup ghee, melted butter, or liquid coconut oil

2 teaspoons chopped chipotle peppers in adobo sauce (use more or less, as desired)

¼ cup chicken broth

¼ cup plain Greek yogurt, sour cream, or cream cheese

Pinch cumin powder

Salt and pepper, to taste

1. In a pot over medium-low heat, melt the ghee or butter, or heat the liquid coconut oil until warm.

2. Stir in the chipotle peppers and broth.

3. Reduce the heat to low and stir in the yogurt, cumin, salt, and pepper until all ingredients are combined.

4. Remove from heat and allow to cool.

5. Store in an airtight container in the fridge for up to 4 days.

PER SERVING (2 tablespoons): 32 calories, 0.8g net carbs, 1.2g total carbs, 0.4g fiber, 1g sugars, 2.9g fat, 0.6g protein

TIP: For something different, replace the chipotle with 1 or 2 teaspoons of your favorite prepared mustard and omit the cumin.

EASY-PEASY KETCHUP

Makes about 1½ cups

This no-sugar, low-carb ketchup is not as sweet as commercially prepared products, but it's every bit as tasty! Adjust the spices to your palate, if desired.

1 (6-ounce) can tomato paste

2 tablespoons white wine vinegar, apple cider vinegar, or red wine vinegar

¼ teaspoon dry mustard powder

⅓ cup water, at room temperature

¼ teaspoon cinnamon

¼ teaspoon salt

Pinch ground cloves

Pinch ground allspice

OPTIONAL: ⅛ teaspoon cayenne pepper

OPTIONAL: Pinch black pepper

1. Combine all ingredients in a medium bowl. Whisk together until smooth.

2. Allow the ketchup to sit for 30 minutes to blend the flavors. Taste, and adjust vinegar, spices, and salt.

3. Store the ketchup in an airtight container in the refrigerator for up to 3 weeks.

PER SERVING (1 tablespoon, made with white wine vinegar): 7 calories, 0.6g net carbs, 0.9g total carbs, 0.3g fiber, 0.9g sugars, 0.1g fat, 0.3g protein

EASY-PEASY MUSTARD

Makes about 1 cup

Mustard is so easy to make in a home kitchen that I've always wondered why people purchase it. This is the most basic of mustard recipes. To switch it up, consider tossing in a handful of your favorite herbs, some lemon zest, a shake or two of a beloved spice, or subbing vinegar or wine for the water.

½ cup dried mustard powder

½ cup water, at room temperature

Salt, to taste

1. Combine the mustard powder and water in a medium bowl. Whisk together until smooth.

2. Add salt to taste.

3. Allow mustard to sit for 30 minutes before using. Store in an airtight jar in the refrigerator for up to 3 weeks.

PER SERVING (1 tablespoon): 39 calories, 1.3g net carbs, 1.8g total carbs, 0.5g fiber, 0g sugars, 2.6g fat, 2g protein

KETO SALSA

Makes about 4 cups

Salsa is such a healthy, delicious way to brighten up your meals. This version—which is sweetener-free—is easy to make using ingredients found in your local grocery store.

2 tablespoons lime or lemon juice

2 tablespoons avocado oil

2 cloves garlic, minced

⅓–½ cup cilantro, roughly chopped

Salt and pepper, to taste

1 small sweet onion, such as Vidalia or Walla Walla

2 fresh jalapeño chili peppers, seeds removed, minced

1 (28-ounce) can diced tomatoes, drained (Save the liquid for another recipe.)

1. In a medium bowl, whisk together the lime juice, avocado oil, garlic, cilantro, salt, and pepper.

2. Stir in the onion, jalapeño, and tomatoes.

3. Store in an airtight container in the refrigerator for up to 1 week.

PER SERVING (1 tablespoon): 10 calories, 0.5g net carbs, 0.8g total carbs, 0.3g fiber, 0.4g sugars, 0.5g fat, 0.2g protein

TIP: Personalize this salsa by using a different type of chili for more heat or add other spices, like a bit of cumin or oregano.

KETO QUICHE

Makes 6 servings

Quiche is a breakfast, brunch, lunch, and dinner staple. It's easy, fast, keeps well, and is as flexible as your palate and the ingredients in your kitchen. This classic recipe is made without a crust—a smart way to keep carb counts low.

6 large eggs

½ cup heavy cream

¼ grated Parmesan cheese

½ cup grated cheese (cheddar, Swiss, Monterey Jack, etc.)

OPTIONAL: 1 tablespoon minced fresh parsley

Salt and pepper, to taste

1 cup cooked broccoli, spinach, chard, or any leftover cooked low-carb vegetables, chopped

1. Preheat the oven to 350°F.

2. Lightly grease a 10-inch tart or quiche pan with butter or your favorite oil. Set aside.

3. In a large bowl, whisk together eggs, cream, and Parmesan cheese. Once combined, fold in grated cheese, parsley, if using, and salt and pepper.

4. Pour the egg mixture into the prepared tart pan.

5. Distribute the vegetables evenly throughout the pan.

6. Place the pan in the oven and cook for 40–50 minutes, or until the egg mixture sets.

7. When the eggs are cooked, remove the pan from the oven. Let the quiche cool for 15 minutes before slicing.

PER SERVING (made with cheddar and broccoli): 205 calories, 2.2g net carbs, 2.5g total carbs, 0.3g fiber, 0.6g sugars, 16.5g fat, 13.1g protein

KETO BROCCOLI RABE SAUTÉ

Makes 4 servings

You might think throwing a bunch of veggies in a pan with a splash of oil, and cooking until tender-crisp, is a healthy side dish. However, if you choose a high-carb veggie, you can throw your progress off track. This classic Italian recipe, featuring broccoli rabe (one of the lowest net-carb veggies), and olive oil (a good healthy fat), is an excellent choice and a quick accompaniment to any meal.

2 pounds broccoli rabe (about 2 medium bunches), ends trimmed

1 pound sweet or spicy Italian sausage links, cut into 1-inch pieces.

3 tablespoons extra-virgin olive oil

3 garlic cloves, minced

Salt and pepper, to taste

OPTIONAL: Red pepper flakes

1. Fill a large stockpot with salted water, place it on the stove on high heat, and bring the water to a rolling boil. While the water boils, put a colander in a clean sink.

2. Once the water boils, plunge the broccoli rabe into the pot, cook for 30 seconds, and then quickly remove it with a slotted spoon or tongs. Place the broccoli rabe in the colander in the sink, and rinse immediately with cold water to stop any residual cooking.

3. Once cool, pick up a small bunch of broccoli rabe and squeeze out excess water with your hands. Place the squeezed broccoli rabe on a cutting board. Continue with the remaining broccoli rabe. Cut broccoli rabe into 2-inch sections, from stem to leaves. Set aside.

4. In a large skillet over medium-high heat, add 1 tablespoon of olive oil and the sausage. Cook the sausage until browned on all sides and cooked through the middle. Remove the sausage from the pan and place in a bowl. Set aside.

5. With the heat still on and oil in the skillet, add the remaining two tablespoons of olive oil. Add the broccoli rabe to the pan and toss in the oil. Season with salt, pepper, and red pepper flakes, if desired.

6. Sauté the broccoli rabe until fork-tender. Add the sausage to the skillet, toss, and heat through before serving.

PER SERVING: 391 calories, 2.3g net carbs, 26.4 total carbs, 24.1g fiber, 3g sugars, 23.4g fat, 32.6g protein

ROASTED LOW-CARB ROOTS

Makes 4 servings

Roasted roots are a culinary staple in many home kitchens. With good reason: They are easy, delicious, and incredibly nutritious. However, many roots have high amounts of carbohydrates. Stick with the keto-compliant roots below and enjoy a fine, fiber-and-nutrient-filled side dish.

2 bunches of radishes, cleaned, trimmed, and cut in half

2 turnips, cut into 1-inch cubes

2 kohlrabi bulbs, cut into 1-inch cubes

3 tablespoons extra-virgin olive oil

Salt and pepper, to taste

1. Preheat the oven to 425°F.

2. In a large bowl, combine the prepared vegetables. Drizzle the olive oil over the vegetables and add salt and pepper, to taste. Toss the vegetables to distribute oil and seasoning evenly.

3. Arrange the vegetables in a single layer on one or two ungreased, rimmed baking sheets and place in the oven.

4. After 20 minutes, open the oven door and gently toss the veggies, making sure they are in a single layer when you are finished.

5. Close the oven door and allow the vegetables to bake for another 20 minutes, or until they are fork-tender.

PER SERVING: 145 calories, 5g net carbs, 12g total carbs, 7g fiber, 5g sugars, 10.6g fat, 2.6g protein

RADISH SLAW

Makes 8 servings

Coleslaw is such a fast, nutritious dish. But when made with high quantities of cabbage and sweetener it can also be high in carbs. This version, which features radishes and omits the sweetener, is bright, bold, and delicious.

¼ cup apple cider vinegar

¼ cup sour cream

¼ cup mayonnaise

1 teaspoon celery seed

1 teaspoon onion powder

½ teaspoon dried mustard

Salt and pepper, to taste

2 bunches radishes, julienned

3 cups shredded green cabbage

OPTIONAL: 1—2 tablespoons minced fresh dill, parsley, chives, or cilantro

1. In a large bowl, whisk together vinegar, sour cream, mayonnaise, celery seed, onion powder, dried mustard, and salt and pepper.

2. Add radishes, cabbage, and optional herbs to the bowl. Toss to combine.

3. Cover tightly and chill the slaw in the refrigerator for 2–4 hours, so flavors can marry. Stir well before serving.

PER SERVING (made without optional herbs): 49 calories, 2.9g net carbs, 3.7g total carbs, 0.8g fiber, 1g sugars, 3.8g fat, 0.6g protein

Keto Sauces

These accompaniments are tasty, keto-compliant diet staples to have on-hand in your keto kitchen.

. . . .

CHIPOTLE CREAM SAUCE

Makes 1 cup

This delicious sauce is addictive! You'll love it on poultry, meats, and fish; as a sandwich spread; on nachos and tacos; swirled in soups; as a dip; and more.

1 canned chipotle chili in adobo sauce

1–2 teaspoons adobo sauce from canned chipotle

½ cup mayonnaise

⅓ cup sour cream, coconut cream, or plain full-fat yogurt

¼ cup chopped cilantro

¼ teaspoon ground cumin

Salt, to taste

1. Place all ingredients in a blender or food processor and puree until smooth, about 2–3 minutes or until the mixture is nice and creamy.

2. Place in an airtight jar or container and refrigerate for up to 3 weeks.

PER SERVING (¼ cup, made with sour cream): 169 calories, 4g net carbs, 7.8g total carbs, 3.8g fiber, 2.8g sugars, 13.4g fat, 3.3g protein

KETO HOT SAUCE

Makes about 1½ cups

Many hot sauces contain a bit of sweetener to temper their heat. This homemade version—which is actually super-easy to make—is sweetener-free. Try this with wings or burgers like the Big-O Bacon Burgers (page 88) or Inside-Out Avocado Burger Pockets (page 85).

18 fresh cayenne peppers (ends and stems removed)

1½ cups white vinegar

2 teaspoons garlic, minced

1 teaspoon salt

1 teaspoon garlic powder

1. Place all ingredients in a small saucepan over medium-high heat.

2. When the mixture reaches a boil, lower the heat to medium-low and simmer, uncovered, for 20 minutes

3. Turn off the heat and remove the saucepan from the burner. Let the mixture cool to room temperature. Once cool, transfer the mixture to a blender and process until smooth.

4. Transfer the mixture back to the saucepan and simmer on medium-low for another 15 minutes.

5. Allow to completely cool to room temperature and store in a jar or covered container in the refrigerator for up to 2 months.

PER SERVING (1 teaspoon): 2 calories, 0.2g net carbs, 0.3g total carbs, 0.1g fiber, 0.1g sugars, 0.1g fat, 0.1g protein

KETO BARBECUE SAUCE

Makes about 3 cups

Store-bought barbecue sauces are loaded with sweeteners (and carbs!), making them poor choices for keto-eaters. This easy-to-make recipe is made without sweet ketchup or the stevia that many keto recipes call for. If you must have some sweetness, go ahead and add a few drops of stevia during step 3.

1 tablespoon bacon fat or avocado oil coconut oil, or macadamia nut oil

1 shallot, finely diced

1 or 2 garlic cloves, finely diced

1 (6-ounce) can tomato paste

¼ cup Easy-Peasy Mustard (page 21), Dijon mustard, or brown mustard

1½ cups water or Chicken Bone Broth (page 4)

1 tablespoon apple cider vinegar

2 teaspoons salt

1 tablespoon chili powder

½ tablespoon smoked paprika

½ teaspoon black pepper

1 teaspoon cumin

¼ teaspoon thyme

1. Heat the fat in a sauté pan over medium-high heat. Add the shallot and garlic and sauté until the shallots are translucent.

2. Add all remaining ingredients, stir well, and let simmer for 5 minutes.

3. Puree in a blender or food processor until smooth.

4. Store in an airtight jar or container in the refrigerator for up to 1 month.

PER SERVING (1 tablespoon, made with avocado oil and water): 13 calories, 0.8g net carbs, 1.3g total carbs, 0.5g fiber, 0.5g sugars, 0.9g fat, 0.3g protein

VERSATILE MARINARA SAUCE

Makes 4 cups

This easy recipe can be used to dress Spiralized Veggie Pasta (page 139), as a dipping sauce for your favorite finger foods (I recommend the Sausage Puffs, page 102, or Pizza Pockets on page 92), or in recipes (such as Keto Italiano Lasagna, page 160, or Stuffed Cabbage Rolls, page 148).

1 (28-ounce) can crushed tomatoes or tomato puree

¼ teaspoon black pepper

½ teaspoon red pepper flakes

1 teaspoon onion powder

1 teaspoon garlic powder

1 teaspoon dried basil

1 teaspoon dried oregano

1 teaspoon dried parsley

1 teaspoon salt, or to taste

2 tablespoons red wine vinegar

¼ cup extra-virgin olive oil

1. Place all ingredients into a blender and puree until smooth.

2. Taste and adjust spices and salt, if necessary.

PER SERVING (½ cup, made with canned crushed tomatoes): 79 calories, 1.2g net carbs, 3.8g total carbs, 2.6g fiber, 2g sugars, 7g fat, 1.1g protein

TIP: I like to divide the recipe into a few small dressing-size food containers (for when I want a small amount of the sauce as a dip for pizza rolls and other handheld meals) and some 1-cup containers. I freeze a few and store the others in the refrigerator so I can grab one when needed.

Keto Breakfast Cakes,
page 39

CHAPTER TWO

BREAKFAST

EGG CUP

Makes 1 serving

This easy meal is about as low carb as it gets. Plus, you can switch it up depending on what meats, cheeses, and low-carb veggies you have in your fridge and pantry. For this recipe you'll need a ramekin, a small ovenproof cup.

2 large eggs

1 tablespoon heavy cream, half and half, milk, coconut cream, or coconut milk

Salt and pepper, to taste

OPTIONAL: 1 tablespoon chopped, cooked, low-carb vegetables, such as broccoli, peppers, or mushrooms

OPTIONAL: 1 tablespoon shredded cheese of your choice

OPTIONAL: 1 tablespoon chopped or shredded cooked meat, poultry, fish, or deli meat of your choice

1. Preheat the oven to 350°F.

2. In a large bowl, whisk together the eggs and cream. Season with salt and pepper, to taste.

3. Add any optional ingredients you would like to use. Stir to combine.

4. Pour the egg mixture into a greased ramekin or ovenproof cup.

5. Bake for 15 to 20 minutes, depending upon how you like your eggs.

PER SERVING (made with heavy cream, 1 tablespoon cooked broccoli, 1 tablespoon cheddar, and 1 tablespoon cooked ham): 311 calories, 2.4g net carbs, 2.9g total carbs, 0.5g fiber, 1g sugars, 23.6g fat, 21.9g protein

TIP: Want to make a bigger batch? Increase the ingredients by 12 and use a muffin tin instead of a ramekin. Don't want to make that many? Pour water into unused muffin cups to keep the tin from warping during cooking.

BAKED AVOCADO

Makes 2 servings

Rich, dense, creamy, and incredibly fatty, this dish is delightful. If you have never baked an avocado, you are in for a treat!

1 Hass avocado, cut in half and pit removed

1 slice cooked bacon, or 1 link cooked breakfast sausage, chopped (or use ¼ cup

cooked chopped ham, chicken, or another meat)

2 large eggs

Salt and pepper, to taste

1. Preheat the oven to 425°F.

2. Using a cookie scoop, melon baller or small spoon, gently enlarge the indentation left by the pit. Place the scooped-out avocado flesh in a small freezer-safe container and freeze it to use later in smoothies. Arrange prepared avocados on a baking pan or in a muffin tin, cradling each avocado half in a muffin cup.

3. Sprinkle half of the bacon or whatever meat you are using into the indentation of each avocado half.

4. Crack one egg in a small bowl. Gently pour the egg into the avocado indentation on top of the crumbled bacon, being careful not to break the yolk. Repeat this step with the second egg and avocado half.

5. Season the eggs with salt and pepper.

6. Gently arrange the remaining bacon or meat on top of the egg, again being careful not to break the yolk.

7. Bake the avocados for 13–15 minutes, depending upon how you like your eggs.

8. Remove from the oven and serve immediately.

PER SERVING (made with 1 slice bacon): 328 calories, 2.5g net carbs, 9.2g total carbs, 6.7g fiber, 0.9g sugars, 28.5g fat, 11.7g protein

BLT STACK

Makes 1 serving

Bacon, lettuce, and tomato sandwiches are my personal favorite, but bread and tomatoes are high in carbs. This is my solution for a lower carb count with the same great flavor.

1 large romaine lettuce leaf

1 tablespoon mayonnaise, divided

6 slices bacon, cooked

1 thin slice of tomato

Salt and pepper, to taste

1. On a cutting board, cut the lettuce leaf in half horizontally. You should have two square-like shapes of lettuce. Spread each leaf half with a ½ tablespoon of mayonnaise.

2. On top of one of the lettuce leaf halves, arrange three slices of bacon. Add the tomato slice and season the tomato with salt and pepper. Repeat this step with the remaining bacon.

3. Place the remaining lettuce leaf, mayonnaise-side down, on top of the bacon. Eat immediately.

PER SERVING: 506 calories, 1.8g net carbs, 2g total carbs, 0.2g fiber, 0.4g sugars, 41.8g fat, 28.4g protein

KETO BREAKFAST CAKES

Makes 2 servings or 4–6 pancakes

These are a bit like pancakes or (as my grandparents used to say) hotcakes. Any that you don't use can be saved in freezer wrap and frozen, or stored in the fridge for up to three days. My favorite toppings are a dollop of yogurt and raspberries as pictured on page 32.

4 ounces cream cheese

4 eggs, lightly beaten

2 tablespoons coconut flour

OPTIONAL: 1 teaspoon cinnamon, or a spice blend, such as pumpkin pie spice or apple pie spice blend

Butter or coconut oil, to grease the skillet

1. Add cream cheese, eggs, coconut flour, and optional spice to the bowl of an electric mixer fitted with the paddle attachment. Mix on medium-low speed until all ingredients are blended and the batter is smooth.

2. Add a pat of butter or coconut oil to a large skillet over medium-high heat. When the fat is melted, pour about 2 tablespoons of batter into the skillet to form a pancake. (It is easier to make 1 pancake at a time.) It will be a bit thinner than a traditional pancake, but will cook in a similar way. When the pancake begins to bubble, it is ready to flip.

3. Repeat step 2, adding a bit more butter or coconut oil to the pan, then pouring in about 2 tablespoons of batter to form a pancake until no batter remains. Place finished pancakes on a covered plate to keep warm.

4. To serve, divide the pancakes among 2 plates and eat plain or dress with nut butter, whipped cream, or the topping of your choice.

PER SERVING (with no topping): 365 calories, 5g net carbs, 8g total carbs, 3g fiber, 1g sugars, 19g fat, 17g protein

TIP: This recipe makes 2 servings so if making these pancakes for the whole family or friends make sure to double or triple the recipe.

Keto Hotcake Toppers

Maple syrup, jelly, honey—all of the traditional pancake, waffle, and French toast toppers we love so much are incredibly sugary and carb-heavy. Fortunately, there are yummy keto-friendly toppings you can use!

- -

Whipped Coconut Cream

Chill a can of coconut cream (or chill a few tablespoons of coconut cream) overnight. Open the can and empty the coconut cream into the bowl of an electric mixer. Using the whisk attachment, whip the coconut cream on the highest speed until it resembles whipped cream. You can add your favorite sweetener if you'd like—just make sure to drizzle it into the bowl as the mixer is on. Plus, note that most sweeteners (with the exception of stevia) do contain carbs.

- -

Whipped Dairy Cream

It is hard to believe that this delicious topping is allowed on a keto diet. Add chilled heavy cream to the bowl of an electric mixer. You can add a few tablespoons for a single serving, or a half cup for enough whipped cream to top eight servings of pancakes. Using the whisk attachment, whip the mixture on high until the cream turns firm and billowy. This won't take long, so make sure you're standing nearby.

- -

Full-Fat Yogurt or Greek Yogurt

This is probably the easiest topper there is. If you want to sweeten it up a bit, add a touch of Stevia.

. . . .

Nut Butter

Be it almond, peanut, or hazelnut, nut and seed butter is a great, straight-from-the jar option for pancakes, waffles, and French toast. Just make sure to check the carb count of your nut butter. Or, better yet, toss a handful of nuts in a blender or food processor and process until they are ground into a creamy, homemade spread.

. . . .

Whipped Nut Butter

Place a tablespoon or two of your favorite nut butter in the bowl of an electric mixer. Using the whisk attachment, whip the mixture on high, slowly drizzling in a quarter cup of chilled heavy cream or coconut cream as you go.

. . . .

Raspberries

This tart, fiber-filled fruit is one of the lower-carb fruit offerings out there. Topping a pancake with 10 fresh raspberries will set you back about 1.1 grams of net carbs.

. . . .

TEX-MEX KETO HASH

Makes 4 servings

Hash is a great way to use up small amounts of keto-safe ingredients left over from other meals. This recipe features Mexican-style chorizo, but if you have leftover pot roast, Italian sausage, pork shoulder, pulled chicken or another protein, use it instead.

1 pound Mexican-style chorizo, removed from casings

2 garlic cloves, minced

1 jalapeño, minced

1 bunch radishes, diced

2 small zucchini, diced

Salt and pepper, to taste

½ teaspoon chili powder

OPTIONAL: Chopped cilantro for garnish

OPTIONAL: Sour cream for garnish

OPTIONAL: Hot sauce

1. Place a large skillet over medium-high heat. Add chorizo, breaking up the meat with a spoon. Add garlic and cook until it is translucent.

2. Stir in jalapeño and radishes. Cook about 3 or 4 minutes, until the vegetables have softened.

3. Add zucchini, salt, pepper, and chili powder and stir to distribute spices evenly. Cook until zucchini is just softened, about 5 minutes.

4. Remove the skillet from heat. Transfer the hash to 4 plates. Garnish, if desired, with a dollop of sour cream and cilantro. Serve with your favorite hot sauce.

PER SERVING: 532 calories, 4.3g net carbs, 5.6g total carbs, 1.3g fiber, 1.7g sugars, 43.5g fat, 28.3g protein

TIP: Add an extra boost of energy with a fried egg on top. It will add 72 calories, 0.4g net carbs, 0.4g total carbs, 0g fiber, 0.4g sugars, 5g fat, and 6.3g protein to your meal.

Italian Veggie-Protein Soup,
page 50

SOUPS & SALADS

LEEK-AND-SALMON COMFORT CHOWDER

Makes 6 servings

Leeks and salmon together are a winning combination. This creamy chowder is healthy, delicious, comforting, and easy, with only 3 steps.

2 tablespoons extra-virgin olive oil

4 leeks, washed, trimmed, and sliced into crescents

3 cloves garlic, minced

6 cups Chicken Bone Broth (page 4)

1½ teaspoons dried thyme leaves

1 teaspoon fresh chopped dill (or ½ teaspoon dried)

Salt and pepper, to taste

1 pound salmon fillets or pieces, cut into bite-size pieces (You can use fresh or frozen fish.)

1 (15-ounce) can of coconut milk (about 1¾ cup)

1. Heat the oil in a large saucepan over medium-low heat. Add the leeks and garlic, and cook until slightly softened.

2. Add the broth, thyme, and dill. Simmer for about 15 minutes. Season to taste with salt and pepper.

3. Add the salmon and coconut milk to the pan. Bring back to a gentle simmer and cook just until the fish is opaque and tender. Serve immediately.

PER SERVING (1½ cups): 663 calories, 4.4g net carbs, 6.2g total carbs, 1.8g fiber, 2.9g sugars, 38.4g fat, 72.9g protein

Make-It-Your-Own Chowder

Makes 4 servings

This easy fish chowder can be made with fish from last night's dinner, like Fish Baked in Coconut Milk (page 11), or with canned tuna or salmon. You'll come back to this one often!

¼ cup butter or bacon fat

½ cup chopped onion

½ cup chopped celery

½ cup chopped green, red, yellow, or orange bell pepper

1 teaspoon minced garlic

3 cups Chicken Bone Broth (page 4)

1 tablespoon dill, minced (or ½ teaspoon dried)

2 cups heavy cream or coconut cream

3 (6-ounce) cans of tuna or salmon, in oil, or 2 cups of chopped leftover cooked fish of your choice

OPTIONAL: 3 cooked bacon slices, chopped, and/or ¼ cup of cooked ham, diced

Salt and pepper, to taste

1. Place the butter in a large saucepan over medium heat. When the butter is melted, add the onion, celery, peppers, and garlic, and cook about 5 minutes to soften the vegetables.

2. Add the broth and dill and bring to a boil. Lower the heat, cover, and let simmer for 15–30 minutes.

3. Add the cream and fish—as well as the bacon or ham, if using—and stir to combine. Adjust the salt and pepper to taste. Cook for 5 minutes to combine the flavors.

Calorie, fat, protein, and carbohydrate counts will vary.

TIP: Consider using crab, shrimp, or other shellfish as the fish in this dish. Feel free to play with the veggies, as well.

CAULIFLOWER-LEEK BISQUE

Makes 4 large servings

Cauliflower soup is one of my absolute favorite soups. Feel free to experiment using your favorite spices or fresh herbs.

2 tablespoons coconut oil

3 tablespoons butter

3 leeks, cleaned and cut into 1-inch pieces

1 large head cauliflower, chopped

3 cloves garlic, finely chopped

8 cups Chicken Bone Broth (page 4)

Salt and freshly ground black pepper, to taste

1 cup heavy cream

1. Add the oil and butter to a large soup pot over medium heat. Add the leeks, cauliflower, and garlic, and sauté for about 10 minutes, or until the vegetables are softened.

2. Stir in the broth and increase the heat to medium-high.

3. Bring the mixture to a boil; then reduce the heat to medium-low, cover, and simmer for 45 minutes.

4. Remove the soup from the heat. Blend the soup with an immersion blender or a handheld mixer. Season to taste with salt and pepper. Mix in the cream, and continue blending until smooth.

PER SERVING (2½ cups): 257 calories, 5g net carbs, 9g total carbs, 4g fiber, 3.7g sugars, 18.5g fat, 11.8g protein

MAKE IT VEGAN!

Replace the butter with extra-virgin olive oil or coconut oil, the chicken broth with veggie broth, and heavy cream with coconut cream for a plant-based recipe.

ITALIAN VEGGIE-PROTEIN SOUP

Makes 8 servings

The veggies listed below are especially low-carb, but this soup (pictured on page 44) can be made with whatever veggies you have on hand. The soup freezes well, making it a great choice for those of you who like to have prepared meals.

---

2 slices uncooked bacon, chopped

½ tablespoon extra-virgin olive oil

¼ cup chopped onion

1 tablespoon minced fresh garlic

¼ cup chopped sun-dried tomatoes in oil

½ cup sliced white or baby bella mushrooms

4 cups Chicken Bone Broth (page 4)

1½ cups water

1 cup peeled and chopped celery root (½-inch cubes)

2 cups chopped cooked chicken breast

1 cup sliced and quartered yellow squash (They will look like small triangles.)

½ cup sliced green beans (1-inch pieces)

2 cups chopped chard (any color)

1 tablespoon red wine vinegar

Salt and pepper, to taste

¼ cup chopped fresh basil

---

1. In a large soup pot, cook the bacon in the olive oil over medium heat for 2 minutes.

2. Add the onion, garlic, sun-dried tomatoes (with any oil), and mushrooms. Cook for 5 minutes.

3. Pour in the broth and water, then add the celery root and chicken. Simmer for 15 minutes.

4. Add the squash, green beans, and chard and simmer for 10 minutes.

5. Add the red wine vinegar and season with salt and pepper to taste.

6. Stir in the fresh basil just before serving

PER SERVING (1 cup): 253 calories, 4.5g net carbs, 6g total carbs, 1.5g fiber, 2g sugars, 7.2g fat, 38.2g protein

ITALIAN WEDDING SOUP

The lovely soup of white beans, escarole, and sausage or meatballs can be easily ketofied. Follow the recipe for Italian Veggie-Protein Soup, replacing 1 pound of bulk Italian sausage (sweet or hot) for the bacon in step 1. Increase the onion to ½ cup, and omit the sun-dried tomatoes, chopped celery root, chicken breast, yellow squash, green beans, and chopped chard. Instead, add 3 or 4 cups chopped escarole and 1 cup chopped fresh basil leaves in step 4. Enjoy as is or with as much grated Parmesan cheese as you like.

BEEF STROGANOFF STEW

Makes 6 servings

My husband loves Hungarian food, and I spoil him with this delicious stew. When enjoyed for lunch at work, it will make your officemates swoon.

---

2 (8-ounce) sirloin steaks

Salt and pepper, to taste

¼ cup extra-virgin olive oil or ghee, divided

1 medium onion, chopped

2 cloves garlic, minced

1½ pounds white or brown mushrooms, thinly sliced (about 8 cups)

2 teaspoons sweet paprika

1 tablespoon Dijon mustard

5 cups beef bone broth

Juice from 1 large lemon, about ¼ cup

1½ cups whipping cream, coconut cream, or sour cream

¼ cup chopped fresh parsley

---

1. Slice the steaks into thin, bite-size strips (see tip).

2. Season the steaks with salt and pepper to taste.

3. Add half of the olive oil to a large frying pan over medium-high heat. Working in batches, quickly brown the meat on both sides and remove to a waiting plate. Repeat until all the meat has been browned. Set aside.

4. Heat the remaining oil in a heavy soup pot over medium-high heat. Add the chopped onion and minced garlic, and cook until lightly browned and fragrant, about 2–3 minutes.

5. Add the mushrooms and cook for 3–4 more minutes, stirring occasionally.

6. Whisk in the paprika, mustard, broth, and lemon juice and bring to a boil. Immediately lower the heat to medium and cook for 2–3 minutes.

7. Add the browned beef slices and whipping cream, and immediately remove the pot from the heat.

8. Stir in the chopped parsley and adjust the seasonings.

PER SERVING: 439 calories, 3.9g net carbs, 4.4g total carbs, 0.5g fiber, 3g sugars, 33.3g fat, 25g protein

TIP: Raw beef is easier to slice thinly when it is partially frozen. Place the beef, unwrapped and in a single layer, in the freezer for 45 minutes before slicing.

CREAMY SPINACH SOUP

Makes 4 servings

It's easy for keto-eaters to forget how important vegetables are to a healthy diet. Spinach is a great low-carb veggie and blends beautifully into soups, like this creamy version.

½ cup butter

½ cup onion, chopped

2 cloves garlic, minced

1 (10-ounce) package frozen, chopped spinach

4 cups Chicken Bone Broth (page 4)

2 teaspoons dried basil

1 teaspoon pepper

1 teaspoon salt

½ cup heavy cream

1. Add the butter to a large soup pot over medium heat.

2. Add the onion and garlic, and cook until tender.

3. Stir in the frozen spinach (no need to defrost), chicken broth, basil, pepper, and salt. Increase the heat to medium-high and bring the mixture to a boil.

4. Once the mixture is boiling, decrease the heat to medium-low and allow to simmer for about 10 minutes, or until thickened.

5. Remove the soup from the heat. Blend the soup with an immersion blender or a handheld mixer. Mix in the cream and continue blending until smooth.

PER SERVING (1½ cups): 317 calories, 3.2g net carbs, 5.4g total carbs, 2.2g fiber, 1.5g sugars, 28.3g fat, 11.6g protein

MAKE IT VEGAN!

If you'd like to try a vegan, keto-friendly version of this recipe, replace the butter with coconut oil, the Chicken Bone Broth with veggie broth, and the heavy cream with coconut cream.

BACON-GUACAMOLE SOUP

Makes about 8 servings

This fresh-tasting soup is a bit exotic. Light and refreshing, yet filling and satisfying, it is great for a light meal or enjoyed as a first course. Try it warm, at room temperature, or chilled.

---

4 cups Chicken Bone Broth (page 4), divided

⅓ cup fresh chopped cilantro, loosely packed

1 large garlic clove, minced

2 medium avocados, peeled and pitted

½ medium lime, juiced

Pinch of cumin

Pinch of chili powder

½ pound bacon, cooked and broken into small pieces

Salt and pepper, to taste

---

1. Add the broth to a large soup pot over medium-high heat. Bring to a boil, cover the pot, and turn off the heat while prepping the remaining ingredients.

2. Place the cilantro, garlic, avocados, and lime juice in a blender, and pulse a few times until chunky.

3. To the blender, add 1 cup of the chicken broth, the cumin, and the chili powder. Blend until smooth.

4. Add the blended mixture to the soup pot with the rest of the broth.

5. Add the bacon to the soup pot.

6. Season with salt and pepper to taste, and serve.

7. To serve chilled, allow soup to rest in the refrigerator for a minimum of 90 minutes.

PER SERVING (¾ cup): 252 calories, 2.3g net carbs, 5.1g total carbs, 2.8g fiber, 0.7g sugars, 19.9g fat, 13.7g protein

NEW MEXICAN PORK STEW

Makes about 8 servings

This delicious green chili–laced pork stew is very filling. Plus, the recipe makes a lot, which is actually a good thing: You'll want to freeze some for later.

---

3 tablespoons extra-virgin olive oil

2 pounds pork loin, cubed

½ cup chopped onion

2 cloves garlic, minced

1 (2-ounce) can whole Hatch green chilies with liquid

2 teaspoons ground cumin

2 teaspoons granulated garlic

1 teaspoon pure powdered chilies, such as chipotle, ancho, etc.

2 cups low-sodium chicken broth (Regular chicken broth will make the stew too salty.)

Salt and pepper, to taste

OPTIONAL: Chopped cilantro

---

1. Add the oil to a large sauté pan over medium-high heat.

2. Working in small batches, add the cubed pork loin, browning on all sides but not cooking through. Remove to a waiting platter.

3. Meanwhile, add the onion, minced garlic, and chilies with their liquid to a food processor and pulse into a chunky paste. Set aside.

4. Place a large saucepan on the stove over medium-low heat. Add the browned pork, cumin, granulated garlic, and powdered chilies. Add the pureed chili mixture and broth.

5. Cover the pot with the lid ajar and turn the heat down to low. Cook for 1½ hours or until the liquid has cooked down and the pork is tender.

6. Adjust the seasonings, if desired. Garnish with cilantro and serve.

PER SERVING: 224 calories, 1.3g net carbs, 1.8g total carbs, 0.5g fiber, 0.8g sugars, 9.6g fat, 31g protein

Keto Slow-Cooker Stew Blueprint

People who often make fantastic homemade soups with no recipes are sometimes afraid to try their hands at stew-making, but it is quite easy—especially if you let your slow cooker do most of the work. Here's a quick blueprint for a 4- to 6-serving stew to get you started.

2 pounds beef, lamb, pork, or venison stew meat, cut into 1-inch cubes

OPTIONAL: 1–4 slices uncooked bacon, roughly chopped

½ teaspoon salt

½ teaspoon ground black pepper

1–4 cloves garlic, minced

1 teaspoon Worcestershire sauce or soy sauce

1 cup chopped onion, leeks, or shallots

1½ cups Chicken, Bone Broth (page 4), beef broth, or pork broth

2 cups cauliflower, cut into small florets

2 cups chopped turnip, kohlrabi, rutabaga, or radish (or a combination)

2 stalks celery, chopped

1–2 cups roughly chopped or sliced mushrooms, any kind

1 bay leaf

1 teaspoon paprika

OPTIONAL: ½–1 teaspoon cumin, basil, thyme, oregano

1. Place all ingredients in a slow cooker and stir.

2. Cover, and cook on low for 10–12 hours.

Calorie, fat, protein, and carbohydrate counts will vary.

SIGNATURE TOMATO SOUP

Makes 8 servings

Customiz this soup with your favorite spices. Try basil and extra garlic, cumin and curry, or chili powder and fresh cilantro.

2 tablespoons extra-virgin olive oil, butter, coconut oil, or another fat

1 medium onion, chopped

1 stalk celery, chopped

2 cloves garlic, chopped

OPTIONAL: 1 teaspoon or more chopped fresh herb of choice, such as thyme, parsley, dill, or cilantro

OPTIONAL: 1 teaspoon or more of your favorite spice, such as cumin, chili powder, or coriander

3 (14-ounce) cans whole peeled tomatoes, with juice

4 cups Chicken Bone Broth (page 4)

½ cup coconut cream

Salt and pepper, to taste

1. Heat the oil in a Dutch oven over medium heat. Add the onion and celery, and cook, stirring occasionally, until softened, 4–6 minutes. Add the garlic, herbs (if using), and spice (if using), and cook, stirring, until fragrant, about 10 seconds.

2. Stir in the tomatoes. Add the broth, and bring to a lively simmer over high heat. Reduce the heat to maintain a lively simmer and cook for 10 minutes.

3. Stir in the coconut cream, salt, and pepper.

4. Puree the soup in the pot using an immersion blender or in batches if using a blender.

PER SERVING (2 cups, made with olive oil): 100 calories, 3.5g net carbs, 4.9g total carbs, 1.4g fiber, 2.7g sugars, 7.2g fat, 5.6g protein

TIP: Use caution when pureeing hot liquids, always adding to a blender or food processor in small amounts and processing on lower speeds.

THAI COCONUT SOUP

Makes 6 servings

This recipe for *Tom Kha Gai*, one of Thailand's famous chicken soups, also tastes great with shrimp or pork. You can purchase makrut leaves in a well-stocked grocery store or online.

6 cups Chicken Bone Broth (page 4)

2 stalks lemongrass

10 makrut lime leaves (or 1 lime)

1 (1-inch) piece fresh ginger, peeled and grated or minced

1 teaspoon soy sauce, or to taste

¾ cup sliced white or mixed mushrooms

½ serrano or jalapeño chili, chopped

2 cups shredded chicken thigh meat, or chopped cooked shrimp or pork

1½ cups coconut cream

1 tablespoon fish sauce

2 tablespoons chopped cilantro

OPTIONAL: Lime wedges for serving

1. Add the broth to a large soup pot over medium-high heat.

2. Whack the lemongrass stalks with the blunt end of a knife a few times to help release their aroma, then cut the stalks into 1-inch pieces. Add them to the chicken broth along with the makrut lime leaves, ginger, and soy sauce.

3. Simmer the broth for about 20 minutes. Strain out the solids using a strainer, such as a spider, or pour the broth into a colander set over a large bowl and then return the strained broth to the soup pot.

4. Add the mushrooms and chili to the broth and cook for 10 minutes.

5. Add the chicken, coconut cream, and fish sauce and cook for about 5 minutes.

6. Stir in the cilantro and adjust the seasonings, if necessary. Divide soup among 4 bowls and serve with lime wedges, if using.

PER SERVING (1½ cups, made with serrano chili and chicken thigh meat): 365 calories, 6g net carbs, 16g total carbs, 10g fiber, 10g sugars, 14.8g fat, 23.4g protein

CREAM OF TURKEY SOUP WITH BACON

Makes 4 servings

Can you ever have enough cream-based soups? You can use turkey or chicken for this one—I often use it with leftovers from our Thanksgiving bird.

6 slices bacon

2 tablespoons butter

2 cloves garlic, minced

¼ cup sliced mushrooms (button, cremini, shiitake, etc.)

4 ribs celery, chopped

½ cup coconut milk or almond milk

½ cup heavy cream

3 cups Chicken Bone Broth (page 4)

2–4 cups chopped cooked dark meat turkey

Salt and pepper, to taste

2 tablespoons chopped fresh parsley

1. Add the bacon to a large soup pot over medium heat. Cook until crisp.

2. Remove the bacon, keeping as much grease as possible in the pot. Set the bacon aside.

3. Add the butter, garlic, mushrooms, and celery to the pot, and cook until the vegetables are softened.

4. Stir in the coconut milk, heavy cream, and broth.

5. Add the turkey, and salt and pepper to taste. Simmer until heated throughout.

6. Chop the bacon and add it, along with the parsley, to the soup.

PER SERVING (1½ cups, made with coconut milk and 2 cups of dark meat turkey): 499 calories, 3.8g net carbs, 5.6g total carbs, 1.8g fiber, 2.1g sugars, 36.7g fat, 36.3g protein

Fatabulous Keto Cream Soup Blueprint

Makes about 2 to 4 servings

Here's a fast and easy four-serving blueprint. Personalize it however you'd like or ad-lib based on what you have on hand.

3 tablespoons fat of choice, such as butter, ghee, avocado oil, coconut oil, lard, bacon grease, olive oil, etc.

1–3 garlic cloves, minced

¼–½ cup chopped leeks, onions, or shallots

¼ cup chopped celery, carrots, and/or bell peppers

2½ cups Chicken Bone Broth (page 4) or beef broth or another type of broth

1 cup of heavy cream or coconut cream

Salt and pepper, to taste

¼–1 teaspoon spices, such as cumin, paprika, basil, oregano, etc.

1–3 cups chopped cooked seafood, poultry, or meat

OPTIONAL: 1–3 tablespoons chopped fresh herbs of choice

1. Heat the fat in a large soup pot over medium heat. Add the garlic, leeks, and celery (and/or carrots and/or bell peppers) and cook until soft.

2. Add the broth and allow to simmer for 15–20 minutes.

3. Stir in the cream, salt, pepper, spices, and chopped seafood, poultry, or meat. Adjust the seasonings and cook for 5–10 minutes to blend the flavors.

4. Remove from the heat and stir in the herbs, if using.

Calorie, fat, protein, and carbohydrate counts will vary.

BEEF BURGER CHOWDER

Makes 6 servings

Chowder is comfort food at its best. This beef version is rich enough to serve alone—or dish out in smaller portions for an easy starter.

1 pound ground beef or bison

2 tablespoons butter or coconut oil

½ of a small onion, diced (about ¼ cup)

2 garlic cloves, minced

1 cup cooked, riced or mashed cauliflower

3 cups chicken broth

1¼ cups heavy cream, half and half, or coconut cream

1 teaspoon fresh chives, minced (or ½ teaspoon dried chives)

1 teaspoon fresh parsley, minced (or ½ teaspoon dried)

Salt and black pepper, to taste

OPTIONAL: Pinch of sweet or hot paprika, chili powder, cayenne, red chili flakes, or chipotle powder

1. In a large sauté pan over medium-high heat, brown the ground meat. Set aside and allow to cool. (Don't drain the fat. You can add it to the soup.)

2. In a large soup pot over medium-high heat, melt the butter. Add the onion and garlic and sauté until they are softened and translucent.

3. Add in the cooked ground meat, including any fat, cauliflower, broth, cream, herbs, and spices. Stir to combine.

4. When the soup begins to boil, reduce heat to low and simmer for 25 minutes.

PER SERVING (1¼ cup, made with ground beef [chuck], butter, and heavy cream): 288 calories, 2.4g net carbs, 3g total carbs, 0.6g fiber, 1.1g sugars, 18.5g fat, 26.4g protein

TIP: If you have leftover seasoned riced or mashed cauliflower from another meal, use it here!

AVOCADO BISQUE

Makes 4 servings

This fat-filled soup is elegant, luxurious, and so good for you, thanks to the brain-healthy fats and glutathione found in avocados. Be sure not to let the soup boil—it will separate.

2 large ripe Hass avocados, cut in half, pit and skin removed

2 teaspoons lemon juice

¼ teaspoon cayenne, chipotle powder, chili powder, or another spice

¼ teaspoon garlic powder

¼ teaspoon cumin

OPTIONAL: 1 or 2 teaspoons minced fresh cilantro, parsley, or chives

Salt and pepper, to taste

3 cups chicken stock

1 cup full-fat buttermilk, yogurt (either regular or Greek), or sour cream

1. Add the avocado, lemon juice, spices, optional herbs, and salt and pepper to a blender. Process until the avocado mixture is smooth. If it is too thick to process easily, add a few tablespoons of the stock. Set aside.

2. Add the stock to a large saucepan over medium-high heat. Bring the stock to a boil. Once boiling, turn the stovetop to the lowest heat setting.

3. Whisk in the blended avocado mixture and buttermilk, using a large fork, a wire whisk, or an immersion blender. Whisk until the soup is silky smooth. Serve immediately.

PER SERVING (1 cup, made with buttermilk and without optional herbs): 150 calories, 5.6g net carbs, 8.1g total carbs, 2.5g fiber, 0.6g sugars, 11.7g fat, 3g protein

TIP: This soup does not keep well, so you'll want to eat it shortly after making it.

AVOCADO-SHRIMP SALAD

Makes 2 servings

Shrimp and avocado are a beautiful pairing of protein and fat and great for keto-eaters. This luxurious salad travels well and can be customized with the addition of extra veggies.

¼ cup chopped red onion

Juice of 2 limes

1 tablespoon avocado oil or extra-virgin olive oil

Pinch of salt

Pinch of pepper

1 pound cooked large or jumbo shrimp, peeled, deveined, and tails removed

1 avocado, diced

1 medium tomato, cored, seeded, and diced

1 jalapeño, seeds removed, minced

1 tablespoon chopped cilantro

1. In a small bowl, combine the onion, lime juice, oil, salt, and pepper. Let the onion marinate for at least 5 minutes to mellow its flavor.

2. In a large bowl, combine the shrimp, avocado, tomato, and jalapeño.

3. Add the onion–lime juice mixture to the shrimp mixture. Add the cilantro and gently toss. Adjust the salt and pepper to taste.

PER SERVING (made with avocado oil): 445 calories, 4.5g net carbs, 15g total carbs, 10.5g fiber, 3g sugars, 28.2g fat, 34.1g protein

TIP: You can use the shrimp whole, but I like to chop them so I get a piece of shrimp in each bite.

KETO GREEK SALAD

Makes 2 servings

Greek salad is a universal favorite—plus it is keto-friendly! If you'd like more protein, feel free to add a cup of grilled chicken, lamb, or squid.

½ large, seedless English cucumber (about 6–7 ounces), chopped

½ red bell pepper, chopped

1 cup halved cherry or grape tomatoes

⅓ cup Kalamata olives

¼ small red onion, thinly sliced

3 ounces feta, cubed

2 tablespoons extra-virgin olive oil, or more to taste

1 tablespoon red wine vinegar

1 teaspoon fresh oregano (or ½ teaspoon dried)

Salt and freshly ground black pepper, to taste

1. In a large bowl, combine the cucumber, pepper, tomatoes, olives, onion, and feta.

2. In a small bowl, whisk together the olive oil, vinegar, oregano, salt, and pepper to make a dressing.

3. Pour the dressing over the salad right before serving. If packing the salad, store the salad and dressing separately.

PER SERVING: 312 calories, 5.5g net carbs, 12g total carbs, 6.5g fiber, 5g sugars, 26g fat, 7.9g protein

CAULIFLOWER-TABBOULEH SALAD

Makes 6 servings

Traditional tabbouleh uses bulgur, a wheat product that's filled with gluten, which can set off eczema—not to mention all the carbs. This fun, yummy version uses riced cauliflower. Feel free to add chopped poultry or salmon.

Florets from 1 large head cauliflower

½ cup lemon juice

¾ cup extra-virgin olive oil

1 bunch parsley or cilantro, washed and chopped

1 bunch green onions (also known as scallions), chopped

2 cups chopped Roma tomatoes

1 teaspoon salt

1 teaspoon pepper

1. Add the cauliflower florets to a food processor and pulse until they resemble rice.

2. In a large bowl, combine the riced cauliflower and lemon juice, and stir well.

3. Add the olive oil, parsley, green onions, tomatoes, salt, and pepper.

4. Stir well.

5. Taste and add more salt and pepper, if needed.

6. Cover and refrigerate for at least 4 hours, stirring once each hour.

PER SERVING (made with cilantro): 257 calories, 4g net carbs, 7.1g total carbs, 3.1g fiber, 3.9g sugars, 25.4g fat, 2.7g protein

TIP: Look for prepared cauliflower rice at your supermarket in the produce section for a time-saver.

BARBECUE SALAD

Makes 2 servings

This fun salad is for all of you pulled-chicken- and pulled-pork-sandwich aficionados. Feel free to fatify this further by adding a diced avocado or ½ cup of cheese.

¼ cup Keto Barbecue Sauce (page 30)

1 tablespoon mayonnaise

Salt and pepper, to taste

OPTIONAL: Hot sauce, to taste

2 cups Pulled Pork (page 8) or Big Batch Chicken Thighs (page 3), chopped

2 cups shredded green or savoy cabbage

2 carrots, grated

¼ cup diced red onion

1. In a small bowl, whisk together the barbecue sauce, mayo, salt, pepper, and hot sauce, if using, until emulsified.

2. If you are packing the salad, divide the salad dressing between two lunch containers, pouring half the dressing into the bottom of each container.

3. Next, layer the pork in each container.

4. Place the cabbage, carrots, and onion in a large bowl and toss gently to combine.

5. Place the tossed salad on top of the dressing and pork in each lunch container.

6. Seal immediately and store in the refrigerator.

7. Before eating, shake the container gently to distribute the dressing.

PER SERVING (made with pulled pork and savoy cabbage): 475 calories, 5.5g net carbs, 10.5g total carbs, 5g fiber, 4g sugars, 24.4g fat, 67g protein

CHEESEBURGER SALAD

Makes 2 servings

Ground beef is not normally seen on a salad. But as we keto-eaters know, ground beef belongs anywhere you want it to. Feel free to use ground bison, pork, sausage, lamb, or venison in place of the beef.

½ pound ground beef

1 garlic clove, minced

Salt and pepper, to taste

¼ cup mayonnaise

1 tablespoon white wine vinegar

1 teaspoon brown or yellow mustard

1 head romaine lettuce, roughly chopped

2 plum tomatoes, roughly chopped

2 scallions, chopped, or ¼ cup diced red onion

½ cup shredded cheddar cheese

¼ cup chopped dill pickles, or chopped pickled jalapeños

1. In a large sauté pan over medium-high heat, cook the ground beef and garlic, seasoning with salt and pepper to taste. Cook until the beef is browned and cooked through, about 8–10 minutes.

2. Using a slotted spoon, remove the beef mixture from the sauté pan and place on a plate or in a bowl. Set aside. Reserve the fat from the pan to use in the dressing.

3. Place the leftover beef drippings, mayonnaise, vinegar, and mustard in a blender or food processor. Pulse until smooth. Add salt and pepper to taste.

4. If taking the salad to work, divide the salad dressing between two lunch containers, pouring half the dressing into the bottom of each container.

5. Place the lettuce, tomatoes, scallions, cheese, and pickles in a large bowl and toss gently to combine.

(continued)

6. Place the tossed salad on top of the dressing. Add half of the reserved beef mixture on top of the salad ingredients in each container.

7. Seal immediately and store in the refrigerator.

8. Before eating, shake the container gently to distribute the dressing.

PER SERVING (made with yellow mustard and dill pickles): 322 calories, 5g net carbs, 10g total carbs, 5g fiber, 3g sugars, 22.7g fat, 14.2 protein

TIP: If you've ever wondered, yes, the different grades of ground beef contain different amounts of fat. Sirloin, typically the most expensive, is also the leanest, weighing in at 5–10 percent total fat. The next lean is round, with 10–15 percent total fat. The fattiest (and usually least expensive) is the keto favorite, known as ground chuck. It contains 15–20 percent fat. When buying beef, I often opt for the least expensive. If you're a hard-core keto-eater, you'll purchase chuck.

Keto Cobb Salad

KETO COBB SALAD

Makes 2 servings

The dish was created in the 1930s when a hungry restaurant owner named Robert Howard Cobb wanted something to eat. The only ingredients available at his Hollywood restaurant, the Brown Derby, were assembled into a quick salad. It was so delicious, he gave it his name and placed it on the menu.

- 2 tablespoons extra-virgin olive oil or avocado oil
- 1 tablespoon apple cider vinegar
- Salt and pepper, to taste
- 1 medium avocado, diced
- 3 slices cooked bacon, minced
- 1 cup cubed cooked chicken breast
- ½ cup cubed cheddar cheese
- 1 large hard-boiled egg, roughly chopped (see the Perfect Hard-Boiled Egg, page 2)
- 1 head romaine lettuce, roughly chopped

1. Whisk together the oil, vinegar, salt, and pepper until emulsified. Set aside.

2. If packing the salad, divide the salad dressing between two lunch containers, pouring half the dressing into the bottom of each container.

3. Add the diced avocado to the salad dressing in each container.

4. Place all remaining salad ingredients in a large bowl and toss gently to combine.

5. Place the tossed salad on top of the dressing and avocado in each lunch container.

6. Seal immediately and store in the refrigerator.

7. Before eating, shake the container gently to distribute the dressing.

PER SERVING: 706 calories, 5g net carbs, 12g total carbs, 7g fiber, 2g sugars, 64.4g fat, 47.1g protein

Big-O Bacon Burgers,
page 88

HANDHELD MEALS

Keto Wraps

Here are a few easy wrap recipes to play with.
Fill with whatever keto-friendly fillings you'd like!

. . . .

ICEBERG WRAPS

Makes varying amounts

Iceberg lettuce is the butt of many culinary jokes. True, it's mostly water and some fiber, but, wow, does it make an excellent keto sandwich wrapper. As hardy as iceberg is, however, it can be a bit fussy in the wrap department. Here is a quick rundown on how to use the leaves:

1. Choose a head that is large and unblemished; its leaves will be the best. Without cutting into the lettuce leaves, remove the core at the base of the head. You can do this by turning the head of lettuce upside down and carving the core out from the bottom of the head. You can then simply pull the core out from the intact head.

2. If there are any withered or torn leaves on the outside of the head, gently remove those as well.

3. Fill a large mixing bowl or pot with cold water. Gently submerge the head of lettuce, holding it under the water if it floats up. Your goal is to get water between the layers of leaves. This helps separate them in a way that keeps the leaves large and tear-free. (You can also do this by simply turning your faucet on and allowing water to run into and through the lettuce.)

4. While the lettuce is underwater, gently remove the leaves, stacking them in a waiting colander or laying them flat on a clean dish towel.

5. To use as a wrap, place the filling in the lower third of the leaf, fold in the sides, then roll the same way you'd roll a burrito.

6. Unused leaves can be stacked between dry paper towels.

PER SERVING: 2 calories, 0.1g net carbs, 0.2g total carbs, 0.1g fiber, 0.2g sugars, 0g fat, 0.1g protein

PALEO-STYLE KETO WRAP

Makes 4 wraps

I got this recipe from a paleo-loving friend. It uses coconut flour and ground psyllium husks (you can whir psyllium husk in your coffee grinder) to make a puffy, soft, low-carb wrap. I find they are easier to fill and wrap when they are warm or room temperature. Play with the spices to make flavored wraps.

¼ cup coconut oil, plus more for greasing

½ cup coconut flour

2 tablespoons ground psyllium husks

½ teaspoon salt

OPTIONAL: ¼–½ teaspoon onion or garlic powder

OPTIONAL: ½ teaspoon dried basil, oregano, chili powder, curry powder, or any other spice or spice mix you like

1 cup boiling water

1. Preheat the oven to 350°F.

2. Lightly grease a sheet of parchment paper (the size of a baking sheet) with coconut oil. Set aside.

3. In the bowl of a stand mixer, whisk together the coconut flour, ground psyllium, salt, and any optional spices.

4. Add ¼ cup of coconut oil and mix on low just until combined.

5. With the mixer on, slowly pour in the hot water. Continue mixing until the dough is smooth and well-combined

6. Cover the mixing bowl with plastic wrap or foil and place in the refrigerator for 15 minutes to cool.

7. Remove the mixing bowl from the refrigerator and divide the dough into four balls. Place the balls of dough on the greased parchment, leaving a lot of space between them.

8. Using a rolling pin, roll each ball into a circle between ⅛ and ¼ inch thick.

9. Lift the parchment onto a baking sheet and bake for 18–20 minutes.

(continued)

10. Remove and let cool for 15 minutes before removing each wrap with a spatula. Store unused wraps in the refrigerator for up to 2 days.

> **PER SERVING:** 200 calories, 4g net carbs, 19g total carbs, 15g fiber, 2g sugars, 15.8g fat, 4g protein

OMELET WRAP

Makes about 6 (8-inch) wraps

Here's another coconut-based wrap, this one made with mostly eggs. It cooks up on the stove, almost like an omelet. Feel free to spice things up with ¼–½ teaspoon of your favorite dried herbs or spices.

½ cup coconut flour

6 large eggs

1¼ cup coconut milk

½ teaspoon of salt

1 teaspoon coconut oil

1. In the bowl of a stand mixer, combine the flour, eggs, milk, and salt. Mix on a low speed until smooth.

2. Turn off the mixer and allow the batter to sit for 5 minutes to help the coconut flour absorb the moisture. The batter should be runny. If not, add an extra tablespoon of milk.

3. Place the oil in a skillet with a cover over medium-high heat. Pour ¼ cup of batter onto the skillet and immediately tilt it in different directions to create an 8-inch circle.

4. Place the lid on the skillet and cook for 1–2 minutes, until the edges are golden and slightly turned inward and bubbles form in the middle.

5. Flip the wrap, cover again, and cook another 1–2 minutes or until browned on the other side.

6. Repeat until the batter is used up.

> **PER SERVING:** 260 calories, 4.7g net carbs, 12.5g total carbs, 7.8g fiber, 3g sugars, 19.6g fat, 10.1g protein

CHEESY FAUX TORTILLAS

Makes 1 wrap

This is one of the simplest wraps ever! Plus, it is absolutely no carb. While the type of cheese you use for this recipe does not matter, you will need to use deli-style slices. The recipe won't work with chunks carved off blocks of cheese.

2 deli slices of cheese

1. Fold a sheet of parchment paper in half. (You can use a single layer of parchment, but it may be too thin and flimsy to hold the wrap in place when removing it from the microwave.)

2. Open the parchment paper and place a single slice of cheese in the center.

3. Slice the second slice of cheese into 8 ribbons. Then position the 8 pieces of cheese on the parchment around the large piece of cheese.

4. Lift the parchment with the cheese into a microwave and warm it on medium-high for 12 seconds or until the cheese is barely warm and pliable but not melted.

5. Remove the parchment paper and cheese from the microwave. Using your hand or an oiled rolling pin, fashion the soft cheese into a circle.

6. Place the cheese circle in the refrigerator to cool, about 10 minutes.

7. To use, remove the cheese tortilla from the refrigerator and layer it with your favorite fillings, such as homemade Sandwich Salad (page 96). Roll up as you would a regular tortilla.

PER SERVING (using American cheese): 140 calories, 3.3g net carbs, 3.3g total carbs, 0g fiber, 3.1g sugars, 10.6g fat, 7.7g protein

TIP: If you don't have a microwave, turn your oven to 150–200°F and place the cheese and parchment paper in just until the cheese looks soft. Continue with steps 5–7.

Keto Buns

A lot of people like their sandwiches on rolls or buns—myself included! There are many keto-friendly sandwich buns. Here are my go-to recipes.

. . . .

EGGPLANT BUNS

Makes 2+ servings

Eggplant is a fun, economical, easy-to-use vegetable for bun-making. This recipe will most likely make more than 2 servings, depending upon how large the eggplant is.

1 eggplant

3 tablespoons ghee, extra-virgin olive oil, avocado oil, or coconut oil, divided

½ teaspoon salt

½ teaspoon pepper

OPTIONAL: ¼ teaspoon of your favorite dried herb or spice

1. Preheat the oven to 425°F. Line a baking sheet with foil and set aside.

2. Slice the eggplant evenly into rounds ¾ inch thick. Arrange in a single layer on the prepared pan.

3. Drizzle half of the ghee evenly over the eggplant, then flip each eggplant slice and drizzle the remaining ghee on the other side. Season with the salt and pepper and optional herbs or spices.

4. Bake the eggplant slices for 18–20 minutes, or until each slice is browned on the outside and just fork-tender. (You don't want to allow these to get mushy or too soft.)

5. Remove from the oven and allow to cool before using. Extras can be stored in an airtight container in the refrigerator for up to 2 days.

PER SERVING (2 slices, made with ghee): 143 calories, 2.9g net carbs, 7.2g total carbs, 4.3g fiber, 3g sugars, 13g fat, 1.3g protein

PORTOBELLO BUNS

Makes 1 serving

Mushroom buns are very popular in the keto community. If you've never made your own, you're in for a treat: They are easy, come together quickly with few ingredients, and, most important, are outrageously yummy.

½ tablespoon extra-virgin olive oil, avocado oil, or coconut oil

1 clove garlic, minced

1 teaspoon dried oregano

Salt and pepper, to taste

2 portobello mushroom caps, gills removed

1. In a large bowl, whisk together the oil, garlic, oregano, salt, and pepper.

2. Add the mushroom caps to the bowl, and rub the seasoned oil into the caps.

3. Preheat a frying pan to high heat. (You could also use a ridged grill pan.) Add the mushroom caps and cook for 4–5 minutes on each side, or until fork-tender.

4. Use immediately, or allow to cool before filling with your favorite fillings.

5. Store unused caps in an airtight container in the refrigerator for up to 2 days.

PER SERVING (made with extra-virgin olive oil): 80 calories, 2g net carbs, 2g total carbs, 0g fiber, 0g sugars, 7g fat, 2g protein

TIP: It is important to clean portobello caps by scraping out the gills. These frills on the underside of the mushroom cap can turn slimy when cooked, and they often hide grit. Using the side of a small spoon, simply scrape them off and discard.

GRILLED ZUCCHINI BUNS

Makes 2 servings

This easy veggie bun recipe uses an indoor grill pan, but you may also choose to use an outdoor grill.

1 tablespoon ghee, extra-virgin olive oil, avocado oil, or coconut oil

¼ teaspoon salt

¼ teaspoon pepper

OPTIONAL: ¼ teaspoon of your favorite dried herb or spice

4 (½-inch-thick) slices of a large zucchini

1. In a large bowl, whisk together the ghee, salt, pepper, and optional herbs or spice.

2. Add the zucchini slices and turn to coat.

3. Heat a grill pan over medium-high heat. Lay the zucchini slices on the grill and cook for 2 minutes on each side, or until grill marks are visible and the zucchini is barely fork-tender.

4. Layer with your favorite sandwich fillings.

5. Store unused buns in an airtight container in the refrigerator for up to 2 days.

PER SERVING (made with ghee): 82 calories, 3.6g net carbs, 5.4g total carbs, 1.8g fiber, 2.8g sugars, 6.7g fat, 2g protein

SWEET POTATO SLIDER "BUNS"

Makes 4 or 5 servings

Because they have a higher carb content, root veggies aren't eaten often on the keto diet. However, using two slices of sweet potato in place of traditional slider rolls will save you carbs and give you your daily requirement for vitamin A.

1 tablespoon coconut oil, avocado oil, olive oil, or another oil

Salt and pepper, to taste

OPTIONAL: Dash of cayenne or chili powder

1–2 large sweet potatoes, sliced ⅓ inch thick

1. Preheat the oven to 400°F.

2. In a large bowl, whisk together the oil, salt, pepper, and optional spice.

3. Add the sweet potato slices and turn to coat.

4. Arrange the sweet potato slices on a baking sheet.

5. Bake for 12 minutes. Using an offset spatula, turn the slices.

6. Bake for another 12 minutes, or just until fork-tender.

7. Allow to cool before using. Store extra buns in an airtight container in the refrigerator for up to 2 days.

PER SERVING (2 slices, made with coconut oil): 58 calories, 4.8g net carbs, 6g total carbs, 1.2g fiber, 2g sugars, 2.8g fat, 7.5g protein

TIP: When buying sweet potatoes for this recipe, search for ones with a rounder shape and a wider diameter, as they will make better buns.

DELI COUNTER LETTUCE SUB

Makes 1 serving

The deli sub, a favorite lunchtime option, is a keto no-no when made with a carb-heavy sandwich roll. Use lettuce wraps as the base for a blueprint—feel free to use whatever meats, cheeses, or keto-friendly toppings you have on hand or prefer.

1 large iceberg or butter lettuce leaf (see Iceberg Wraps page 76)

1 slice of Muenster or American cheese

1 slice deli ham or roast beef

1 slice deli chicken or turkey

2 pepperoncini peppers, well drained

1 teaspoon Keto Salad Dressing (page 16)

1. Lay the lettuce leaf on a flat surface. Layer the cheese, ham, and chicken on the lower third of the lettuce leaf.

2. Top with the pepperoncini peppers, then drizzle the salad dressing over the stack of meat and cheese.

3. Fold in the sides, as if you were making a burrito. Starting at the bottom, roll the leaf as you would a burrito.

4. Wrap in foil or food wrap and store in the refrigerator until ready to eat.

PER SERVING (made with iceberg lettuce, muenster cheese, deli ham, and deli turkey): 224 calories, 4.6g net carbs, 5g total carbs, 0.4g fiber, 3.8g sugars, 13.2g fat, 21.2g protein

INSIDE-OUT AVOCADO BURGER POCKETS

Makes 4 servings

This yummy burger features a hidden fatty surprise: avocado! Eat these without a bun or try the Eggplant Buns (page 80).

2 pounds ground beef, bison, or turkey

Salt and pepper, to taste

2 ripe avocados

1 scallion, sliced

½ lemon, juiced

1. In a large mixing bowl, gently combine the ground meat, salt, and pepper. Form 8 very thin patties and lay them flat on a tray. Set aside.

2. In another mixing bowl, mash together the avocados, scallion, lemon juice, salt, and pepper.

3. Divide the avocado mixture among 4 patties, placing a dollop of the mixture in the center of each.

4. Gently position each of the remaining 4 patties over the avocado-dressed patties to create a burger. Seal the edges of the 2 patties together, creating 4 stuffed burgers.

5. Heat a frying pan over medium-high heat. If using turkey, lightly grease the pan with your favorite oil, leftover fat, or butter. Bison and beef have enough fat to keep them from sticking to the pan.

6. When the pan is hot, add the 4 stuffed burgers. Cook about 7–8 minutes or until browned. Gently turn the burger and cook another 7–8 minutes or until done.

7. Remove the burgers from the pan and allow them to rest for 15 minutes. Eat immediately, or wrap with food wrap and refrigerate for up to 2 days.

PER SERVING (made with ground beef): 628 calories, 2.6g net carbs, 8.6g total carbs, 6g fiber, 1.7g sugars, 47.7g fat, 43.8g protein

KETO SOFT TACOS

Makes 4 servings

A favorite from my childhood in northern California, tacos often wind up in my kids' lunch boxes. Look at the tip for the best way to pack them.

2 egg whites

Pinch of cream of tartar

Dash of cumin or chili powder

½ tablespoon avocado oil, coconut oil, or lard, if cooking poultry

1 pound ground bison, beef, chicken, or turkey

1 garlic clove, minced

1 tablespoon chili powder

1 teaspoon ground cumin

½ teaspoon dried oregano

½ teaspoon salt

OPTIONAL TOPPINGS: Keto Salsa (page 22), Perfect Guacamole (page 13), shredded cheese, and sour cream

1. Make the tortillas: In the bowl of a stand mixer, whisk together the egg whites, cream of tartar, and a dash of cumin or chili powder until the mixture is light. Set aside.

2. Heat a large nonstick skillet over medium heat for 1 minute. Pour in 2 tablespoons of tortilla batter and rotate the pan to help distribute the batter.

3. Cover the pan and cook for 2 minutes. Flip, cover, and cook the tortilla for 2 more minutes.

4. Remove the tortilla and set on a plate. Fold the tortilla in half so it resembles a taco shell and allow to cool.

5. Repeat with the remaining batter. Wipe down the skillet.

6. Make the taco filling: Return the skillet to medium-high heat. If you will be using ground chicken or turkey, add the avocado oil.

7. Add the ground meat, garlic, chili powder, cumin, oregano, and salt to the skillet and sauté until meat is fully cooked through.

8. Assemble the tacos by holding a tortilla with 1 hand and filling it with taco meat. Top with optional toppings and eat immediately.

> **PER SERVING** (made with avocado oil and ground beef): 264 calories, 0.3g net carbs, 0.3g total carbs, 0g fiber, 0.1g sugars, 19g fat, 22.2g protein

TIP: If packing these tacos for lunch, wrap the tacos without toppings in foil or food wrap. Store in the refrigerator until ready to eat. Pack the optional toppings in separate small containers.

BIG-O BACON BURGERS

Makes 4 servings

This burger (pictured on page 74) uses bacon in a whole new way: inside the burger, to give it flavor and a moist texture. Serve this burger on a warm Portobello Bun (page 81).

2 tablespoons olive oil, avocado oil, or ghee, divided

½ pound white or cremini (aka baby bella) mushrooms, minced

1 small garlic clove, minced

4 ounces uncooked bacon, roughly chopped

1 pound ground beef, bison, or turkey

1½ teaspoons kosher salt

Freshly ground black pepper

FOR SERVING: lettuce, tomato, red onion, and Easy-Peasy Ketchup (page 20)

1. In a large skillet over medium-high heat, warm 1 tablespoon of the oil. Add the mushrooms and garlic, and sauté until the liquid they release has cooked off. Set mushrooms aside to cool to room temperature. Wipe down the skillet with a paper towel.

2. Add the bacon to the bowl of a food processor and pulse just until ground.

3. In a large bowl, combine the mushrooms, bacon, and ground bison with salt and pepper. Gently use a spatula or your hands to combine the ingredients.

4. Separate the mixture into 4 portions and create patties.

5. Return the skillet to the stove over medium heat. Add the remaining oil to the skillet, and when warm, add the 4 patties. Cook the patties until browned, about 3–4 minutes, and then flip. Cook on the other side about 3–4 minutes or until done.

6. Eat immediately, or place in a covered container in the refrigerator for up to 2 days.

PER SERVING (made with ground beef): 494 calories, 2.6g net carbs, 8.6g total carbs, 6g fiber, 1.7g sugars, 47.7g fat, 43.8g protein

TRIFLE SANDWICHES

Makes 1 serving

Served in a style similar to the layered dessert, this recipe uses savory sandwich ingredients instead. It's a perfect way to get the taste of a sandwich without wraps, buns, or bread.

1 cup Sandwich Salad (page 96), Pulled Pork (page 8), diced Big Batch Chicken Thighs (page 3), or diced cooked meat of choice

1 cup shredded romaine lettuce or green cabbage

½ cup Perfect Guacamole (page 13)

½ cup cubed or shredded cheese

OPTIONAL: 1 hard-boiled egg, chopped (see the Perfect Hard-Boiled Egg, page 2)

OPTIONAL: 1 or 2 slices cooked bacon, chopped

1. In a jar, layer ½ cup of the Sandwich Salad or meat, ½ cup of the romaine lettuce, ¼ cup of the guacamole, ¼ cup of the cheese, and all of the optional ingredients, if using.

2. Finish with a second layer of the remaining Sandwich Salad or meat, romaine lettuce, guacamole, and cheese.

Calorie, fat, protein, and carbohydrate counts will vary.

CUCUMBER SUB

Makes 1 serving

Think of this as a ketofied tea sandwich. Feel free to try an equal amount of another protein, such as smoked whitefish, hard-boiled egg (see the Perfect Hard-Boiled Egg on page 2), or leftover chicken.

½ cup chopped smoked trout or smoked salmon

2 tablespoons Homemade Mayo (page 17)

1 teaspoon Dijon mustard

2 teaspoons minced fresh dill

Salt and pepper, to taste

1 cucumber, peeled, halved lengthwise, and seeded

1. In a large bowl, combine all ingredients except the cucumber. Mix gently until combined and adjust seasoning to taste.

2. Fill the center depression in each cucumber half with the fish mixture. Place cucumber halves together, as if they were a hoagie roll. Wrap in food wrap and store in the refrigerator until ready to eat.

PER SERVING (made with smoked trout): 454 calories, 5g net carbs, 10g total carbs, 5g fiber, 3g sugars, 21.6g fat, 51g protein

TIP: To seed a cucumber with ease, run a spoon down the center to scoop out the seedy "marrow."

PIZZA POCKETS

Makes 2 servings

It is important to use low-moisture cheese when making this pizza-inspired dish. I also suggest using preshredded mozzarella for best results. The instructions seem a bit involved, but these are actually quite easy to make—I promise!

¾ cup shredded mozzarella

1 tablespoon cream cheese

1 tablespoon grated Parmesan

½ teaspoon dried basil

¼ cup flax meal (you can make your own by whirring 1 ounce of flax seeds in a coffee grinder)

4 slices deli salami

2 deli slices provolone

1. Preheat the oven to 400°F.

2. Place a large piece of parchment or waxed paper on the counter or another flat surface and have a second, same-size, sheet of parchment or waxed paper ready.

3. Place the mozzarella, cream cheese, Parmesan, and basil in a microwave-safe bowl. Microwave on high for about 30 seconds to melt. Check, and if not thoroughly melted, microwave for another 10 seconds, repeating as necessary to melt.

4. Remove from the microwave and stir in the flax meal.

5. Place the dough on the parchment or waxed paper. Place the second piece of parchment or waxed paper directly on top of the dough.

6. Using a rolling pin, roll the dough out between the two sheets of parchment or waxed paper. The dough should be a large rectangle between ⅛ and ¼ inch thick.

7. Cut the rectangle into 2 squares.

8. Layer the salami and cheese slices on the lower half of each dough square.

9. Fold each square over like an envelope, encasing the ingredients. Press the edges of the dough together to seal.

10. Prick the pockets in a few places to allow the steam to escape while baking.

11. Gently place the parchment with the sealed pizza pockets on an ungreased baking sheet and bake at 400°F for 15–20 minutes, or until golden brown and firm to the touch.

12. Allow to cool on the baking sheet for 15 minutes before cutting in half. Store uneaten pizza pockets in a sealed container in the refrigerator for up to 2 days.

PER SERVING: 352 calories, 1.7g net carbs, 9.8g total carbs, 8.1g fiber, 0.2g sugars, 28.5g fat, 21.1g protein

CHARD LEAF MEATBALL HOAGIE WRAP

Makes 1 serving

Chard is related to beet leaves and makes a great sandwich wrapper. You can also use a lettuce wrap if you prefer.

---

1 large chard leaf

4 Keto Meatballs (page 7)

1 tablespoon Versatile Marinara Sauce (page 31)

1 or 2 slices cheese of your choice

---

1. Lay the chard leaf on a flat surface. Using a pair of kitchen shears or a knife, remove the stem and about 2 inches of the spine from the leaf. Discard the stem and spine, or chop and sauté as a vegetable for use in another dish.

2. Arrange the meatballs in a horizontal line on the lower third of the leaf, above where you've removed the spine.

3. Top with marinara sauce and cheese.

4. Fold in the 2 sides, as if you were rolling a burrito.

5. Begin rolling the leaf from the bottom.

6. If necessary, use a toothpick to keep the wrap together.

PER SERVING (made with 1 slice of provolone cheese): 480 calories, 3.4g net carbs, 4.6g total carbs, 1.2g fiber, 2.1g sugars, 29.4g fat, 47.1g protein

CHARD LEAF BBQ PULLED PORK HOAGIE WRAP

This wrap works well with Pulled Pork (page 8) as well. Omit the cheese and use a tablespoon of Keto Barbecue Sauce (page 30) in place of the marinara.

TIP: Avoid chard leaves if you have thyroid issues, as they slightly (although temporarily) reduce thyroid function.

Sandwich Salad Blueprint

Makes 2 cups, or 4 (½-cup) servings

Do you know what Sandwich Salad is? It's not really salad; it's a filling. Think tuna salad, egg salad, chicken salad, or any other kind of chopped-protein-with-fixings kind of sandwich filling. This easy blueprint lets you make a tasty, nutritious, keto-approved sandwich salad no matter what kind of protein you have on hand.

- 2 tablespoons Homemade Mayo (page 17)
- 1–3 teaspoons Easy-Peasy Mustard (page 21) or prepared mustard of choice
- 1–2 tablespoons minced sweet onion (such as Vidalia) or red onion
- 1–2 tablespoons relish or chopped dill pickles
- Salt and pepper, to taste

- OPTIONAL: 1 or 2 celery stalks, finely chopped
- OPTIONAL: 1 or 2 fresh herbs, minced (dill, parsley, cilantro, chives, etc.)
- OPTIONAL: Pinch of cayenne, curry, chili powder, or another spice
- 1½ cups cooked and chopped or flaked protein of choice (such as canned poultry, fish, seafood, red meat, or hard-boiled eggs)

1. In a large bowl, whisk together all ingredients except the protein.

2. Gently fold in protein of choice, until all ingredients are combined.

3. Serve with a keto-approved wraps or buns or on top of salad greens. Store the remaining Sandwich Salad in a container in the refrigerator for up to 2 days.

Calorie, fat, protein and carbohydrate counts will vary.

TIP: If you do not like mayo, consider using 2 tablespoons smashed avocado or Perfect Guacamole (page 13) instead.

Sausage Puffs, page 102

SNACKS

Fat Bombs 101

Fat bombs are mini meals, snacks, or treats that are high in fat and low in carbs and that you can enjoy as a quick midafternoon snack, use as a pre- or post-workout energizer, or munch on any time you need a hit of energy. Here are four facts about fat bombs:

1. Fat bombs are often small. They are high in fat and often very filling, and come in the shape of balls, nuggets, patties, plops, or mini-muffins.

2. They can be savory or sweet. Sweeter fat bombs use stevia as opposed to traditional sweeteners (think sugar, molasses, honey, apple juice concentrate) that contain carbohydrates.

    FUN FACT: Stevia causes fewer stomach problems than sugar alcohols and culinary glycerins, which are often used in mainstream low-carb treats.

3. Fat bombs contain a ton of healthy fats. On a ketogenic diet eating healthy fat is highly important to lower inflammation in your body. Most fat bombs contain coconut oil, coconut butter, cacao butter, and/or avocado for this reason—plus these ingredients are solid at cooler temperatures and therefore act, as a binder in most recipes. They often last five days in the refrigerator in an airtight container.

4. Fat bombs often contain nuts and seeds. Many keto dieters avoid consuming too many nuts and seeds because they tend to be high in carbs and, if heated, can easily become oxidized. That being said, nuts and seeds add wonderful texture, healthy fats, and flavor, so use sparingly.

BACON-LIVERWURST BALLS

Makes about 12 balls

Liverwurst is high in iron and protein and has a good amount of fat, which is why it's a keto staple. If you like Braunschweiger, you'll love this no-cook recipe!

---

8 ounces liverwurst, at room temperature

6 ounces cream cheese, softened

¼ cup chopped pecans

1–2 teaspoons mustard

Salt and pepper, to taste

8 slices crisp cooked bacon, finely chopped

---

1. Place the liverwurst, cream cheese, pecans, mustard, salt, and pepper in a food processor and pulse until just combined.

2. Using a small cookie scoop or a large spoon, scoop out 12 portions and roll into balls.

3. Place the balls on a plate or baking sheet, and chill in the refrigerator for at least 30 minutes.

4. Roll each ball in bacon. Eat immediately or store in a covered container for up to a 5 days. Serve cold or at room temperature.

PER SERVING (1 ball, made with pecans and 1 teaspoon mustard): 194 calories, 1.3g net carbs, 1.6g total carbs, 0.3g fiber, 0.8g sugars, 16.9g fat, 9g protein

SAUSAGE PUFFS

Makes about 20 puffs

These yummy puffs (pictured on page 98) make a great appetizer at your next party. Buy bulk ground sausage, or buy links and remove the casings.

1 pound pork breakfast or Italian sausage, uncooked

1 egg

1 cup finely ground pecans, almonds, or nut of choice

8 ounces extra-sharp cheddar cheese

¼ cup grated Parmesan cheese

1 tablespoon butter, coconut oil, lard, or another fat

2 teaspoons baking powder

Salt and pepper, to taste

1. Preheat the oven to 350°F.

2. Add all ingredients to the bowl of a stand mixer and mix on a low speed until completely combined. The sausage will be chunky.

3. Using a small cookie scoop or a large spoon, scoop out 20 portions and roll into balls.

4. Place the balls on a cookie sheet lined with foil or parchment paper.

5. Bake for 16–20 minutes or until browned and just firm to the touch.

6. Eat immediately or store in the refrigerator for up to 3 days.

PER SERVING (1 puff, made with whipping cream): 153 calories, 0.3g net carbs, 0.4g total carbs, 0.1g fiber, 0g sugars, 12.5g fat, 9.4g protein

MEATY JALAPEÑO POPPERS

Makes 16 poppers

This keto-friendly version of the beloved appetizer uses fresh peppers and cream cheese. If you have leftover meat loaf or meatballs (like Keto Meatballs page 7), or leftover bacon, you can crumble it up and substitute it for the ground meat, garlic, and spices, skipping step 2 and adding the leftover meat at step 3.

---

coconut oil, avocado oil, olive oil, lard, or bacon fat, for greasing

6 ounces ground beef, bison, chorizo, or another ground meat

1 garlic clove, minced

1 teaspoon cumin

1 teaspoon dried oregano

Salt and black pepper, to taste

8 medium jalapeños, cut in half and seeds removed

2 ounces cream cheese

---

1. Preheat the oven to 350°F and lightly grease a baking sheet with a bit of coconut oil, avocado oil, olive oil, lard, or bacon fat.

2. Add the meat, garlic, cumin, and oregano to a large pan over medium heat. Cook until browned, and season with salt and pepper. Set aside.

3. Smear each jalapeño half with cream cheese, leaving room for the meat mixture. Once the meat has cooled, spoon the meat mixture into each prepared jalapeño half.

4. Place the poppers on a baking rack and bake for 30 minutes.

5. Eat immediately or store in the refrigerator for up to 5 days.

PER SERVING (2 poppers): 80 calories, 0.8g net carbs, 1.2g total carbs, 0.4g fiber, 0.5g sugars, 5.6g fat, 6g protein

SALMON DAIRY BLOBS

Makes about 8 blobs

This recipe is an easy way to add fish and its omega-3's into your diet. It is ideal for brunch or even a dinner appetizer.

½ cup cream cheese

⅓ cup butter

8 ounces smoked salmon

1 tablespoon fresh lemon juice

1–2 tablespoons freshly chopped dill (or 1 teaspoon dried), plus more for garnish

Pinch of salt

1. Line a tray with parchment paper. Set aside.

2. Place all ingredients into a food processor. Pulse until smooth.

3. Using a cookie scoop or a large spoon, create small fat bombs using about 2½ tablespoons of the mixture per portion. Garnish with more dill and place in the refrigerator for 1–2 hours or until firm.

4. Eat as is or on top of crunchy lettuce leaves, or enjoy as a spread on cucumber slices or with spears of endive or romaine lettuce. Store in the refrigerator for up to 5 days.

PER SERVING (1 blob): 162 calories, 0.9g net carbs, 0.9g total carbs, 0g fiber, 0.8g sugars, 14.9g fat, 6.4g protein

TIP: Instead of creating blobs, spoon the mixture into an airtight container. Eat immediately or store in the refrigerator for up to 1 week. Spoon out about 2½ tablespoons per serving.

BACON AVOCADO PLOPS

Makes 6 plops

If you love bacon and avocado sandwiches, you'll love these addictive goodies. Feel free to adjust the spiciness.

4 large slices bacon

½ large avocado, pit and peel removed

¼ cup coconut oil, room temperature

1 small chili pepper, minced

⅓ cup finely chopped onion

2 tablespoons freshly chopped cilantro

1 tablespoon fresh lime juice

¼ teaspoon salt or more, to taste

Black pepper, to taste

1. Preheat the oven to 375°F. Line a baking tray with parchment paper. Lay out the bacon strips, leaving space so they don't overlap. Place the tray in the oven and cook for about 10–15 minutes, until golden brown. Remove from the oven and set aside to cool. Reserve the bacon grease.

2. Place the avocado, coconut oil, chili pepper, onion, cilantro, and lime juice into a bowl, and season with salt and pepper. Mash with a potato masher or a fork until well combined.

3. Add the bacon grease into the avocado mixture, and mix well. Cover with foil and place in the refrigerator for 20–30 minutes to firm up.

4. Crumble the bacon into small pieces and spread on a plate or baking tray.

5. Remove the guacamole mixture from the refrigerator and create 6 balls, using an cookie scoop or large spoon. Roll each ball in the bacon crumbles, wrap, and place on a tray. Eat immediately.

6. If not eating immediately, wrap each in plastic wrap and store in the refrigerator in an airtight container for up to 5 days.

PER SERVING (1 plop): 169 calories, 1.01g net carbs, 1.9g total carbs, 0.8g fiber, 0.3g sugars, 16.2g fat, 5g protein

PIZZA BOMBS

Makes 16 bombs

Pizza is one of the world's favorite foods, so there is a good chance that this may be one of your favorite fat bombs!

3½ ounces cream cheese

¼ cup butter, softened

1 tablespoon chopped fresh basil (or 1 teaspoon dried)

2 teaspoons chopped fresh oregano leaves (or 1 teaspoon dried)

¼ cup oil-packed, sun-dried tomatoes, drained and chopped

¼ cup pitted Kalamata olives, chopped

2 cloves garlic, minced

Salt and pepper, to taste

¼ cup grated Parmesan cheese

1. Place all the ingredients in the bowl of a food processor and pulse a few times until just combined.

2. Chill the mixture in the refrigerator for 30 minutes, or until firm.

3. Using a small cookie scoop or a large spoon, scoop out 8 portions and roll into balls.

4. Eat immediately or store in the refrigerator in an airtight container for up to 5 days.

PER SERVING (1 bomb): 77 calories, 0.7g net carbs, 0.8g total carbs, 0.1g fiber, 0.2g sugars, 7.1g fat, 2.9g protein

MATCHA AND COCONUT FAT BALLS

Makes about 32 balls

Containing antioxidant-rich matcha, this healthy, delicious treat is just different enough to catch your attention. Sometimes I like to add ⅛ teaspoon of ground star anise, or cardamom.

1 cup firm coconut oil (refrigerate to harden, if necessary)

1 cup creamy coconut butter, at room temperature

½ cup coconut cream, refrigerated overnight

1 tablespoon + ½ teaspoon matcha green tea powder, divided

¼ teaspoon ground ginger

¼ teaspoon salt

1 teaspoon pure vanilla extract

1 cup finely shredded unsweetened coconut

1. In the bowl of a stand mixer fitted with a paddle attachment, add the coconut oil, coconut butter, coconut cream, ½ teaspoon of the matcha green tea powder, ginger, salt, and vanilla extract.

2. Mix on high speed until light and fluffy. Remove the bowl from the mixer and stash in the refrigerator for 1 hour or more to firm up.

3. While the mixture is firming up, whisk together the shredded coconut and the remaining 1 tablespoon of matcha powder in a large mixing bowl. Set aside.

4. Remove the mixture from the refrigerator. Using a small cookie scoop or a large spoon, form 32 little balls, roughly the size of a gum ball.

5. Roll the balls quickly between the palms of your hands to smooth them into perfect balls. Then drop each ball into the bowl with the coconut-matcha mixture. Roll gently until completely coated.

6. Transfer your finished fat balls to an airtight container and keep refrigerated for up to 10 days.

7. These can be eaten straight out of the refrigerator, but they are even better when you let them sit at room temperature for 10–15 minutes before eating them.

> **PER SERVING** (1 ball): 194 calories, 4g net carbs, 7g total carbs, 3g fiber, 3.7g sugars, 19.1g fat, 1.3g protein

TIP: For this recipe, it's important that the coconut oil and coconut cream be firm. Refrigerate both for at least 2 hours before you begin.

BLACKBERRY-NUT FAT SQUARES

Makes 12 squares

Try this with raspberries for a more tart (and pink) fat bomb.

---

2 ounces ground macadamia nuts, cashews, pistachios, or another nut or mixture of nuts

3½ ounces cream cheese, at room temperature

1 cup blackberries

¼ cup mascarpone cheese

½ cup butter

½ cup coconut oil

1 cup coconut butter

1 teaspoon lime juice

Stevia, to taste

---

1. Preheat the oven to 325°F.

2. Press the ground nuts into the bottom of an 8-inch baking pan. Bake 5–7 minutes or until golden brown.

3. Remove from the oven and allow to cool slightly.

4. Spread the cream cheese over the nut crust.

5. In the bowl of a stand mixer set to low, mix together the blackberries, mascarpone cheese, butter, coconut oil, coconut butter, lime juice, and stevia until smooth.

6. Smooth the mixture over the cream cheese layer. Freeze for 30–60 minutes. Remove and eat immediately or store in an airtight container in the refrigerator for up to 10 days.

PER SERVING (1 square, made with macadamia nuts): 478 calories, 3.6g net carbs, 11.3g total carbs, 7.7g fiber, 3.4g sugars, 48.9g fat, 4.2g protein

TIP: You can use a food processor or a coffee grinder to make the nut crust.

WHITE CHOCOLATE BOMBS

Makes about 12 balls

White chocolate is a creamy, fatty, thoroughly addictive substance. Personalize this recipe with spices, extracts, or add-ins like dried coconut, chocolate chips, or nuts.

¼ cup cocoa butter

¼ cup coconut oil

¼ finely shredded unsweetened coconut

10 drops liquid stevia

½ teaspoon vanilla extract

1. In the bowl of a double boiler set over low heat, melt together the cocoa butter and coconut oil.

2. Remove from the heat and stir in the shredded coconut, stevia, and vanilla extract.

3. Pour into molds or mini muffin cups.

4. Chill until hardened.

5. Remove from the molds. Eat immediately or store in a covered container in the refrigerator for up to 10 days.

PER SERVING (1 bomb): 183 calories, 2.5g net carbs, 5g total carbs, 2.5g fiber, 1.3g sugars, 19.3g fat, 1.3g protein

DIY Sweet Bomb Blueprint

Makes about 12 servings

If you have a blueprint, you can make anything your own, using what you have on hand. Yummy sweet fat bombs are no exception. Use this easy blueprint to come up with endless combinations of delish, healthy, fatabulous bombs. Try it!

1 cup fat, or a mixture of two or three fats (These may include coconut oil, coconut cream, coconut butter, cocoa butter, avocado oil, avocado, ghee, butter, heavy cream, cream cheese, sour cream, or nut butter.)

1 tablespoon or more flavoring (If you're making sweet bombs, this most often means dark chocolate, but it can also be a teaspoon of vanilla extract, spices, a few drops of peppermint extract, or the like.)

2 tablespoons to ¼ cup texture-giving, "bulkifying" ingredients, such as shredded coconut, chia, cacao nibs, nuts, or seeds

1. Add all ingredients to a large bowl. Whisk together until thoroughly blended. If it makes sense to use a food processor or blender, do so, pulsing the ingredients together until blended.

2. Pour the mixture into small cups or molds. I like to use mini muffin cups.

3. Freeze or refrigerate until solid.

4. Store in a cool place or refrigerate in an airtight container for up to 10 days.

NOTE: If you're using nuts or seeds, less is more. These ingredients are best used in small amounts because they tend to be high in carbohydrates.

SIMPLE NUT BUTTER FUDGE

Makes 12 pieces

This treat is made with nut butter and coconut oil. Change things up by adding your favorite spices or extracts.

1 cup unsweetened peanut butter, almond butter, or another nut or seed butter of choice

1 cup coconut oil

¼ cup unsweetened coconut milk, coconut cream, dairy cream, or almond milk

OPTIONAL: Pinch of salt, only if needed

OPTIONAL: Dash of vanilla extract, or a sprinkle of cinnamon or nutmeg

OPTIONAL: 1–2 teaspoons liquid stevia

OPTIONAL: Unsweetened shredded coconut

1. Slightly melt or soften the peanut butter and coconut oil together in a small pot over low heat or in the microwave.

2. Add the warm mixture, along with all remaining ingredients except the shredded coconut, to the bowl of a food processor or stand mixer and process until combined and smooth.

3. Pour into the paper cups of a mini-muffin tray. Sprinkle a pinch of shredded coconut on each serving.

4. Refrigerate until set, for about 2 hours. Eat immediately or store in an airtight container in the refrigerator for up to 10 days.

PER SERVING (1 piece, made with coconut milk): 294 calories, 3.1g net carbs, 4.5g total carbs, 1.4g fiber, 2.2g sugars, 30.2g fat, 5.5g protein

COCOA-COCONUT BALLS

Makes 12 balls

Have some powdered peanut butter on hand that you don't know what to do with? Use it to make this recipe. If you can find it, powdered almond butter also works.

½ cup coconut oil

¼ cup finely chopped dark chocolate

¼ cup peanut butter powder

6 tablespoons shelled hemp seeds

2 tablespoons heavy cream or coconut cream

1 teaspoon vanilla extract

15–28 drops liquid stevia, or to taste

¼ cup unsweetened shredded coconut

1. In the bowl of a stand mixer or food processor, place the coconut oil, dark chocolate, peanut butter powder, and hemp seeds, and process until it forms a paste.

2. Add the heavy cream, vanilla, and stevia, and process until everything is combined and smooth. Store in the refrigerator for 30 minutes or more to chill.

3. Place the coconut on a plate or tray.

4. Using a small cookie scoop or a large spoon, scoop out 12 portions and roll them into balls.

5. Roll each ball into the coconut to coat. Eat immediately or store in an airtight container in the refrigerator or freezer for up to 10 days.

PER SERVING (1 ball, made with heavy cream): 181 calories, 2.8g net carbs, 4.2g total carbs, 1.4g fiber, 2.6g sugars, 17.3g fat, 3.6g protein

ORANGE-SCENTED CHOCOLATES

Makes 12 chocolates

If you are also an orange-chocolate fan, you will adore these fatabulous chocolates. If you're not as excited by the citrus-cocoa pairing, simply leave out the orange peel.

---

4 to 5 ounces of dark chocolate, 85% cocoa

¼ cup coconut oil

OPTIONAL: ½ teaspoon or more vanilla extract

OPTIONAL: 10–15 drops of stevia

½–1 tablespoon finely chopped fresh orange peel (just the orange part)

1 cup finely chopped pecans

---

1. Melt the chocolate in a double boiler over low heat.

2. Stir in coconut oil and, if using, vanilla extract and stevia.

3. Add the fresh orange peel.

4. Add the pecans and stir until coated.

5. Spoon the mixture into paper mini muffin or candy cups.

6. Place in the refrigerator for a couple of hours or until solid. Store in a covered container in the refrigerator or at room temperature for up to 10 days.

PER SERVING (1 chocolate): 101 calories, 5.5g net carbs, 7g total carbs, 1.5g fiber, 6.3g sugars, 8.8g fat, 0.9g protein

ALMOND-PISTACHIO SQUARES

Makes 36 squares

Nuts are used sparingly in keto recipes. Here, a sprinkling of pistachios (or another nuts) provide texture and flavor.

1 cup all-natural almond butter

1 cup coconut butter

1 cup coconut oil, chilled until semisolid

½ cup coconut cream, chilled overnight

¼ cup liquid coconut oil, pistachio oil, or ghee

1 teaspoon pure almond extract

2 teaspoons apple pie spice blend, chai spice blend, or pumpkin pie spice blend

¼ teaspoon salt

½ cup cacao butter, chopped and melted

¼ cup chopped pistachios, almonds, macadamia nuts, or walnuts

1. Grease and line a 9-inch-square baking pan with foil or parchment paper, leaving 2 inches hanging on either side for easy unmolding. Set aside.

2. Add the almond butter, coconut butter, semisolid coconut oil, coconut cream, liquid oil, almond extract, spice blend, and salt to the bowl of a large stand mixer. Mix on low speed for 30 seconds to incorporate the ingredients.

3. Switch the mixer speed to high and mix until the mixture becomes airy and lighter in color, for about 3 minutes.

4. Reduce the mixer speed to low and slowly pour in the melted cacao butter. Mix for about 1 minute, or until well blended.

5. Transfer the mixture to the prepared pan and spread as evenly as possible. Press the chopped nuts into the top of the mixture.

6. Refrigerate for 4 hours, or until firm. Then cut into 36 squares.

7. Eat immediately or store in an airtight container in the refrigerator for up to 10 days.

PER SERVING (1 square, made with ghee and chopped pistachios): 225 calories, 4.1g net carbs, 6.9g total carbs, 2.8g fiber, 3.5g sugars, 21.7g fat, 3.3g protein

NUTTY 3-INGREDIENT CRACKERS

Makes 6 servings (about thirty 1½- × 2½-inch crackers)

Crackers are one of those things you may hesitate to make at home. But if you are a keto-eater who loves crispy snacks, you know how expensive store-bought low-carb crackers can be. This delicious (and simple!) recipe can help save your wallet!

1 large egg

2 cups almond flour (or almond meal), or another nut flour, such as pecan, peanut, walnut, or hazelnut flour

½ teaspoon salt

OPTIONAL: ⅛–¼ teaspoon of cayenne, sesame seeds, poppy seeds, garlic salt, or another favorite spice

1. Preheat the oven to 350°F.

2. In a large bowl, add an egg and beat with a whisk.

3. Gently stir in the almond flour and salt, as well as any optional spice you may be using. Stir until blended.

4. Place 1 long sheet of waxed or parchment paper on a countertop or table. Empty the dough out of the bowl onto the waxed paper and form the dough into a disk.

5. Place another long sheet of waxed or parchment paper over the disk of dough. Using a rolling pin, roll the dough through the waxed paper into a large rectangle. The dough should be about ¹⁄₁₆–⅛ of an inch thick.

6. Gently lift the parchment paper and dough and place in the refrigerator. Let the dough chill for at least 15 minutes. This will make it easier to handle in the next steps.

7. Remove the chilled dough from the fridge and peel away the top layer of waxed paper.

8. Using a paring knife or a pizza cutter, cut the dough into squares or rectangles. (I prefer to cut my crackers into 1½- × 2½-inch rectangles.)

9. Prick each cracker 2 or 3 times with the tines of a fork.

10. Using an offset spatula, gently transfer the crackers to an ungreased, rimless baking sheet that has been lined with a piece of foil.

11. Bake the crackers for 10–12 minutes, or until golden and slightly firm to the touch (they'll firm up further once they're removed from the oven).

12. Enjoy immediately or store in an airtight container for 10 days.

PER SERVING (5 crackers, using almond flour and no optional spice): 224 calories, 4g net carbs, 8g total carbs, 4g fiber, 1g sugars, 19.5g fat, 9.5g protein

KETO CHEESE DIP

Makes about 2½ cups

Cheese dip is a fun food. Use whatever you'd like as a dipper, from spears of asparagus to chunks of chicken. It can also be used as a sandwich spread or as a sauce for poultry or veggies.

1 cup canned coconut cream

1½ cups cheddar cheese (sharp or mild), finely shredded/grated

OPTIONAL: A pinch of chipotle or chili powder or a tablespoon minced jalapeño or poblano chilies

1. Add the coconut cream to a small saucepan over medium heat. Heat until just warm, about 3 minutes.

2. Slowly stir in the cheese, a tablespoon at a time. Keep stirring until the cheese is fully incorporated.

3. If using the optional spice, add to the cheese dip and mix in thoroughly.

4. Using a spatula, scrape the cheese dip into a serving bowl and serve immediately.

PER SERVING (2 tablespoons, made with a pinch of chipotle powder): 59 calories, 0.5 net carbs, 0.8g total carbs, 0.3g fiber, 0.4g sugars, 5.5g fat, 2.2g protein

TIP: Wish you had something crunchy? The Nutty 3-Ingredient Crackers (page 120) are keto-approved and make a great substitute for mainstream crackers.

TUNA-STUFFED CELERY

Make 4 servings

Celery is such an overlooked food, but as a low-calorie, low-carb veggie, it needs to be in every keto-eater's fridge. Here, it is dressed up with a tasty, tuna-based stuffing.

1 tablespoon cream cheese, room temperature

2 tablespoons mayonnaise

1 (4-ounce) can of white or pink tuna in oil

¼ cup chopped olives (any variety)

8 celery stalks, trimmed

1. In a large bowl, mix together the cream cheese and mayonnaise.

2. Add the tuna and chopped olives to the bowl and stir to combine.

3. Using a small spoon, fill each stalk of celery with the tuna salad stuffing.

4. Serve immediately, or arrange on a plate, cover with food wrap, and refrigerate for up to 8 hours.

PER SERVING (made with white tuna packed in oil): 235 calories, 3.3g net carbs, 4.9g total carbs, 1.6g fiber, 1.6g sugars, 12.9g fat, 23.8g protein

STUFFED MUSHROOMS

Makes 5–6 servings

These sausage-stuffed bites are a great holiday appetizer. This version is similar to the one my husband's family makes, but without the carb-heavy breadcrumbs.

---

1 pound white, button mushrooms, about 20–24 mushrooms

3 tablespoons extra-virgin olive oil

3 cloves garlic, minced

1 pound bulk spicy Italian sausage

Salt and pepper, to taste

½ cup finely grated Parmesan cheese

4 ounces cream cheese, at room temperature

1 teaspoon dried basil or ½ tablespoon fresh minced basil

1 teaspoon dried parsley or ½ tablespoon fresh minced parsley

---

1. Preheat the oven to 375°F.

2. Remove stems from mushrooms and roughly chop the stems, reserving mushroom caps for stuffing.

3. Heat olive oil in a large sauté pan over medium-high heat. Add garlic and chopped mushroom stems to the pan and sauté for 3 minutes, or until softened.

4. Add sausage to the pan and cook for about 5 minutes, or until browned, breaking up the sausage into small bits with a spatula or a wooden spoon.

5. With a slotted spoon, transfer sausage-mushroom mixture from the pan into a large mixing bowl. Adjust salt and pepper to taste.

6. To the bowl, add Parmesan cheese, cream cheese, salt and pepper, basil, and parsley, and stir to blend.

7. Using a teaspoon, spoon the filling into each mushroom cap. When all mushroom caps have been filled, place them gently, filling-side up, on a baking tray.

8. Bake for 15 minutes, or until mushrooms are fork-tender all the way through. Remove from the oven and serve.

PER SERVING (4 mushrooms): 525 calories, 5g net carbs, 6g total carbs, 1g fiber, 1g sugars, 45g fat, 19g protein

CUCUMBER BITES

Makes 4 servings

Cucumber is a refreshing, satisfying low-carb veggie that can be paired with almost any food. Here, Persian cucumbers—sometimes called "salad cucumbers"—are served as the vehicle for a fat-fueled savory salmon filling.

4 ounces cream cheese, room temperature

1 tablespoon minced fresh chives

1 tablespoon minced fresh dill

Salt and pepper, to taste

4 to 6 ounces cooked salmon (leftover salmon is fine, or use salmon from a can or a pouch; most of these come in 4-ounce, 5-ounce, or 6-ounce sizes)

4 small Persian-style cucumbers

1. Place cream cheese, chives, dill, salt, and pepper in the stand mixer bowl. Using the whisk attachment, whip the mixture to combine and aerate.

2. Add the salmon to the bowl and slowly mix just to combine. Set aside.

3. Trim the ends off each cucumber, and slice them in half lengthwise.

4. Using a small spoon, gently scrape out any seeds from each cucumber half, creating a well to hold the filling.

5. Spoon the filling into each cucumber half.

6. Serve immediately or arrange on a plate, cover with food wrap, and refrigerate for up to 6 hours.

PER SERVING (using 4 ounces of leftover salmon): 200 calories, 2.5g net carbs, 3g total carbs, 0.5 fiber, 1.3g sugars, 15.4g fat, 19.5g protein

KETO COLD CUT ROLL-UP

Makes 1 serving

This is kind of like a wrap, made without the carbs. In fact, the cheese and meat become the wraps themselves. You can use whatever you have in the fridge for this easy, creative, and fun snack.

1 slice deli poultry, such as smoked turkey, roast turkey, or chicken

1 slice deli pork-based or beef-based meat, such as ham, prosciutto, roast beef, pastrami, etc.

1 large piece iceberg lettuce

1 slice deli cheese, such as American, cheddar, Swiss, provolone, etc.

1 teaspoon mustard

1 teaspoon mayonnaise

1. Place a piece of deli poultry on a flat surface. Add a slice of pork- or beef-based deli meat on top.

2. Next, stack the lettuce, and cheese.

3. Spread the mustard and mayonnaise evenly on top of the cheese.

4. Starting at the outer, longer edge of the stack, roll the ingredients into a tube. If you need something to secure the wrap, pierce the rolled ingredients with a toothpick.

5. Eat immediately, or wrap tightly in food wrap and store for up to 12 hours.

PER SERVING (using turkey breast, ham, and provolone cheese): 273 calories, 2.6g net carbs, 3.3g total carbs, 0.7g fiber, 1.1g sugars, 21.8g fat, 15.7g protein

CHAPTER SIX

ENTRÉES

KETO ITALIANO STUFFED PEPPERS

Makes 2 servings

When I was growing up, my mom would occasionally make stuffed peppers using green bell peppers, leftover meat loaf, and instant rice. I like them . . . but I love these even more. Feel free to use a different color pepper if you'd like (pictured on page 128).

1½ cups small cauliflower florets, raw

1 tablespoon olive oil

1 teaspoon dried basil, or a combination of dried basil and oregano, divided

Salt and pepper, to taste

6 ounces Italian sweet or hot sausage, casing removed

2 large red bell peppers

½ cup grated provolone cheese, divided

1. Preheat the oven to 350°F.

2. Place the cauliflower in a food processor and pulse until it resembles rice. Or use a box grater and grate the cauliflower.

3. Combine the cauliflower rice, olive oil, ½ teaspoon of the basil, salt, and pepper in a sauté pan with a lid and let it steam over medium heat until the cauliflower is tender, for about 6 minutes. Remove the pan from the heat and set aside.

4. In another sauté pan, cook the sausage, the remaining basil, salt and pepper to taste until the sausage is no longer pink. Set aside.

5. Remove the sausage from the pan with a slotted spoon and let drain on paper towels. Reserve the grease.

6. Add the sausage, sausage grease, and cauliflower rice to a large bowl with ¼ cup of the cheese. Stir to combine. Adjust seasonings if necessary. Set aside.

7. Prepare the peppers by carefully cutting off the tops. Then place the peppers on their sides and cut them in half lengthwise. Remove the seeds. You will have 4 pepper halves.

8. Place the peppers, cut side up, in a lightly greased baking dish and spoon the sausage-cauliflower mixture into each pepper half. Top with the remaining cheese.

9. Cover the dish with foil and bake for 25 minutes.

10. Remove the foil and bake for 10 more minutes or until the cheese is bubbly.

PER SERVING: 334 calories, 5g net carbs, 8.5g total carbs, 3.5g fiber, 3.5g sugars, 23g fat, 24.2g protein

TIP: For a stand-alone recipe for Cauliflower Rice, see page 138.

CILANTRO-LIME SHRIMP SCAMPI WITH ZUCCHINI NOODLES

Makes 4 servings

This is a traditional, special-occasion recipe that is perfect for your workday lunch. Serve over Cauliflower Rice (page 138) or spiralized zucchini noodles.

2 tablespoons coconut oil, extra-virgin olive oil, or butter

1 pound jumbo shrimp (16–24), shelled and deveined

4 cloves garlic, chopped

OPTIONAL: Pinch-red pepper flakes

¼ cup Chicken Bone Broth (page 4)

Juice of 1 lime (about 2 tablespoons)

Salt and pepper, to taste

2 tablespoons chopped cilantro

Base of choice, such as spiralized zucchini noodles or Cauliflower Rice

1. Warm the oil in a large sauté pan over medium-high heat. Add the shrimp, cook for 2 minutes, then flip. Add the garlic and red pepper flakes, if using, and cook for 1 more minute before setting the shrimp aside.

2. Add the broth, lime juice, salt, and pepper to the pan, scrape any browned bits from the bottom of the pan, and simmer for 2 minutes.

3. Return the shrimp to the pan with the cilantro, and toss to combine. Remove from the heat and pour over your base of choice.

PER SERVING (made with coconut oil and zucchini noodles): 213 calories, 2.4g net carbs, 3.7g total carbs, 1.3g fiber, 1.3g sugars, 9.1g fat, 30.1g protein

TIP: Don't own a spiralizer? You can purchase spiralized veggie noodles in the produce section of most grocery stores.

MEATY FRIED "RICE"

Makes 4 servings

Substitute any type of poultry, red meat, or seafood you have on hand for the pork, if desired.

---

1 large head cauliflower, separated into florets

2 tablespoons avocado or coconut oil, divided

2 cloves garlic minced

½ medium onion, chopped

1 pound pork chops or pork loin, minced

1 celery stalk, chopped

OPTIONAL: ½ cup frozen peas

OPTIONAL: ½ cup diced red bell pepper

OPTIONAL: ½ cup finely shredded cabbage

1 large egg, beaten

2 tablespoons soy sauce

1 teaspoon toasted sesame oil

---

1. In the bowl of a food processor, process the cauliflower until it resembles rice. Or use a box grater and grate the cauliflower. Set aside.

2. Add the oil to a large skillet over medium-high heat. Add the garlic and onion and cook until softened, about 4–5 minutes. Add the pork and cook until barely opaque. Do not overcook at this early stage, as pork will continue to cook as you add the remaining ingredients.

3. Add the riced cauliflower and sauté for 2–3 minutes. Add the celery and any optional vegetables and cook for 1–2 minutes, being careful not to overcook. (You don't want mushy fried rice!)

4. Add the egg, soy sauce, and sesame oil and cook until the egg is scrambled, for about 1 minute.

5. Enjoy immediately, or pack in an airtight container and store in the refrigerator for up to 2 days.

PER SERVING (made with avocado oil and without optional ingredients): 450 calories, 4g net carbs, 6.2g total carbs, 2.2g fiber, 2.6g sugars, 37.5g fat, 28.9g protein

CREAMY FISH CASSEROLE

Makes 4 servings

This casserole, while reminiscent of Mom's tuna casseroles, is not only dressier. It's keto-friendly. If you don't have fish, use shrimp, chicken, or turkey. If you don't have broccoli, use asparagus, zucchini, or cauliflower.

1 tablespoon butter

½ pound of broccoli tops, separated into small florets

1 shallot, minced

1 tablespoon small capers

Salt and pepper, to taste

¾ pound whitefish, salmon, tuna, or another uncooked fish, cut into bite-size pieces

⅔ cup heavy cream

½ tablespoon Dijon mustard

2 teaspoons dried herb of choice, such as parsley, dill, or cilantro (or 2 tablespoons fresh)

1. Preheat the oven to 400°F.

2. Add the butter to a large frying pan over medium-high heat. Add the broccoli and shallot, and sauté until the broccoli is just barely tender, for about 5 minutes.

3. Add the capers, salt, and pepper, and sauté for 1 minute.

4. Transfer the sautéed vegetables to a casserole dish.

5. Gently stir the fish into the vegetables and set aside.

6. In a large bowl, whisk together the cream, mustard, herbs, salt, and pepper. Pour over the fish and vegetables.

7. Bake, uncovered, for 20 minutes, or until the fish is cooked through and flakes easily with a fork.

PER SERVING: 479 calories, 4.4g net carbs, 8.6g total carbs, 4.2g fiber, 2.1g sugars, 16.4g fat, 67.2g protein

MIXED KETO PAELLA

Makes 4 servings

This take on traditional paella features all the things my family loves about paella, with none of the carb-heavy rice. This recipe can be adjusted, based on the proteins and vegetables you have on hand.

1 head cauliflower, separated into florets

¾ cup Chicken Bone Broth (page 4)

2 tablespoons extra-virgin olive oil, divided

4 boneless, skinless chicken thighs, cubed

1 medium yellow onion, chopped

2 cloves garlic, minced

½ red bell pepper, diced

2 Roma tomatoes, chopped

Salt and pepper, to taste

1 teaspoon saffron threads

¼ teaspoon smoked paprika

8 ounces chorizo sausage

½ pound jumbo shrimp, peeled and deveined

¼ cup fresh parsley

Lemon wedges, for garnish

1. In the bowl of a food processor, process the cauliflower until it resembles rice. Or use a box grater and grate the cauliflower. Set aside.

2. Add the broth to a large saucepan over medium heat.

3. Heat 1 tablespoon of the olive oil in a large skillet over medium-high heat. Add the chicken pieces and cook for 5 minutes, stirring occasionally to brown the chicken on all sides.

4. Add the remaining 1 tablespoon of oil, onion, garlic, red pepper, tomatoes, salt, pepper, saffron, paprika, and chorizo. Continue to sauté for another 7 minutes, until the onions have softened.

5. Pour the warm broth into the skillet, stirring to scrape up the browned bits from the bottom of the skillet.

6. Stir in the shrimp and the riced cauliflower and simmer for 5 minutes, or until the shrimp looks done.

7. Sprinkle the parsley over the top. Garnish with lemon wedges.

8. Enjoy immediately or store in an airtight container in the refrigerator for up to 2 days.

PER SERVING: 468 calories, 5g net carbs, 8g total carbs, 3g fiber, 4g sugars, 17.9g fat, 72g protein

Faux Rice, Pasta, and Potatoes

If you're like me, one of your favorite parts of a saucy, comfort food meal is the starchy side. Here are some keto-approved side dish substitutions.

CAULIFLOWER RICE

Makes 4 servings

This recipe can be personalized with additional herbs or spices. Have fun with it!

1 large head cauliflower, separated into 1-inch florets

3 tablespoons butter

2 garlic cloves, minced

Salt and pepper, to taste

OPTIONAL: 1–2 teaspoons lemon juice, to keep the cauliflower white

OPTIONAL: 2 tablespoons fresh herbs, such as parsley or chives

1. Add the cauliflower to the bowl of a food processor and pulse until the cauliflower resembles rice. Depending on the size of your food processor, you will probably need to work in 2 or 3 batches. Or use a box grater and grate the cauliflower. Set aside.

2. Add the butter to a large skillet over medium-high heat. Add the garlic and cauliflower and stir to combine. Season with salt and pepper.

3. Cook the cauliflower mixture until the cauliflower just begins to soften, for about 4–5 minutes.

4. Remove from the heat, adjust the seasonings, and stir in the lemon juice and fresh herbs, if using.

PER SERVING (without optional ingredients): 113 calories, 3.4g net carbs, 7g total carbs, 3.6g fiber, 3.5g sugars, 8.8g fat, 3g protein

BROCCOLI RICE

Makes 2 servings

This recipe is a brilliant way to use up broccoli stalks. If you don't have a food processor, simply grate the broccoli on the coarsest side of a box grater.

4 uncooked broccoli stalks (the dried ends trimmed), cut into large chunks

1½ tablespoons butter

1–4 garlic cloves, minced

Salt and pepper, to taste

1. Place the broccoli stalks in the bowl of a food processor and pulse until they resemble rice grains. Do not overprocess.

2. In a large sauté pan over medium heat, add the butter and garlic. Cook for 1–2 minutes, until the garlic is softened.

3. Add the broccoli rice, salt, and pepper, and cook just until tender, for about 8–10 minutes.

PER SERVING (made with 1 clove garlic): 172 calories, 6g net carbs, 13.5g total carbs, 7.5g fiber, 3.7g sugars, 9.6g fat, 7.8g protein

SPIRALIZED VEGGIE PASTA

Makes 1 or 2 servings

This is a fun recipe if you have a spiralizer attachment for your stand mixer or food processor. You can also use a handheld version or —the easiest option—simply purchase a tub of already spiralized veggies in the produce section of your local grocery store.

1 peeled and trimmed root, bulb, or marrow vegetable, or 2–4 ounces spiralized vegetables

1 tablespoon butter or another fat (Bacon fat is nice.)

Salt and pepper, to taste

(continued)

1. Using a spiralizer attachment on your food processor or stand mixer, or a mechanical spiralizer or handheld spiralizer, spiralize one vegetable per serving. (Large vegetables, such as rutabagas and eggplants, will make 2 servings.) If using prepared spiralized vegetables, skip this step.

2. Place a large sauté pan over medium-high heat and add the butter. When it melts, add the spiralized veggies and sauté for 5 minutes, stirring gently to coat all strands with butter.

3. Season with salt and pepper to taste.

4. Use in your favorite recipe or store in an airtight container for up to 2 days in the refrigerator.

Calorie, fat, protein, and carbohydrate counts will vary.

TIP: Vegetables are important in your diet but can be carb-heavy. Stick to low-carb veggies, such as jicama, white-fleshed sweet potato, turnip, rutabaga, kohlrabi, zucchini, or eggplant for this dish.

CAULIFLOWER MASH

Makes about 4 servings

You'll never know the difference with all the delicious Keto-friendly fat added to the mash.

1 large head cauliflower, cut into florets

3 tablespoons butter

2 tablespoons cream

Salt and pepper, to taste

OPTIONAL: 1–2 teaspoons lemon juice, to keep the cauliflower white

OPTIONAL: 2 tablespoons fresh herbs, such as parsley or chives

1. Place a saucepan of salted water over high heat and bring to a boil Add the cauliflower and boil until fork-tender.

2. Transfer to a food processor and puree with butter, cream, salt, pepper, and lemon juice, if using. Process until smooth.

3. Adjust the seasoning and top with herbs, if using.

PER SERVING (without optional ingredients): 137 calories, 4g net carbs, 7.6g total carbs, 3.6g fiber, 3g sugars, 11.3g fat, 2.9g protein

CHEDDAR CAULIFLOWER MASH

Omit the lemon juice and herbs. Stir in 1½ cups shredded cheddar cheese before step 3.

BROCCOLI MASH

Makes 2 servings

This bright green dish looks nothing like mashed potatoes, but it has that same smooth, creamy texture.

---

2 cups broccoli florets and/or peeled stalks

1½ tablespoons butter

1 small garlic clove

Salt and pepper, to taste

OPTIONAL: 1 tablespoon fresh chives, parsley, basil, or other herb

---

1. Place a saucepan of salted water over high heat and bring to a boil. Add the broccoli and boil until fork-tender.

2. Remove the broccoli and while it is still warm, place it in the bowl of a food processor with the remaining ingredients and pulse until smooth.

3. Alternately, you could use an immersion blender to blend the remaining ingredients into the cooked broccoli.

4. Adjust the seasonings and serve immediately, or place in an airtight container in the refrigerator for up to 2 days.

PER SERVING (without optional ingredients): 110 calories, 4.2g net carbs, 6.6g total carbs, 2.4g fiber, 4g sugars, 9g fat, 2.7g protein

KETO INDI CURRY

Makes 4 servings

Indian-style curries are the ultimate comfort foods, both soothing and exciting at the same time. Feel free to add a cup of greens (such as spinach) or another veggie to this recipe.

3 tablespoons coconut oil

1½ pounds boneless, skinless chicken thighs, chopped

1 tablespoon (or more) Madras-style curry powder

½ onion, chopped

2 garlic cloves, minced

1 (1-inch) slice of ginger, peeled and minced (or grated)

1 (14-ounce) can coconut milk

1 cup chicken broth

Salt and pepper, to taste

Broccoli Rice (page 139)

1. Add the oil to a large saucepan over medium-high heat.

2. Add the chicken and let brown for 5 minutes. Do not let the chicken cook completely.

3. Add the curry powder, onion, garlic, and ginger to the pan with the chicken and cook for 2 minutes.

4. Stir in the coconut milk and broth. Season with salt and pepper to taste. Allow to simmer for 30-40 minutes, until slightly reduced and thickened.

5. Enjoy with Broccoli Rice.

PER SERVING: 470 calories, 4.3g net carbs, 6g total carbs, 1.7g fiber, 2.7g sugars, 38.4g fat, 31.6g protein

TIP: If bringing this recipe for lunch, store the curry and broccoli separately to prevent mushy "rice."

THAI RED CURRY CHICKEN

Makes 4 servings

If you don't have chicken, use pork. If you can't find red curry paste, use green. This recipe is more of a guide than a set of iron-clad culinary rules.

1 tablespoon coconut oil

1 onion, thinly sliced into half moons

1½ pounds boneless, skinless chicken thighs, chopped

2 cloves minced garlic

1 red bell pepper, sliced lengthwise

1 small zucchini, cut into half-moon slices

1 cup fresh mushrooms, sliced

1 (14-ounce) can coconut milk

3 tablespoons Thai red curry paste

½ tablespoon soy sauce

OPTIONAL: 2 tablespoons minced fresh cilantro, mint, or holy basil (or a combination)

Cauliflower Rice (page 138) or Broccoli Rice (page 139)

1. Add the oil to a large frying pan over medium-high heat. When warm, add the onions and sauté until just starting to soften.

2. Add the chicken and minced garlic. Cook until the chicken is nearly cooked through, about 5–7 minutes. Add the red pepper, zucchini, and mushrooms, and sauté just until the red peppers are tender-crisp.

3. Lower the heat to medium-low and stir in the coconut milk, red curry paste, and soy sauce, and simmer for 10 minutes or until thickened.

4. Stir in the herbs, if using, and remove from the heat.

5. Enjoy with Cauliflower Rice or Broccoli Rice.

PER SERVING (without optional ingredients): 137 calories, 4g net carbs, 7.6g total carbs, 3.6g fiber, 3g sugars, 11.3g fat, 2.9g protein

KETO SHEPHERD'S PIE

Makes 8 servings

Shepherd's pie is a popular pub casserole featuring seasoned ground meat resting beneath a blanket of mashed potatoes. This yummy keto version replaces the carb-heavy potatoes with (you guessed it!) cauliflower.

1 pound ground lamb

1 pound ground beef

½ cup chopped onion

Salt and pepper, to taste

1 clove garlic, minced

½ cup dry red wine

2 tablespoons chopped fresh rosemary (or 2 teaspoons dried)

1 recipe Cheddar Cauliflower Mash (page 141)

1. Preheat the oven to 400°F.

2. In a large skillet over medium heat, brown the lamb and beef until cooked through, about 10–12 minutes. Using a slotted spoon, remove the meat to a separate plate or bowl. Drain the grease that has collected in the pan, leaving 1–2 tablespoons of oil behind in the pan. Return the pan to the heat and add the onion, salt, and pepper. Cook until the onion is translucent, about 5 minutes. Add the garlic and cook until fragrant, 1 minute more.

3. Return the meat to the pan, and add the wine and rosemary. Cook until the wine is mostly evaporated and the juices have thickened, 4–5 minutes. Transfer the meat mixture to a 2-quart casserole dish

4. Spread the Cheddar Cauliflower Mash over the meat mixture in the casserole dish, and bake for 20 minutes or until bubbling and golden.

5. Allow the casserole to sit for 10 minutes once removed from the oven.

PER SERVING: 439 calories, 3g net carbs, 3g total carbs, 0g fiber, 1.1g sugars, 30.4g fat, 32.1g protein

PIZZA SPAGHETTI CASSEROLE

Makes 4 servings

Spaghetti squash gets its name from its stringy flesh, which resembles pasta. Yet, unlike pasta, it is gluten-free and great for keto-eaters. Enjoy it in this meaty, pizza-like casserole.

1 pound ground beef

1 pound bulk Italian sausage, sweet or hot

1 or 2 garlic cloves, minced

1 tablespoon dried oregano

½ tablespoon dried basil

Pinch of crushed red pepper flakes

Salt and pepper, to taste

1½ cups tomato puree

½ cup grated Parmesan cheese

Coconut oil, avocado oil, olive oil, lard, or bacon fat, for greasing

1 (2-pound) spaghetti squash, cooked and flesh removed (see "How to Cook Spaghetti Squash," page 147)

2 cups mozzarella cheese, divided

1. Place a large skillet over medium-high heat and add the ground beef, Italian sausage, garlic, oregano, basil, red pepper flakes, salt, and pepper. Cook until the meat is browned and no longer pink. Drain the grease, if desired.

2. Stir in the tomato puree and Parmesan and allow to cook until thickened, for about 10 minutes.

3. In the meantime, preheat the oven to 375°F.

4. Grease a casserole dish with a bit of coconut oil, avocado oil, olive oil, lard, or bacon fat. Add the cooked spaghetti squash to the bottom of the dish and sprinkle with salt and pepper to taste.

5. Layer 1½ cups of the mozzarella directly on top of the spaghetti squash.

6. Pour the meat mixture on top.

THE KETO COOKBOOK

7. Top with the remaining ½ cup of mozzarella and bake until bubbly, for about 20 minutes.

8. Remove the casserole from the oven and let it rest for at least 10 minutes before serving.

PER SERVING: 626 calories, 5.1g net carbs, 10.7g total carbs, 5.6g fiber, 4g sugars, 9g fat, 67.4g protein

- -

How to Cook Spaghetti Squash

If you've never cooked a spaghetti squash before, here is how I like to do it: Preheat the oven to 400°F. Slice the spaghetti squash in half down its length. Remove the seeds. Rub ½–I tablespoon of your favorite oil or fat (such as bacon fat, lard, or butter) on the exposed interior flesh of the squash. Add salt and pepper to taste. If desired, add your favorite spices or dried herbs. Place the squash, cut side down, on an ungreased baking sheet. Bake for about 45 minutes, or until the vegetable is fork-tender. Remove from the oven, and allow to cool to room temperature. Using a fork, scrape out the spaghetti-like strands into a bowl. Use immediately or store in an airtight container in your refrigerator for 2–3 days.

- -

STUFFED CABBAGE ROLLS

Makes 6 servings

Cabbage rolls are easy, healthy, and versatile. You can use ground pork, turkey, or chicken in place of beef.

1 medium head cabbage (about 2 pounds)

1 pound ground beef

1½ cups Cauliflower Rice (page 138)

⅓ cup chopped fresh parsley

3 garlic cloves, minced

Salt and pepper, to taste

1 teaspoon sweet paprika

Coconut oil, avocado oil, olive oil, lard, or bacon fat, for greasing

4 cups tomato sauce or Versatile Marinara Sauce (page 31)

OPTIONAL: Parsley, for garnish

1. Remove any dry or broken outer leaves from the cabbage head before coring it, being careful not to split the head or tear any of the leaves. Set aside.

2. Place a large pot of salted water over high heat and bring to a boil.

3. Lower the prepared cabbage head into the boiling water, making sure the entire head is submerged. Boil for 8–10 minutes, or until the head is softened, but not soft or soggy or mushy.

4. Place the cabbage in a colander in the sink and allow cold water to run over it to stop the cooking process. Let the cabbage head drain while you continue with the recipe.

5. In a large sauté pan, combine the beef, cauliflower rice, parsley, garlic, salt, pepper, and paprika. Cook over medium-high heat until the meat is browned.

6. Lightly grease a 9×12-inch baking dish with a bit of coconut oil, avocado oil, olive oil, lard, or bacon fat. Set aside.

7. Preheat the oven to 350°F.

8. Gently peel the outer 6 leaves from the prepared cabbage head to use for the cabbage rolls. With a sharp paring knife, shave off any thick ribs from the outside of the leaves.

9. Lay a cabbage leaf out in front of you, placing the base side at the bottom.

10. Place 2 tablespoons of the beef mixture about 2 inches above the bottom edge and roll. Place, seam-side down, in the prepared baking dish. Continue with the remaining 5 cabbage leaves.

11. Pour the tomato sauce over the cabbage rolls, cover dish with foil, and bake for 45–60 minutes, or until the rolls are tender.

12. Remove the baking dish from the oven and let the cabbage rolls rest for 20 minutes. Garnish with parsley, if desired, and serve.

> **PER SERVING:** 230 calories, 5.1g net carbs, 12g total carbs, 6.9g fiber, 10g sugars, 9g fat, 26.7g protein

Keto Bowl Blueprint

Makes 1 serving

As a keto eater, you know that those trendy grain and bean bowls are way too carb-heavy to fit into your eating plan. Fortunately, there is an easy way to enjoy a lunch bowl in a keto-approved way: make your own!

You can put together a bowl with just about anything you have in your kitchen—even if you only have small amounts of this and that. Plus, bowls are super portable—just layer the ingredients in a Mason jar or a grab-and-go container and toss it into your bag, and you've got an easy lunch. Follow this blueprint.

¼ cup (or more) Keto Salad Dressing (page 16), or your favorite salad dressing

1 tablespoon (or more) favorite herb or mix of herbs

1 garlic clove, minced

¼ cup minced red onion, scallions, or shallots

Salt and pepper, to taste

1 avocado, chopped

2 cups cooked (or canned) fish, seafood, poultry, or red meat of your choice

2 cups chopped cooked or raw vegetables, such as Cauliflower Rice (page 144) or broccoli stems

OPTIONAL: ½ cup shredded or cubed cheese

OPTIONAL: 1 hard-boiled egg, chopped (see the Perfect Hard-Boiled Egg, page 2)

OPTIONAL: 1–2 slices of bacon, cooked and chopped

OPTIONAL: ½ cup or more shredded unsweetened coconut

1. In a lunch container or jar, add the salad dressing, herbs, garlic, onion, salt, and pepper and whisk or shake until the ingredients are combined.

2. Add the avocado to the dressing and toss gently until coated. Adjust the salt and pepper to taste.

3. Add all the other ingredients on top of the dressing. Do not stir! Allow the dressing and avocado to sit at the bottom of the container until you're ready to eat.

4. Place the lid on the container and store in the refrigerator.

5. Before eating, shake the container gently to distribute the dressing.

Calorie, fat, protein and carbohydrate counts will vary.

KETO CHICKEN ENCHILADA BOWL

Makes 2 servings

Go ahead and personalize this dish by changing the veggies and seasonings.

---

2 (4-ounce) uncooked chicken breasts

¾ cups prepared red enchilada sauce

1 (4-ounce) can green chilies

¼ cup chopped red onion

¼ cup Chicken Bone Broth (page 4)

1 (12-ounce) bag cauliflower rice (or see recipe on page 138)

Salt and pepper, to taste

Preferred toppings, such as chopped cilantro, sliced avocado, Perfect Guacamole (page 13), shredded cheese, Keto Salsa (page 22), etc.

---

1. Place a sauté pan over medium heat. In the dry, hot pan, sear all sides of the chicken breasts until lightly browned.

2. Add the enchilada sauce, chilies, onions, and chicken broth to the sauté pan with the chicken. When the mixture begins to simmer, lower the heat to medium-low and cover the pan. Cook until the chicken is tender, about 10 minutes. Turn off the heat and remove just the chicken.

3. Place the chicken in a large bowl. Shred the chicken using two forks. Add the shredded chicken back to the sauce in the sauté pan and turn the heat to medium. Allow the mixture to simmer for 10 minutes or until any liquid has disappeared. Remove from the heat and set aside.

4. Meanwhile, prepare the cauliflower rice per the bag's instructions and add salt and pepper to taste. Then dice your preferred toppings.

5. To assemble the bowls: Place the cauliflower rice in the bottom of a sealable food container. Layer with the chicken mixture. Top with toppings of your choice. Seal and place in the refrigerator for up to 3 days.

PER SERVING: 485 calories, 5g net carbs, 7g total carbs, 2g fiber, 3g sugars, 5.4g fat, 106.4g protein

KETO POKE-ISH BOWL

Makes 2 servings

This keto-friendly version of the trendy Hawaiian dish does not use raw fish, which may not store well in your refrigerator. Instead, it uses cooked salmon or tuna. Canned fish also works.

1 tablespoon rice wine vinegar

2 tablespoon sesame oil

1 teaspoon fish sauce

Salt and pepper, to taste

2 cups cooked Broccoli Rice (page 139)

1 English cucumber, peeled and chopped

1 celery stalk, chopped

1 cup sliced snow peas

2 radishes, sliced

1 carrot, peeled and shredded

1 cup watercress or other greens

2 cups cooked salmon, such as leftover Fish Baked in Coconut Milk (page 11), cut or flaked into bite-size pieces

OPTIONAL: 2 tablespoons chopped cilantro, parsley, or dill

1. In a small bowl, whisk together the vinegar, oil, fish sauce, salt, and pepper. Set the dressing aside.

2. To assemble the bowls: Divide the broccoli rice between two dishes. Layer the cucumber, celery, snow peas, radishes, carrots, and watercress, dividing between the two dishes as well.

3. Drizzle the dressing over the contents of both dishes.

4. Divide the fish between the two dishes, placing it directly on top of the dressed vegetables.

5. Sprinkle the herbs, if using, over the top of each dish before serving.

PER SERVING (without optional ingredients): 272 calories, 4.5g net carbs, 10g total carbs, 5.5g fiber, 4g sugars, 14.1g fat, 26.1 protein

ITALIAN SAUSAGE BOWL

Makes 2 servings

This salad is based on the popular Italian sausage, onion, and pepper sandwich. This yummy salad offers up that delicious, familiar taste we love in a low-carb, keto-friendly bowl.

1 small sweet onion, such as Walla Walla or Vidalia, roughly chopped

1 red, green, or orange bell pepper, roughly chopped

OPTIONAL: ¼ teaspoon dried basil

OPTIONAL: ¼ teaspoon dried oregano

3 tablespoons extra-virgin olive oil, divided

Salt and pepper, to taste

½ pound Italian sausage links, sweet or hot, sliced into coins

1 garlic clove, minced

2 tablespoons red wine vinegar

1 head romaine lettuce, roughly chopped

1. Preheat the oven to 375°F and set out a large rimmed baking pan.

2. In a large bowl, toss the onions, peppers, and herbs, if using, with 1 tablespoon of the olive oil, and salt and pepper to taste. Transfer the mixture to the baking pan. Add the sausage pieces.

3. Bake for 15 minutes or until the sausage is browned and the vegetables are soft and beginning to caramelize. Remove from the oven, pour off the drippings (reserve them to be used for the dressing), and set aside the vegetables and sausage.

4. Add the garlic, salt and pepper to taste, the remaining 2 tablespoons of olive oil, red wine vinegar, and the drippings from the baking pan to a blender, and process until smooth.

5. If packing the salad, divide the salad dressing between two lunch containers, pouring half the dressing into the bottom of each container.

6. Place the roasted sausage and vegetables in the containers, on top of the salad dressing.

7. Add the lettuce, dividing between the 2 containers.

8. Seal immediately and store in the refrigerator.

9. Before eating, shake the container gently to distribute the dressing.

PER SERVING (made with green bell pepper): 509 calories, 5.6g net carbs, 10.4g total carbs, 4.8g fiber, 3g sugars, 52g fat, 22g protein

TEX-MEX BOWL

Makes 1 serving

Bowls continue to be popular for lunch, dinner—and even breakfast! They are a great way to use up small portions of ingredients, like those few avocado slivers, and the baggie of cubed chicken breasts. Double this recipe (or triple it) to serve more people.

1 cup chopped romaine lettuce, spring mix greens, iceberg, or baby spinach

1 cup dark meat chicken, roughly chopped (or diced cooked steak, pork chops, brisket, etc.)

¼ Hass avocado, cubed

¼ cup shredded cheese of your choice

¼ cup chopped cucumber, radish, celery, or another low-carb veggie—see tip, page 140 for a list

½ tablespoon vinegar of your choice (balsamic, apple cider, red wine, etc.)

1 tablespoon avocado oil or extra-virgin olive oil

Salt and pepper, to taste

1. In a large sealable food container or serving bowl, add lettuce, chicken, avocado, cheese, and cucumber. Set aside.

2. In a small bowl, whisk together vinegar, oil, and salt and pepper.

3. Drizzle the dressing over the contents of the container or bowl. Toss to combine and serve. If packing the bowl, store the salad and dressing separately.

PER SERVING (made with dark meat chicken, cheddar cheese, and cucumber): 317 calories, 3.8g net carbs, 4.6g total carbs, 0.8g fiber, 1.6g total sugars, 22.5g fat, 26.8g protein

PORTOBELLO STEAK

Makes 2 servings

This meaty mushroom makes for a great plant-based entrée that's delicious, too. Many recipes for portobello steaks are grilled, but this one is baked in the oven.

2 tablespoons soy sauce

1 tablespoon balsamic vinegar

½ teaspoon minced garlic

¼ teaspoon black pepper

½ tablespoon extra-virgin olive oil

2 large portobello mushrooms, stems removed

1. Preheat the oven to 400°F.

2. In a 9×11-inch glass baking dish, combine the soy sauce, vinegar, garlic, pepper, and olive oil.

3. Massage sauce into the top and bottom of the mushroom caps and place stem-side down in the baking dish with the remaining sauce. Allow the mushroom caps to marinate for about 20 minutes.

4. After 20 minutes, place the pan in the oven and bake for about 12 minutes. Turn the mushrooms over and spoon any sauce over the new "top side" of the mushroom cap.

5. Continue baking for another 10 minutes, or until mushrooms are fork-tender.

6. Remove the baking dish from the oven. Allow the mushrooms to rest for 5 minutes before slicing and serving.

PER SERVING: 70 calories, 4g net carbs, 5g total carbs, 1g fiber, 3g sugars, 4g fat, 3g protein

KETO ITALIANO LASAGNA

Makes 4 servings

This alternative lasagna uses kale leaves instead of sheets of pasta. If you can't eat kale—or just don't like it—you can use chard (just reduce the cooking time by half).

---

1 tablespoon extra-virgin olive oil

1 pound Italian sausage, sweet or hot, casings removed

3 cups Versatile Marinara Sauce (page 31), divided

1 tablespoon fresh basil, minced (or 1 teaspoon dried)

Salt and pepper, to taste

2 medium bunches of kale, stems and ribs removed, roughly chopped

¼ cup finely grated Parmesan cheese, divided

2 cups grated mozzarella cheese, divided

---

1. Preheat the oven to 375°F.

2. Prepare a 9×12-inch baking dish by rubbing it with olive oil. Set aside.

3. Place the oil in a large frying pan over medium-high heat. Add the sausage and cook until browned, breaking it up with a spoon.

4. Add the marinara sauce, basil, and salt and pepper to taste, and let simmer for about 20 minutes until slightly reduced.

5. While the sauce is cooking, place a large pot of salted water over high heat and bring to a vigorous boil. Add the kale and cook for 4 minutes, or just until bright and wilted. Be sure to not overcook.

6. Immediately drain the kale into a colander and allow cold water to run over the kale to stop the cooking process. Let the kale drain in the sink while you attend to the sauce. (You want the kale as dry as possible. If it still seems wet when you are ready to cook with it, lay it on paper towels to absorb excess water, or run it through a salad spinner.)

7. In the baking dish, layer half of the kale, half of the sauce, half of the Parmesan, and half of the mozzarella.

8. Repeat with another layer of the remaining kale, sauce, Parmesan, and mozzarella. Cover the dish with foil and bake for about 15 minutes, then remove the foil and bake for another 20 minutes, or until the casserole is bubbling and the cheese is starting to brown.

9. Let the lasagna sit for about 10 minutes before serving.

PER SERVING: 574 calories, 5.2g net carbs, 10.5g total carbs, 5.3g fiber, 3g sugars, 41.4g fat, 33.5g protein

STUFFED SALMON

Makes 4 servings

Salmon is a keto-eater's dream food because it has healthy fats such as omega-3 fatty acids, and it's packed with protein. Here, salmon is stuffed with a creamy, low-carb mixture in a simple fish dish you're sure to love.

4 skinless salmon fillets (frozen and thawed is fine)

Salt and pepper, to taste

2 tablespoons extra-virgin olive oil, divided

3 tablespoons lemon juice, divided

½ cup cooked and chopped spinach, chard, or escarole

4 ounces cream cheese at room temperature (do not used whipped cream cheese)

¼ cup finely grated Parmesan or Parmesan-Reggiano cheese

2 tablespoons butter, divided

4 teaspoons minced garlic, divided

1. Preheat the oven to 350°F. Grease a shallow baking pan and set aside.

2. Place each salmon fillet on a flat surface. In a small bowl, whisk together salt, pepper, 1 tablespoon of the olive oil, and 2 tablespoons of the lemon juice. Drizzle the mixture on the tops and bottoms of the salmon fillets.

3. Cut a ¾-inch-deep pocket along the side of each fillet, being careful not to slice all the way through. Set aside.

4. Over a bowl or sink, squeeze out any excess liquid from the spinach or chard before adding it to a medium-sized bowl. Add the cream cheese, Parmesan cheese, 2 teaspoons of the minced garlic, and salt and pepper. Stir to combine.

5. Insert 1–2 tablespoons of the cheese filling into each of the salmon pockets. You can use the back of a spoon or an offset spatula to spread the mixture evenly.

6. Carefully place the stuffed salmon fillets into the greased pan.

7. Bake for 10–12 minutes or until salmon is opaque and can be flaked easily with a fork. Remove from the oven and set aside to make the pan sauce.

8. Add butter, garlic, and the remaining lemon juice to a small sauté pan over medium-high heat. Sauté for about 20 seconds until the garlic becomes fragrant. Remove the pan from the stovetop and drizzle the sauce over stuffed salmon fillets before serving.

PER SERVING (using spinach, Parmesan, and pan sauce): 435 calories, 2g net carbs, 2.1g total carbs, 0.1g fiber, 0.1g sugars, 24g fat, 41g protein

STIR-FRIED BEEF

Makes 4 servings

One thing that many low-carb eaters miss most is Chinese food. While this stir-fried beef dish is not completely authentic, it is incredibly delicious. Serve it with riced cauliflower or broccoli.

1 pound sirloin steak

2 cups broccoli florets, or another green vegetable, such as chopped bok choy, cabbage, snow peas, snap peas, or long beans

1 poblano pepper or two jalapeño peppers

2 tablespoons sesame oil

1 onion, cut in half and sliced

¼ cup soy sauce

¼ cup rice wine vinegar

2 tablespoons honey

1 clove garlic, minced

½ tablespoon minced fresh ginger

OPTIONAL: 1 or 2 teaspoons sriracha hot sauce or Asian chili paste

1. Slice the steak across the grain into thin strips. Then slice the strips into bite-sized pieces. Set aside.

2. Cut the broccoli, or whatever veggie you use, into bite-sized pieces. Set aside.

3. Remove the stem and seeds from the poblano or jalapeño, and slice into very thin ribbons. Set aside.

4. Add sesame oil to a large skillet over high heat. Add the steak, and cook until browned, stirring occasionally, about 3 minutes.

5. Add the broccoli, peppers, and onion to the pan with the beef. Cook the veggies for about 5 minutes or until tender-crisp, stirring often.

6. In a medium-sized bowl, whisk together the soy sauce, rice wine vinegar, honey, garlic, ginger, and hot sauce, if using. Pour the sauce into the pan and stir to coat the beef and vegetables. Cook for an additional 3 minutes, stirring often.

7. Remove the pan from the heat and serve the stir-fry immediately.

PER SERVING: 355 calories, 8g net carbs, 14g total carbs, 6g fiber, 11g sugars, 14g fat, 37g protein

TIP: If you can find it, bison steak makes a nice substitution for beef. You could even use pork or dark meat chicken, if preferred.

CAULIFLOWER KETO STEAK

Makes 4 servings

Cauliflower steaks are all the rage right now—you've probably seen them on a menu, a recipe blog, or in a food magazine. If you've ever wondered if they are as easy to make as everyone says, here's your chance to find out. (Hint: Yes, dinner will be ready in a snap.)

1 large head cauliflower, sliced lengthwise through the core into 4 slabs, or "steaks"

¼ cup extra-virgin olive oil, avocado oil, coconut oil, or another high-quality oil

1 tablespoon fresh lemon juice

2 cloves garlic, minced

Salt and ground black pepper, to taste

OPTIONAL: Any other spice you'd like to use, such as cumin, basil, chili powder, curry powder, etc.

1. Preheat the oven to 400°F. Line a baking sheet with parchment paper or aluminum foil.

2. Place the cauliflower steaks on the prepared baking sheet.

3. In a large bowl, whisk together oil, lemon juice, garlic, salt, pepper, and any optional spices you'd like to use.

4. Brush or rub half of the oil mixture over the tops of the cauliflower steaks and place them in the oven. Set aside the remaining oil mixture for later use.

5. Roast the steaks in the oven for 12 minutes.

6. After 12 minutes, open the oven and carefully flip each steak. Brush the steak with the remaining oil mixture and roast for another 15 minutes, or until cauliflower steaks are golden and fork-tender.

7. Remove from the oven and serve as is or with your favorite topping or sauce.

PER SERVING (using extra-virgin olive oil and no spices): 154 calories, 1.4g net carbs, 6.3g total carbs, 4.9g fiber, 0.9g sugars, 14.4g fat, 3g protein

CHIMICHURRI SAUCE: Makes a little over a ½ cup. Combine ½ cup chopped parsley, 4 cloves chopped garlic, ⅓ cup extra-virgin olive oil, 1 teaspoon lemon zest, 1 teaspoon dried oregano, 1 teaspoon red pepper flakes, ¼ cup red wine vinegar, ½ teaspoon salt, and black pepper to taste in a food processor or blender. Pulse for 20 seconds, or until combined but not completely pureed. You want to be able to see bits of the individual ingredients. Serve at room temperature. Can be stored in an airtight container in the refrigerator for up to a week.

PER SERVING (2 tablespoons): 157 calories, 1.6 g net carbs, 2.2 total carbs, 0.6g fiber, 0.3g sugars, 17.9g fat, 0.5g protein

TIP: For something different, try replacing a ¼ cup of the parsley with ¼ cup cilantro or chives.

Watermelon Cooler, page 179

Keto Coffee

If you can't fathom starting your day without your cup of joe or need a mid-day pick-me-up, these recipes are for you.

· ·

KETO COFFEE LATTE

Makes 2 servings

Keto coffee—aka "bulletproof coffee"—is coffee that's been blended with fat. This lovely version can be made at home and warmed at the office for a late-morning or early-afternoon treat.

2 cups warm coffee of your choice, brewed as you normally would brew your coffee

2 tablespoons unsalted butter, preferably grass-fed

2 tablespoons organic coconut oil

OPTIONAL: 1 or more tablespoons coconut cream or heavy whipping cream

OPTIONAL: 1 teaspoon vanilla extract

Add all ingredients to a blender. Process until smooth and frothy.

PER SERVING (made with 1 tablespoon coconut cream): 248 calories, 4g net carbs, 4g total carbs, 0g fiber, 3.9g sugars, 26.4g fat, 0.5g protein

ICED KETO COFFEE

Makes 2 servings

This strong iced java drink is made keto-friendly with the addition of coconut oil and coconut cream.

12 ounces coffee of your choice, cooled

2 tablespoons organic coconut oil

2 tablespoons coconut cream or whipping cream

Add all ingredients to a blender. Process until smooth and frothy.

PER SERVING (made with whipping cream): 180 calories, 0.4g net carbs, 0.4g total carbs, 0g fiber, 0g sugars, 19.4g fat, 1.6g protein

COCONUT COFFEE SHAKE

Makes 1 serving

This scrumptious shake takes all the good fat of a traditional milkshake, adds a jolt of coffee, and omits the sugary carbs. Enjoy!

6 ounces of cold black coffee

½ cup of full-fat canned coconut milk or coconut cream

¼ medium avocado

1 tablespoon coconut oil

OPTIONAL: Stevia to taste

Place all ingredients in a blender and process until smooth. If you prefer a thinner shake, add a few tablespoons of cold water or additional coffee.

PER SERVING (made with full-fat coconut milk and without optional sweetener): 342 calories, 3.2g net carbs, 3.2g total carbs, 0g fiber, 0g sugars, 37.7g fat, 2.5g protein

BULLETPROOF COFFEE DROPS

Makes 9 drops

These handy fat drops can be kept in your refrigerator and added to hot coffee, hot tea, or hot chocolate—or even tossed into a blender when making a smoothie. Plus, they can turn almost anything into a fat bomb!

½ cup ghee

1 cup organic coconut oil, melted

½ teaspoon cinnamon powder

¼ teaspoon sea salt

1. Combine all ingredients.

2. Whisk and pour into 9 ice-cube tray depressions, filling them to the top (or fill all 12 depressions in a standard ice-cube tray partway). Place the tray in the freezer.

3. Once the drops have set, pop the drops from the tray into a glass container and cover. Store in the refrigerator until you are ready to use.

PER SERVING: 309 calories, 0.1g net carbs, 0.2g total carbs, 0.1g fiber, 0g sugars, 35.5g fat, 2.8g protein

TIP: To make bulletproof coffee: Place one of the cubes and 10 ounces of hot coffee of your choice in a blender. Blend until well combined and foamy.

KETO COCOA

Makes 1 serving

For most people, their cocoa fix comes from an envelope. You can do so much better by whipping this up at home.

1 cup coconut milk

1 ounce unsalted butter, preferably grass-fed

½ tablespoon coconut oil

1 tablespoon cocoa powder

¼ teaspoon vanilla extract

OPTIONAL: Liquid stevia, to taste

1. In a small pot over medium heat, warm the coconut milk, butter, and coconut oil until the mixture begins to simmer.

2. Pour the liquid into a blender, and add the cocoa powder and vanilla extract. Process until blended and frothy.

3. Add stevia, if using, to taste.

PER SERVING: 800 calories, 5g net carbs, 12g total carbs, 7g fiber, 7g sugars, 80g fat, 6.8g protein

What Is Ghee and How to Make it

Ghee is clarified butter that has been relieved of its milk solids and water. To make, melt 1 pound of unsalted organic butter in a small saucepan over medium heat. Once melted, reduce the heat to medium-low and simmer for about 10–12 minutes. Remove the pan from the heat. Remove the foam on the top. Return the pan to the heat and simmer again. The butter will be golden, more foam will appear, and dark milk solids at the bottom of the pan may develop. After 10-12 minutes, remove the foam, turn off the heat, and cool for 3 minutes. Pour the butter through a fine sieve or strainer into a clean glass jar with a tightly fitting lid. Store at room temperature for up to 1 month or in the refrigerator for up to 3 months.

FATTY CHAI LATTE

Makes 2 servings

Chai latte is one of my favorite warm drinks. This version uses a blend of spices for a homemade treat. Yum!

½ teaspoon ground cinnamon

¼ teaspoon powdered ginger (or 1 teaspoon freshly grated)

¼ teaspoon ground allspice

¼ teaspoon whole fennel seeds

¼ teaspoon ground nutmeg

¼ teaspoon ground cloves

4 white cardamom pods

2 teaspoons vanilla extract

2 black tea bags

½ tablespoon coconut oil

1 cup coconut milk

1. In a small pot over medium heat, add 2–3 cups of water. Add the cinnamon, ginger, allspice, fennel, nutmeg, cloves, cardamom, and vanilla extract. Heat until the water boils.

2. Turn heat to the low, add the tea bags, and allow them to steep for 10 minutes.

3. Remove the tea bags and strain the liquid. Return the liquid to the pot and whisk in the coconut oil and coconut milk.

PER SERVING: 321 calories, 4.5g net carbs, 8g total carbs, 3.5g fiber, 4g sugars, 33.1g fat, 2.8g protein

KETO COCOA SHAKE

Makes 2 servings

Smooth and creamy, this superfood smoothie will remind you
of a milkshake, but it's better, thanks to a host of protein-rich,
healthy fats.

1 tablespoon chia seeds

3 tablespoons water

1–1¼ cups full-fat coconut milk

½ small or medium avocado

1 tablespoon nut butter of
choice

1 tablespoon cocoa powder

1 tablespoon coconut oil

1. In a small bowl, combine the chia seeds and 3 tablespoons of water.
Soak for 10 minutes. You probably will have no remaining liquid at the
end of 10 minutes, but if you do, go ahead and use it.

2. Place the chia seeds (and any remaining liquid, if there happens to be
any) and all remaining ingredients in a blender and process until smooth.
Add water, if you'd like a thinner shake.

PER SERVING (made with 1 cup of coconut milk and half a
small avocado): 447 calories, 4.8g net carbs, 11g total carbs,
6.2g fiber, 4g sugars, 45.7g fat, 5.5g protein

ICED KETO TEA

Makes 2 servings

If you've never made your own iced tea before, give it a try. It's fun; it's economical; it's quick; it's easy—and making your own iced tea ensures that you can use whatever kind of tea you'd like.

2–4 bags black, green, or white tea

3 cups boiling water

2 tablespoons unsalted butter

2 tablespoons coconut oil

¼ cup coconut milk, coconut cream, or heavy cream

1. Place the tea bags in a pot or a heatproof bowl and pour the boiling water over them. Let the tea bags steep in the water for 2–4 minutes, depending on how strong you like your tea.

2. Remove the tea bags from the water.

3. Add the butter and coconut oil to the tea and whisk to blend.

4. Place the tea mixture in the fridge to cool.

5. Add the coconut milk to the cooled tea and serve.

PER SERVING (made with heavy cream): 180 calories, 0.4g net carbs, 0.4g total carbs, 0g fiber, 0g sugars, 19.4g fat, 1.6g protein

Keto-Friendly Herbal Teas

Herbal teas—iced or hot—are fantastic, healthy, soothing drinks. But if you're a keto-eater, beware: fruit-flavored teas and teas that include pieces of dried fruit or fruit peel can contain sneaky carbohydrates. If you love herbal tea, stick to leaf-based infusions, such as peppermint.

GREEN KETO LEMONADE

Makes 2 servings

This tart, refreshing cooler is popular with my crowd, who all love the refreshing taste of lemons. Substitute lime juice—or even the juice of Meyer lemons—if that's what you have.

Juice of 2 lemons

1 cup organic spinach

15 drops stevia extract, or to taste

1. Place all ingredients along with 2½ cups of water in a high-powered blender.

2. Process until completely blended.

PER SERVING: 10 calories, 2.6g net carbs, 3g total carbs, 0.4g fiber, 3g sugars, 0.1g fat, 0.5g protein

WATERMELON COOLER

Makes 4 servings

If you're one of the many keto-eaters who desperately miss fruit, this yummy cooler (pictured on page 168) is for you. It's made with low-carb watermelon and is super-refreshing.

1½ pounds seedless watermelon cubes

½ cup coconut water

Juice of 1 lime

Pinch sea salt

Add all ingredients to the blender and puree until smooth.

PER SERVING: 54 calories, 5g net carbs, 10g total carbs, 5g fiber, 9g sugars, 0.3g fat, 0.9g protein

TIP: Wash down a Cocoa-Coconut Ball (page 116) with this refreshing drink.

Separation Anxiety

One complaint keto-eaters often have about creamy drinks is that the fat often separates from the rest of the liquid. While this is not completely unavoidable, there are a few things you can do to keep the drink blended:

* Use frozen or cold ingredients when making drinks.
* Mix drinks using a high-powered blender, and puree the ingredients for at least 2 minutes.
* If you won't be enjoying your drink right away, store it in the refrigerator in a jar or similar container, and shake vigorously before enjoying.

BERRY CREAM SMOOTHIE

Makes 2 servings

This luscious smoothie is filling enough to be a meal, especially when enjoyed with a cup of soup or a salad.

- ½ cup frozen strawberries or raspberries
- ¼ cup frozen blackberries
- ½ cup plain whole-milk Greek yogurt

- 10 drops liquid stevia extract, or to taste
- 1 cup unsweetened coconut milk

Add all ingredients to the blender and puree until smooth.

PER SERVING: 465 calories, 6g net carbs, 20g total carbs, 14g fiber, 19g sugars, 28.9g fat, 33.4g protein

CHIA-BERRY FRESCA

Makes 2 servings

This refreshing cooler features low-carb raspberries and the healthy fat, fiber, and protein of chia seeds.

2 tablespoons chia seeds

¼ cup water

1¾ cups coconut water

¼ cups frozen raspberries

1 tablespoon lemon or lime juice

OPTIONAL: Liquid stevia, to taste

1. Soak the chia seeds in ¼ cup of water for 10 minutes. You probably will have no remaining liquid at the end of 10 minutes, but if you do, go ahead and use it.

2. Place the chia seeds (and any remaining liquid, if there happens to be any), coconut water, raspberries, and lemon juice in a blender and process until smooth.

3. Add liquid stevia, if using, to taste.

PER SERVING (made with lime juice): 108 calories, 5g net carbs, 12g total carbs, 7g fiber, 4g sugars, 4.8g fat, 4.3g protein

KETO MOCKTAIL

Makes 4 servings

When you're trying to stick to an eating plan, alcohol can be dangerous: One drink, and you may find your resolve weakening. I recommend avoiding alcoholic beverages and instead, whipping up a keto-friendly mocktail to enjoy.

1 liter cold water, flat or sparkling

¼ cup unsweetened cranberry, pomegranate, tart cherry, elderberry, or lingonberry juice

Juice of ½ lemon or lime

1 tablespoon minced mint leaves

OPTIONAL: Ice, crushed or cubed

OPTIONAL: Lime slices and mint sprigs, for garnish

1. In a large pitcher, add water, fruit juice, lemon or lime juice, and mint. Stir until combined.

2. If desired, place ice in 4 glasses. Pour mocktail over ice and serve with lime slices and mint sprigs, if desired.

PER SERVING (¼ cup, made with unsweetened cranberry juice): 60 calories, 10g net carbs, 10g total carbs, 0g fiber, 2.03g sugars, 0g fat, 0g protein

KETO GINGER DRINK

Makes 4 generous servings

Ginger is one of those gorgeously warming spices that just make you feel so good. It also helps with digestion and soothes upset tummies—in case you happen to be experiencing any of these symptoms with your new eating plan.

Juice of 1 lemon or lime

1 (2-inch) section of ginger, peeled

1 cup cold tap or flat water

1 liter cold sparkling water such as mineral water, seltzer, or soda water

1. To a blender, add the lemon or lime juice, ginger, and tap water. Process until smooth.

2. Pour the ginger mixture into a large pitcher. Add the seltzer and stir to combine.

3. To serve, pour the drink into glasses and enjoy.

PER SERVING (¾ cup): 6 calories, 1.4g net carbs, 1.5g total carbs, 0.1g fiber, 1.5g sugars, 0g fat, 0.1g protein

TIP: You can use 2 limes or lemons if you prefer a drink with an extra-tart punch.

INDEX

THE KETO KIT

DIET

THE KETO KIT

DIET

STEPHANIE PEDERSEN

STERLING
New York

STERLING
New York

An Imprint of Sterling Publishing Co., Inc.
1166 Avenue of the Americas
New York, NY 10036

This publication is intended for informational purposes only and is not intended to provide or replace conventional medical advice, treatment, or diagnosis or be a substitute to consulting with licensed medical or health-care providers. The publisher does not claim or guarantee any benefits, healing, cure, or any results in any respect and shall not be liable or responsible for any use or application of any content in this publication in any respect including without limitation any adverse effects, consequence, loss, or damage of any type resulting or arising from, directly or indirectly, any use or application of any content herein. Any trademarks are the property of their respective owners, are used for editorial purposes only, and the publisher makes no claim of ownership and shall acquire no right, title, or interest in such trademarks by virtue of this publication.

This publication is a component of the *The Keto Kit*
(ISBN: 978-1-4549-3507-0) and is not to be sold separately.

ISBN 978-1-4549-3509-4

For information about custom editions, special sales, and premium
and corporate purchases, please contact Sterling Special Sales
at 800-805-5489 or specialsales@sterlingpublishing.com.

Manufactured in Canada

2 4 6 8 10 9 7 5 3 1

sterlingpublishing.com

Cover design by David Ter-Avanesyan
Interior design by Christine Heun
Cover photography by Bill Milne

CHAPTER 1

THE HISTORY

There's no doubt that the keto diet can help people lose weight and feel better, but before we learn more about the benefits of keto, let's dive into the diet's fascinating backstory.

Known more formally as the "ketogenic diet," this fat-heavy, carb-shy eating plan was originally created in the 1920s as a therapeutic eating plan to help children with pediatric epilepsy. Anticonvulsant drugs would not be invented for another five decades, so researchers looked to food for help.

These researchers knew that if carbohydrates were removed from the diet, the body would be forced to find a new source of energy. The first energy source the body turns to is its own fat, and during this process the body creates *ketones* (read more about these on page 15). These ketones—paired with another chemical produced by the diet called decanoic acid—were beneficial to brain functioning and lessened the frequency and severity of seizures. With these results, researchers began to recommend the diet to people of all ages with tics and seizure disorders. In time, those on the diet noticed that they not only experienced fewer symptoms, but also easily lost weight—and maintained their weight loss.

It seems counterintuitive, doesn't it? Eat fat—lots of fat—and lose weight. But just how much fat are we talking about? The ketogenic plan encourages you to consume 3 or 4 grams of fat for every single gram of carbohydrate and protein you eat. This amounts to consuming about 75–80 percent of your daily calories as fat. This is why ingredients like bacon, butter, coconut cream, heavy cream, salmon, red meat, avocado, and liverwurst play such important roles in the diet.

So eat fat and lose weight. Seems like a sweet deal? But the diet is a bit more complicated than just adding a lot of fat to your daily meals. In order for your body to enter *ketosis* (the state you're seeking), you must also restrict carbs. A lot. The amount of carbohydrates—as well as fat and protein—you can have each day while on the diet depends on your current body fat levels, as well as your gender, age, and how much activity you generally engage in. We're going to talk more about all these factors in upcoming chapters.

This delicate balancing act may be one reason that the ketogenic diet did not immediately become popular within the health community. Another may simply be that, when the ketogenic diet was developed in the 1920s, the most popular "reducing plan" around was based on counting calories and decreasing fat in your diet. Typical weight loss plans at the time instructed dieters to consume a total of only 600 to 1,200 calories a day. Common low-calorie eating regimens included two apples and a cup of black tea for breakfast, a salad for lunch, and a small piece of fish and celery for dinner. As you can imagine, those adhering to that kind of eating plan were constantly, ravenously hungry.

As time passed, the American diet industry moved toward encouraging a balanced diet with a more vegetable-and-whole-grain–based way of eating. In the 1960s and 1970s, especially, "health food"—including whole-wheat breads and cereals—became an important element of standard weight loss diets. Specialized eating plans grew in popularity through the 1990s, when dieters were experimenting with macrobiotics, vegetarianism, veganism, pescatarianism, and raw foods—none of which included red meat or fatty dairy products. In fact, the no-fat movement of the 1980s was the antithesis of ketogenic eating—people were gorging themselves on carb-heavy meals, such as plain bagels, pasta with tomato sauce, skinless steamed chicken breasts, and salads made with oil-free dressings. By the 1990s, mainstream brands like Kellogg® and Nabisco® had joined the anti-fat movement, creating nonfat crackers, cookies, and snack foods. Incidentally, to make these fat-free foods palatable, companies began to use large amounts of high-carb sweeteners. Thus, people were consuming more carbohydrates than ever.

The upshot of consuming all these carbs? A significant uptick in diabetes, obesity, and metabolic syndrome, leading concerned doctors, nutritionists, scientists, and food journalists to begin exploring other diet alternatives. When one cardiologist, Robert Atkins, found himself overweight after eating a mainstream, carb-heavy diet, he decided to take an academic and scientific approach to his own strategy for losing weight.

In the 1960s, Atkins began reading research studies on weight loss. He decided to follow the carbohydrate-restrictive plan set forth by Dr. Alfred W. Pennington while conducting research at DuPont during World War II. Atkins followed the diet for a little longer than 100 days and lost 20 pounds. He went on to introduce this diet strategy to 65 patients, and all saw positive weight loss results. In 1972, Atkins published a best-selling book, *Dr. Atkins' Diet Revolution* (Bantam). His work sparked decades of research and debates about whether a low-carb and low-sugar diet was better than a diet low in fat and protein. In response to Atkins's diet, similar low-carb diets appeared, including South Beach, The Zone, and Sugar Busters! Diet.

Ketogenic Is the Word

Ketogenic comes from two words: *keto*, which refers to ketones, (chemical substances produced in the body when you burn fat for fuel, instead of glucose) and *genic*, which means producing. The simple science behind the keto diet, is this: Carbohydrates are used to produce energy in the body. When you drastically reduce the amount of carbs you eat, your body begins looking for other sources of energy to fuel its daily functions. In the absence of carbs, your body's own fat is one of its easiest go-to sources of energy. The process of burning the body's fat for fuel is called ketosis, and this process is the basis of the ketogenic diet plan. This way of eating encourages your body to draw on a new fuel source, causes fewer cravings and less hunger, and ultimately helps you shed excess weight. How long you choose to follow a keto eating plan is a personal decision:

A ketogenic diet can be used for several months (until all desired weight is lost or another health goal is reached), or it can be followed for life.

Next-generation diets—which are still popular today—include paleo, primal, Diet360, and Bulletproof. These whole-food plans feature generous amounts of protein, moderately high proportions of fats, moderately low (to quite low) carb counts, and no processed foods. Coming on the tail end of high-protein plans (such as Atkins and South Beach), the popularity of paleo et al. was further boosted by the "wheat belly," gluten-free, and "no grain" movements. These became some of the hottest eating styles in the 21st century. Our culture's growing interest in slow food, old-fashioned foods, and traditional ingredients, together with the trend to avoid processed and mass-produced foods, helped elevate paleo and similar diets to full-fledged diet fads. These diets created the fat-friendly eating environment that allowed mainstream dieters and influencers to embrace the ketogenic diet today.

CHAPTER 2

THE SCIENCE BEHIND THE KETO DIET

Over the course of a woman's lifetime, she will spend an average of six years dieting, according to 2016 research by UK supplements company Forza Supplements. The same research study noted that 26 percent of dieters fall off the wagon after a week. Thirty-one percent lapse after a month. Only 7 percent are still on the diet at the six-month mark. The diets these research subjects tried ranged from raw food to low-fat to veganism, and many other pop culture favorites, including Atkins and South Beach. Each of these diets focuses on consuming—or limiting—very specific foods, and features its own requirements, methodology, and even culture. And most also have their own set of scientific (or pseudoscientific) reasons for working.

In this chapter, we'll delve into the basic science behind the ketogenic diet and why it works.

As we learned in chapter 1, the keto diet encourages fat consumption and discourages the consumption of carbs. In addition, it requires you to count macros and measure ketones daily. As a result of these often-complicated tasks, a dedicated culture—complete with keto food and supplement companies, educational websites, blogs, apps, magazines, trade shows, and even clubs—has cropped up to help keto-eaters establish and maintain *ketosis*, the basis of the diet.

Keep in mind that while you're advised to consult your physician as a matter of course before beginning any weight loss regimen, it is crucial to speak to your medical expert before beginning the keto diet. If you are pregnant or have an underlying health condition, such as diabetes or bipolar depression, the keto diet, or at least the standard version, may not be for you.

With so much information online, including hundreds of keto-related blogs, it is tempting to skip this step or to rely on someone more accessible who knows about the diet, but who is not a medical expert. In the strongest terms, I urge you *not* to start the keto diet until you've met with a certified doctor.

KETOGENIC GLOSSARY

If you've poked around any keto websites or even listened to long-time keto followers talk about their diet, you've probably heard a few words or acronyms that are not familiar to you. Like other eating plans, the ketogenic diet has its own lingo. Here are some of the common terms you may come across as you begin your keto journey, and their definitions.

AS: An acronym for artificial sweetener.

Basal Metabolic Rate (BMR): The number of calories required to keep your body functioning at rest.

BBC: Bulletproof Coffee, aka "keto coffee." Developed and named by David Asprey, developer of bulletproof.com (a healthy living website).

Exogenous Ketones: Ketone supplements. These supplements are either synthetic or naturally derived and are common in the world of athletes and bodybuilders, as they enhance performance. When added to the diet, exogenous ketones are also found to help reduce symptoms for those with epilepsy, Alzheimer's, and Parkinson's. Though they are often marketed as a weight loss aid, there is little proof that they assist in rapid weight loss.

Fat Bomb: Small snack-sized bites that are high in fat. Fat bombs are meant for quick consumption to curb cravings, add a jolt of energy, or reach your daily required fat intake. *The Keto Kit Cookbook* has some outrageously delicious (and super easy) fat bombs in the snacks chapter.

Fat Fast: A restrictive eating plan in which you consume 80–90 percent of your calories from fat. Not recommended for every day, a fat fast is conducted over a two- to five-day period, and is used by experienced keto eaters when they hit a weight loss plateau.

Glucose: A type of sugar in the body. Most carbohydrates we eat are converted to glucose.

Glycogen: The stored form of glucose. When the body doesn't need to use glucose for energy, it stores glycogen in the liver and muscles.

HWC: A common abbreviation in the keto world for heavy whipping cream (or HC, for heavy cream), a common ingredient in keto cooking.

Keto Flu: A syndrome brought on as the body changes its energy source from carbohydrates to fats. Symptoms include fatigue, lethargy, and mild achiness. First-time keto eaters—and those circling back to the diet after falling off the ketogenic wagon—often experience the keto flu. Drinking a no-carb or low-carb electrolyte drink can often alleviate the symptoms.

Ketones: Chemical substances produced by the body when there is not enough insulin in the blood. FYI: There are always a small amount of ketones present in your blood, even on a mainstream, higher carb diet.

Ketosis: The process that occurs when you don't consume enough carbohydrates from food for your cells to burn for energy. As a result, your body begins to burn fat and create ketones. This is the goal of a keto diet.

LCHF: An acronym for low-carb, high-fat, as in a low-carb, high-fat diet.

Metabolic Syndrome: A constellation of symptoms and illnesses brought on by overconsumption of carbs, especially sugar. Among these conditions are obesity, type-2 diabetes, cardiovascular disease, lipid disorders, inflammation, and hypertension.

Medium-Chain Triglyceride (MCT): A type of fat, used by the brain, that is easily and quickly converted to ketones. Coconut oil is an example of an MCT.

Monounsaturated Fatty Acid (MUFA): An unsaturated fat known to support brain health and prevent heart disease. Monounsaturated fatty acids (such as omega-9, oleic acid) are found in avocados, olives, seeds, and nuts, especially macadamias. MUFAs are typically liquid at room temperature and become solid when refrigerated.

NSV: An acronym for non-scale victory, which refers to benefits from the keto diet, such as losing inches around your waist or any other targeted body part.

Paleo Diet: A whole-food eating plan, based on what early humans may have eaten. The paleo diet, also known as the caveman diet, is high in protein, contains a moderate amount of fat, and includes low amounts of carbs. The paleo eating plan does not include dairy products.

Polyunsaturated Fatty Acid (PUFA): An unsaturated type of fat. There are two types of PUFA's: Omega 6 fatty acids and Omega 3 fatty acids. Omega 6 fatty acids are often over-consumed in Western diets, and include corn oil, soy oil, canola oil, sunflower oil, and safflower oil. Excessive intake of omega-6 polyunsaturated fatty acids may increase the risk of several chronic diseases by promoting low-grade inflammation. Omega 3 fatty acids are thought to help lower blood cholesterol levels and triglyceride levels, they are known for reducing inflammation, and help support nervous system health. Omega 3 fatty acids include oils from fish, nuts, and seeds. To make sure you're not over-consuming Omega 6 fatty acids, aim for a 1 to 1 ration between Omega 6 and Omega 3 fatty acids; the average American diet contains 20 times more Omega 6 fatty acids than Omega 3 fatty acids.

Primal Diet: A high-fat diet, with moderate amounts of proteins and low amounts of carbohydrates. Similar to the paleo diet in that it calls for consumption of no processed foods. Unlike the paleo diet, however, it does allow the consumption of full-fat dairy products.

SAD: An acronym for the Standard American Diet, or the typical diet of most Americans. Processed foods and fast food predominate in the Standard American Diet.

Saturated Fats, or Saturated Fatty Acids (SFAs): Sources of fat that are solid at room temperature and are often found in animal products, including red meat, cream, butter, ghee, lard, tallow, and eggs. They are also found in some plant-based oils, such as coconut oil and palm oil.

SF: An acronym for sugar-free. Because sugar is a source of carbs, keto eaters try to eat sugar-free.

Triglycerides: Chemical compounds in the bloodstream that also comprise body fat. They are also known as "lipids."

Very Low Carb Ketogenic Diet (VLCKD): A variation of the keto diet that restricts net carbs (see page 7) to less than 20–35 grams a day. There is much confusion about this term, considering that many on a standard keto diet consume no more than 30 grams of carbs a day. The term is included in this glossary, however, so you'll know what it means, should you come across it.

WOE: An acronym for way of eating. This common phrase is used in reference to an individual's own unique way of "doing the keto thing."

WOL: An acronym for way of life.

Zero-Carb Diet: A meat-and-fat–based diet that contains extremely low amounts of net carbs. This fringe diet is not recommended: Eliminating carb-containing foods completely means restricting all plant foods from your diet. This way of eating deprives the body of fiber, as well as micronutrients, such as vitamins, phytonutrients, enzymes, and more. There is no proof that a zero-carb diet delivers more dramatic results than a low-carb diet.

MACROS: WHAT THEY ARE, AND WHY YOU SHOULD CARE

If you haven't come across the term *macro* yet, you will soon: It's an important word in the keto universe. It is short for "macronutrients," or the energy-producing components that include carbohydrates, protein, and fat.

Macronutrients are fuel. They are the nutrients your body needs—in large amounts—to produce the energy you need to live. If you were a car, macronutrients would be the gasoline that helps your motor run. Too many macros (at least too many carb-based macros) can lead to weight gain, which is one of the reasons ketogenic eaters carefully monitor their macros.

The ketogenic plan requires you to count macronutrients, unlike other diets that may only call for counting calories (or calories, fat grams, and perhaps sugar grams). But counting macros is more complex than simply counting how many grams of carbs, protein, and fat are in each food you consume. Instead, you must take into account the ratio of carb to fat to protein in each meal throughout the day.

Is your head spinning yet? The keto plan isn't the easiest diet to follow in the world, but it is doable, once you get the hang of it. And, luckily, learning how to "calculate your macros," is easier than high school algebra.

How to Calculate Your Macros

Calculating your macros involves figuring out how much of each macronutrient (and in what ratio) *you* should have. Your macros are an individualized component of the diet. If the math seems intimidating (I am raising my hand here), you may be tempted to skip this part of the keto diet. I did that for quite a while. When I was not seeing the results I wanted, I decided to learn how to calculate macros to take my keto plan to the next level. While some individuals choose to obsess over their ratios, I don't make myself crazy with mine. Instead, I use them as a guide because fueling my body with the right ratio of macronutrients made all the difference in my results.

As previously mentioned, ketogenic diets are high in fat, moderate in protein, and low in carbohydrates. Generally speaking, the macronutrient ratio falls within the following ranges:

- 60–75% of your diet is made up of fat (or even more). In *The Keto Kit*, daily food plans aim for 124–132 grams of fat.

- 15–30% of your diet comes from protein. In *The Keto Kit*, daily food plans aim for 80–89 grams of protein.

- 5–10% of your diet is derived from carbs. In *The Keto Kit*, daily food plans aim for 20–28 grams of net carbs.

If you're wondering how you'll ever figure out how to calculate your macros, you're not alone: Calculating macros is so daunting for some of us that we give up before we see results. Before you do the same, let me give you a simple formula, which you can use right now.

> **NOTE:** This formula does not take into account things like your height or gender. It's designed for someone who is overweight and somewhat active (walking a few blocks daily or going to the gym twice a week), and who wants to lose weight. Like many ketogenic macro tracking tools, it does not track calories.

THE MACRO FORMULAS

By using the eating plans I've provided in this book, you can lose weight in a steady way while gently reaching ketosis. You'll find these eating plans in chapter 7 (page 63). But if you're curious about your personal macros, you can figure them out by making the following calculations.

For healthy fat grams: Fat is an important part of the keto diet. There is no formula to find exactly how much fat you need to eat on a ketogenic diet. Instead, followers of the diet are encouraged to consume between 55 percent and 75 percent of their daily diet as fat. If you check out the daily menu plans in chapter 7 (page 63), you'll see we aimed for 119–134 grams of daily fat. A word to the wise: Make sure your fats are healthy fats, including those found in coconut, avocado, nut oils, salmon, high-quality dairy, and animal protein. Avoid cheap and processed fats, such as hydrogenated vegetable shortening, soybean oil, and corn oil. (See chapter 4, page 37, for a list of fats to avoid in your keto diet.)

For carb grams: If you've explored many keto websites, magazines, chat rooms and blogs, you've no doubt come across information on carbs. Specifically, how much of them you should eat each day. Numbers such as 20–30 grams per day are commonly cited, with athletic types needing more carb grams than more sedentary folks. (When you start a keto diet, you'll be more comfortable if your carb intake is a bit on the high side. As your body becomes more comfortable with lower amounts of carbs, you can inch down.) While there is no universal formula used to find your ideal daily carb intake, *The Keto Kit* aims to keep daily carb consumption in the 20–27-gram range. When we talk about carb intake, we're referring to net carbs, not total carbs. For more on this distinction, see page 14.

For protein grams: While there is no single hard-and-fast rule for how much protein you should consume while on a ketogenic diet, it's important not to skimp (or you'll be tired) or consume too much (which will kick you out of ketosis and can put you at risk for kidney stones). A general rule for a sedentary to moderately active woman is 0.6–1 gram of protein for every pound of lean muscle mass. (See below for how to determine that.) If you have 130 pounds of lean muscle mass, this can be figured as follows:

0.6 x 130 = 78 grams of daily protein

Calculating Your Body Fat Percentage, Body Mass Index, and Lean Body Mass

When following a keto diet plan, it helps (but is by no means mandatory) to know your body fat percentage, your body mass index, and your lean body mass. The first is the percentage of your body that is made up of fat—literally, the percentage of fat your body has. The second, is an easy tool used to assess a person's "body fatness," or level of overweightness. It is relatively easy to use and offers fast results. (And while it is a helpful screening tool for body fatness, it isn't precise enough to use as a diagnostic tool.) A person's BMI is calculated by dividing weight (in kilograms) by height (in meters squared): A "healthy weight for your height" BMI is 18.5 to 24.9. A person with a BMI lower than 18.5 is consider underweight, while those with BMI numbers from 24.5 to 29.9 are considered overweight. Individuals with BMI numbers 30 and above are considered obese. The third formula is the number of pounds that comprise your lean body mass—the content of the body (bones, ligaments, organs, muscle, skin) without the stored fat known as "body fat." Depending on the formula you end up using, these can all be used to calculate your macros.

Body Fat Percentage: Most women of average size or who are slightly overweight, have 25–30 percent body fat. A number of websites offer charts, artist's renderings, or actual photos of bodies at various body fat percentages. Looking at these images may be helpful to identify your body fat percentage.

For an estimate of your body fat percentage measure the circumference of your hips, thighs, calves, and wrists using a measuring tape. Make sure to take the measurement at the widest point of each body part. Then use the Covert Bailey Method formula to calculate an estimate.

Body Fat Percentage =
Hips + Thigh − 2 × Calf − Wrist

Though this formula provides a good estimate, the most accurate way to determine your body fat percentage is to have a doctor measure it.

Body Mass Index: There are several ways to calculate your body mass index. One of these is by taking your weight, in pounds, dividing that number by your height in inches squared, and then multiplying the result by 703. For example, someone who is 150 pounds and is 5-foot-6 (66 inches), would divide 150 by 66 squared (which is 4,356), and multiply by 703. Rounded off, this would be about 24.2. If you prefer working within the metric system, you can take weight in kilos and divide it by meters squared. Consult the "healthy weight for your height" BMI stated left to understand your results.

Lean Body Mass: This is the number of pounds in your body that are not fat—your fat-free pounds, if you will. Once you have calculated your body fat percentage you can figure out how much of your weight is fat. Simply multiply your weight by the decimal value of your body fat percentage. Then follow the formula BW (Body Weight) − BF (Body Fat) = LBM (Lean Body Mass). For example, for someone who weighs 160 pounds with a body fat percentage of 30, the formula would be 160 × .30 − 48 pounds of fat. For women, a healthy lean body mass is between 69 and 75 percent.

Regardless of how many macros you choose to consume, you'll need access to a nutritional index that can give you the amounts of fat, protein, and net carbohydrate in the foods you eat. There are pocket-sized nutrient indexes that you can carry with you. Plus, the information is available online, or in many apps. Two online sources that I like are:

* https://www.calorieking.com/foods/
* https://nutritiondata.self.com/ (especially for popular food items from national chain restaurants)

Net Carbs versus Total Carbs

When reviewing the nutrition panel for a packaged food, chances are you've seen an entry called "Total Carbohydrates." Sometimes, this item is labeled simply as "Carbohydrates." In the world of keto, these are not the carbs you count. The only carbs that matter to a keto eater are "net carbs." Measured in grams, net carbs are the total carbohydrates consumed, minus all carbs derived from fiber. The body does not digest fiber, but it is vital for cholesterol control and a healthy digestive tract. All nutrition labels list a food's total carb count. Unfortunately, however, most do not include a listing for net carbs. Luckily, there's an easy way to calculate a food's net carb count: Subtract the fiber grams from the total carb grams. For example, if a food has 20 grams of total carbs and 15 grams of fiber, your net carb total is 5 grams.

Let Your Computer and Phone Help You Calculate Your Macros

There are plenty of online resources to help calculate your macros on the keto diet. Here are some of my tips.

- **Use an online keto macro tracker.** A quick online search will uncover hundreds of keto websites that have macro trackers. These sites will ask you to answer some basic questions (gender, age, height, exercise level) before beginning. Then simply search for your food, and the online source will tally everything up for you and give you an answer. NOTE: These online macro trackers are much more accurate than calculating your macros by yourself. That said, I actually suggest starting out simply and doing the math "by hand" for a few weeks so you can ease into ketogenic eating. If you've been going along for a while on the ketogenic diet and won't be overwhelmed by diving deeper into the world of macros, sites that offer online tracking are:

* https://ketodietapp.com/Blog/page/KetoDiet-Buddy

* https://ketosummit.com/keto-calculator/

- **Install an app on your phone.** Having an app on your phone allows you to punch in numbers wherever you are dining—from the office cafeteria to a local health food restaurant—and get an answer *before* you put anything in your mouth. There are many keto apps available. One of my favorites is: KetoDiet, the original KetoDiet App, by Compumaster.

KETONES: WHAT THEY ARE, AND WHY YOU SHOULD CARE

Ketones, also known as "ketone bodies," are organic compounds produced by your liver as it breaks down fat for energy.

When drawing energy from carbs, your body uses insulin. Insulin, a hormone made by your pancreas, allows your body to produce energy from sugar (*glucose*). This comes from carbohydrates in the food you eat. Insulin also enables you to store this glucose (in the form of *glycogen*) in your muscles, fat cells, and liver to use later, when your body needs it. Without insulin, your body can't use or store glucose for energy. Instead, the glucose stays in your bloodstream. This is bad because too much sugar in the bloodstream can damage the blood vessels that supply blood to vital organs, increasing the risk of heart disease and stroke, and contributing to kidney disease, vision problems, and nerve disorders (see "Ketones and Diabetes," page 16).

However, when your body does not get enough carbs to make into energy, your body draws on stores of fat. Your liver turns this fat into ketones, a type of acid, and sends them into your bloodstream. Your muscles and other tissues then use these ketones as fuel. This is the premise of the ketogenic diet.

KETOSIS VERSUS KETOACIDOSIS

Ketosis is a good thing (unless you are diabetic; see "Ketones and Diabetes," page 16). Also known as "benign nutritional ketosis," ketosis is a sign that your body is burning fat for energy instead of burning carbohydrates.

Ketoacidosis, however, is a bad thing. To reach a state of ketoacidosis, insulin levels must be so low that the body can't regulate blood sugar and ketones in the blood. Without insulin, blood sugar rises to high levels and ketones, which are slightly acidic, build up in the blood. The combination of high blood sugar and high ketone levels can upset the normal pH balance in the blood and become dangerous. Ketoacidosis is extremely rare in those who do not have diabetes. But while ketoacidosis is most often associated with diabetics, it can also occur in connection with these out-of-the-ordinary circumstances:

- extended periods of starvation (a month or more)
- a day or more of constant vomiting and/or diarrhea
- prolonged intensive exercise
- alcoholic binges (known as alcoholic ketoacidosis)

How to Avoid Ketoacidosis

Ketoacidosis is extremely rare in those who do not have diabetes. However, you should know how to avoid it. If you are a keto eater who has experienced an illness that causes diarrhea and/or vomiting, or if you've participated in a vigorous athletic event (a 5K race or triathlon, or even a vigorous basketball game), or have gone on a bender, or haven't eaten in more than a day, you could be at increased risk of ketoacidosis. You can help keep this from happening by ensuring that you are taking in enough fluids, and by continuing to eat regular meals and snacks. If you are vomiting up whatever liquids and food you are consuming, contact your doctor immediately.

Ketones and Diabetes

For individuals with type-1 diabetes, having elevated ketones in the blood can cause diabetic ketoacidosis (DKA), a serious condition that can lead to a diabetic coma, and even death.

When a diabetic's cells don't get the glucose they need for energy, the body begins to burn fat for energy. This, in turn, can produce a buildup of ketones in the blood and urine that is too great for the body to excrete. That's because people with type-1 diabetes may not have enough insulin, which helps to metabolize ketones and helps the body excrete them through urination and by respiration.

In other words, for people with type-1 diabetes, who cannot easily flush these ketones from their bodies, ketosis can lead to an accumulation of acidic ketones in their bloodstream, a condition known as diabetic keto-acidosis (DKA). This buildup, in turn, creates an acidic pH in the blood, which can damage organs so severely that the person might fall into a coma. Ketoacidosis in diabetics is known specifically as diabetic ketoacidosis, and it develops rapidly, sometimes within 24 hours. According to an article in the September 2012 issue of the journal *Diabetes Management*, each year diabetic ketoacidosis is responsible for more than 130,000 admissions to the hospital, as well as 50,000 hospital days, in the United States. So home testing of ketones is crucial for diabetics.

In case you are wondering what this kind of testing looks like for people with diabetes, keep reading. Following we talk about the three ways ketosis is tested for at home. The urine and blood tests discussed are also used by diabetics to test for ketoacidosis.

If you are diabetic, you may be tempted to dive into a keto diet and rely on your home-testing kits to monitor for ketoacidosis. Please don't. Self-monitoring your blood glucose levels and your ketone levels is not a replacement for medical care. If you have diabetes, it is crucial for you to consult with your doctor or a knowledgeable dietitian before starting the ketogenic diet.

How Long Does It Take to Reach Ketosis?

The body can only store a two-day supply of glucose. This means it can take up to two days of consuming no more than 20 to 27 grams of net carbs for the body to start producing ketones and thus reach ketosis.

MONITORING YOUR KETONES

Some ketones are always present in the body, regardless of what you eat or how healthy you are. It is essential for keto-eaters to monitor their ketones every day to know whether they are burning carbs or fat for fuel. If your results show that you are burning carbohydrates, there are a variety of factors that contribute to this, besides the carboyhdrates you consume. For instance, lack of sleep, eating too often, stress, and dehydration can hinder your body's ability to reach a state of ketosis.

When ketosis occurs, water-soluble molecules, called ketones, are released. There are actually three forms of ketones: When in ketosis, acetoacetate is created first, followed by beta-hydroxybutyrate, and lastly, acetone. There are three ways to test your body's ketone levels: Breath, urine, and blood. Each has pros and cons, and each measures ketones in a slightly different way.

Breath: One of the cheapest, easiest, and cleanest ways to measure your ketones is by using a home ketone breathalyzer. These devices measure the acetone levels in your breath. Acetone is one of the components of ketones and a byproduct of ketosis. It naturally diffuses into your lungs so it can exit your body when you exhale. Ketonic breath tests allow you to learn the amount of the acetone ketone in your body in real time, and because they are portable and small, breathalyzers can be stashed in your bag to use whenever you'd like. Breath acetone is measured in parts per million (ppm); adults in ketosis have acetone levels from 4 ppm to 30 ppm.

Urine: Home keto urine tests use a chemical-covered dipstick that reacts with the ketone element acetoacetate. The deeper in color the dipstick turns, the more ketones are present in your urine. Measured in milligrams per deciliter (written as mg/dL), this is a measurement that indicates the amount of a particular substance (such as glucose) in a specific amount of blood. Readings of 10–20 mg/dL show smaller amounts of a substance (in this case, glucose) in blood, 20–50 mg/dL moderate amounts, and 50–90 mg/dL large amounts. While keto urine tests are relatively easy and inexpensive, they aren't completely accurate: They measure the ketones leaving your body, rather than the ketones that are in your body. Further, the results can be distorted if you've had something to drink—be it water, juice, coffee, or anything else—before taking the test.

Blood: Blood ketone testing measures your blood levels of beta-hydroxybutyrate (BHB), an element of ketones. Similar to the testing method that diabetics use to test their blood glucose levels, home blood ketone tests require you to prick your finger and squeeze a drop of blood onto a testing strip. While blood testing is more expensive than urine strips and breathalyzers, and not entirely comfortable, it is extremely reliable.

Did You Know?

* Measuring your ketones first thing in the morning, before eating, will give you the most accurate result. Why? Because you will not have consumed anything that will skew the results.

* Ketone levels drop after exercise.

* Ketone levels rise after consuming medium-chain fatty acids, such as coconut oil, because the body converts them into ketones quickly.

* Regardless of the type of testing method you are using, check your testing kit's expiration date. An expired kit can give you false results.

* How little—or how much—liquid you've consumed before the test can throw off the results. When you are dehydrated, you may get a false positive. When you have consumed liquid in the hour before taking a test, your result may be diluted.

* Regardless of the type of test you use, keep your testing kit tightly sealed in a dry place. Any moisture can give you a false reading.

CHAPTER 3

BENEFITS AND CHALLENGES

P eople derive a variety of benefits from the ketogenic diet. In the intro-
duction and in chapter 1, you learned how the keto diet was originally
developed to help reduce seizures and other symptoms in epileptics.
It was then adopted by others with seizure disorder and tic disorder to lessen
their symptoms. Along the way, researchers found that the diet helped alleviate
other brain-based conditions (such as Alzheimer's), as well as lowering the risk
of cancer, helping with weight loss, and even lowering blood cholesterol. In this
chapter, we will discuss the range of benefits you might experience while on
your keto journey, along with potential challenges that might arise.

WEIGHT LOSS

Weight loss is one of the biggest motivators of any diet. The ketogenic diet
helps facilitate rapid weight loss in several ways. At its most basic, the keto-
eating plan calls for eating healthy, non-processed foods. Although we are not
trained to think that high-fat foods are healthy, the foods consumed while on
the keto diet are made with non-processed, whole ingredients, which helps you
avoid the chemical ingredients found in many convenience foods and fast-food
meals.

The keto diet also requires you to pay close attention to details: For you
to reach ketosis, you must be willing to record what you've eaten, check your
macros, and make choices that will move you toward your goal. One false move
and you can be kicked out of ketosis. This alone keeps people "eating keto,"
because it's hard to justify a cheat meal or snack when you know you'll erase all
the hard work you've put in and the good choices you've made.

Following a low-carb, high-fat regimen also flushes out excess water in our
bodies. This water weight often makes us look puffy, soft, squishy, fat, and

bigger than we really are. One of the most interesting aspects of eating keto (at least in my opinion) is the absence of bloat. Lose the bloat and you quickly drop one or two clothing sizes. For more about water weight, see pages 26 and 39.

Lastly, there is the science of the diet. The keto diet works by using fat—both fat in food, and fat stored in your body—for fuel. As your metabolism eats through your body fat, you grow slimmer and weigh less.

The Case of the Disappearing Cravings

Many low-carb eaters talk enthusiastically about their vanished carb cravings. This common benefit of low-carb, high fat eating occurs because your body no longer burns glucose for fuel, meaning there are no spikes and dips of blood sugar levels. It is these blood sugar highs and lows that cause intense cravings for sugar and carboydrates. When burning fat for fuel, these blood sugar fluctuations don't exist, and neither do the cravings that come with them.

BRAIN-BASED DISORDERS

The ketogenic diet has been used for nearly 100 years as a therapeutic treatment for epilepsy. Recently, researchers have begun to investigate the therapeutic effects of a ketogenic diet in relation to other neurological disorders, such as Parkinson's disease, autism, Alzheimer's, depression, ALS, migraines, brain trauma, and stroke. It is believed that the keto diet helps lessen the symptoms of brain-based disorders and protects the brain from developing further symptoms.

As the body becomes more efficient in metabolizing fat, it also turns fat in the liver into ketones, which enter the bloodstream and supply energy to the brain. This is one way the diet helps protect and improve brain function. In a paper titled "The Ketogenic Diet as a Treatment Paradigm for Diverse Neurological Disorders," published in the April 9, 2012 issue of *Frontiers in Pharmacology*, researchers from the Department of Neurology at the University of Wisconsin and the Department of Clinical Neurosciences at the University of Calgary Faculty of Medicine examined data from a range of clinical studies on the keto diet's effects on 12 different brain-based conditions, from age-related dementia to autism. The data demonstrated that the keto diet improved every condition studied. While the researchers stated that more examination was needed to pinpoint precisely how the keto diet helps keep the brain healthy, they did believe the results demonstrate that metabolic shifts in what we eat, such as adopting a keto-eating plan, may lead to neuroprotective actions.

How Keto Helps Epilepsy: The Science

Epilepsy is a chronic neurological disorder, characterized by unprovoked seizures. During a seizure, the brain's neurons fire abnormally and excessively, which in turn causes any number of unusual (involuntary) behaviors, including lack of bodily control, slumping or crashing to the ground, or even brief periods where an individual seems to have lost consciousness. Epilepsy is the fourth most common neurological disorder and affects people of all ages. It can be genetic or caused by a brain injury, such as a trauma or a stroke.

The ancient Greeks used fasting as a remedy for epilepsy. This method continued to be practiced for hundreds of years until medications for epilepsy were developed in the 20th century. Additionally, it was observed that when epileptics broke their fasts with a carbohydrate-rich meal, seizures recurred. But when they broke their fasts with a meal high in fat, the seizures remained at bay. Doctors in the early 1920s, looking for an easy alternative to fasting that could help their pediatric epilepsy patients, offered a fat-heavy diet as a solution. These physicians hoped that this fat-fueled diet would be easier, and healthier, for their patients than going without food for prolonged periods. And the doctors were correct. Epilepsy Ontario, the epilepsy foundation of the province of Ontario in Canada, states that up to 60 percent of epileptic children who attempt a supervised ketogenic diet experience 50 percent or greater reduction in seizure frequency. Additionally, 40–50 percent of adults with a seizure disorder who try a supervised ketogenic diet experience a 50 percent or greater reduction in seizure frequency.

Scientists do not know all the reasons a high-fat diet helps reduce epilepsy symptoms. That said, researchers have identified a compound called beta-hydroxybutyrate (BHB), which is made in the liver during fat metabolism, that has anticonvulsive properties. More research is currently underway regarding the success of high-fat diets in treating epilepsy.

CARDIOVASCULAR DISORDERS

It seems as if is should not be so: Eat fat and help your heart. It was once thought that eating *saturated fat* left deposits of saturated fat in your bloodstream, leading to high blood cholesterol levels. Today, more and more medical experts point to an overabundance of carbs and sugar as the culprit for high cholesterol. While some believe that the keto diet raises cholesterol, other experts assert—and several studies have shown—that eating healthy fats lowers blood cholesterol or doesn't affect cholesterol levels one way or the other. Some of the most relevant research to compare low-fat and high-fat diets was from a 2006 study. In that study, published in a 2006 issue of *Archives of Internal Medicine*, researchers from Basel Institute for Clinical Epidemiology, University Hospital Basel, Switzerland, monitored the eating habits of about 450 adults for six months. Half of the group were assigned to a moderate-carb, low-fat diet and the other half of the group followed a low-carb, high-fat diet. Both groups lost weight, but the high-fat group experienced five times more weight loss than the low-fat group, plus improved HDL cholesterol and *triglyceride* numbers. This means that the Basel study. shows that a low-carb, high-fat diet is beneficial to the heart and helps address cardiovascular disorders.

METABOLIC SYNDROME

According to both the American Heart Association and the American College of Cardiology, as many as one in three people in the United States have *metabolic syndrome*, a condition characterized by excess weight, elevated blood cholesterol levels, and high blood sugar levels. In fact, you can be diagnosed with metabolic syndrome if you have three or more of the following:

- A waistline, measured across the belly, of 40 inches or more for men and 35 inches or more for women.

- A blood pressure of 130/85 mm Hg or higher or are taking blood pressure medications.

- A triglyceride level above 150 mg/dl.

- A fasting blood glucose (sugar) level greater than 100 mg/dl or are taking glucose-lowering medications.

- A high-density lipoprotein level (HDL) less than 40 mg/dl (men) or under 50 mg/dl (women).

If left untreated, metabolic syndrome can cause heart attacks or strokes. Fortunately, treatment isn't complicated: Regular exercise and weight loss (losing 5–10 percent of body weight can usually restore your body's ability to recognize insulin, reducing the chance that the syndrome will evolve into a more serious illness) and limiting carbohydrates to less than 50 percent of your daily calories. Studies are finding that the keto diet is perfect for helping to treat and reverse metabolic syndrome. One of these, a 2017 study conducted by researchers at Bethel University, in Minnesota, compared the health of three groups of adults diagnosed with metabolic syndrome. One group followed the ketogenic diet without exercise, a second group followed the Standard American Diet (SAD) and did not exercise, and a third group followed the Standard American Diet and did 30 minutes or more of exercise for three to five days per week.

The study revealed that those following the ketogenic diet without exercise were much more successful than the other groups at achieving weight loss, lowering body fat percentage, and decreasing blood glucose control in the long term. Even without exercise, the ketogenic diet produced more dramatic results than the *Standard American Diet* plus exercise.

What Is SAD?

The *Standard American Diet*—known in nutrition circles by its initials, SAD—is a diet that is rich in red meat, dairy products, processed and artificially sweetened foods, and salt, with minimal intake of fruits, vegetables, fish, legumes, and whole grains. Also referred to as the Western Pattern Diet, it is composed of about 50 percent carbohydrates, 15 percent protein, and 35 percent fat.

Metabolic Syndrome versus Metabolic Disorders: What's the Difference?

Metabolism is the process your body uses to get or make energy from the food you eat. There are chemicals in your digestive system that break down food into fuel. The body uses this fuel for everything from regenerating cells to running marathons. Some energy is used right away. However, if you consume more fuel than your body needs at the moment, your body stores that excess fuel in various areas of your body, including your liver, your muscles, and your body fat.

A metabolic disorder occurs when abnormal chemical reactions in your body disrupt this process. There are a number of different metabolic disorders, such as diabetes, Tay-Sachs disease, and cystinosis. A metabolic disorder can be a result of genetics or it may be caused by another disease or deficiency.

Metabolic syndrome, on the other hand, is a collection of risk factors that increase your chance of developing heart disease, stroke, and/or diabetes. The condition is also known as Syndrome X, insulin resistance syndrome, and dysmetabolic syndrome.

Many features of metabolic syndrome are associated with insulin resistance. *Insulin resistance* means that the body doesn't use insulin efficiently to lower glucose and triglyceride levels. Insulin resistance stems from a combination of genetic and lifestyle factors, such as diet, activity level, and perhaps interrupted sleep patterns, including sleep apnea.

KNOWLEDGE IS POWER: KETO CHALLENGES

If you are interested in the keto diet, the last thing I want to do is discourage you from trying it. But, as you've probably already surmised, the keto diet is not the easiest to follow. The philosophy behind the ketogenic diet may seem counterintuitive, tricky, and confusing. These are some of the most common challenges when starting the keto diet.

Dehydration

This will be one of the first symptoms you notice. Dehydration usually occurs after three or four days, when your body enters ketosis. Generally speaking, glycogen encourages the body to store water. (For every gram of glycogen stored in the body, three grams of water are also stored.) When you switch your energy source from glycogen to ketones, your body sheds its water stores. With this initial water weight drop, you might notice more frequent urination and less bloating. You may also experience a loss of electrolytes or important minerals. To prevent dehydration, drink at least a liter of water a day. To counteract potential mineral loss, talk to your doctor about taking a mineral supplement. To read more about lost water weight and for two easy mineral-replacing homemade electrolyte drinks, see chapter 4.

Constipation

Dehydration often causes constipation. Other elements of the keto diet can also lead to constipation, such as consuming fewer fruits and vegetables and the addition of high-fat dairy to your diet. Plus, dairy is notorious for causing digestive upset. Stay hydrated, move around each day by walking, stretching, or engaging in some other type of physical activity, and eat low-carb vegetables with each meal. In time, often within one week, your body will transition to the keto diet and become more regular.

Bad Breath

If you have a partner or an honest friend, he or she might point out the pungent change in your breath. "Keto breath," as it is affectionately called, is another one of the symptoms that occurs when your body switches from burning glycogen to burning fat. Described alternately as smelling like rotting apples, garbage mixed with nail polish remover, or pickled cabbage, you have only the ketones to blame. There is not much you can do about this symptom and still stay in ketosis. Continue to drink water throughout the day to dilute the odor, mask the smell with sugar-free mints or gum, and wait: When the body gets used to ketosis, bad breath often goes away. This usually takes a month.

Hair Loss

Not everyone experiences hair loss while on the keto diet, but it is common enough to warrant a mention. Keto-caused hair loss can be triggered by a lack of protein. Make sure to take the time to figure out how much protein you need so you do not end up coming up short. If you do not consume enough protein, within three months you will notice (temporary) hair loss.

Another, less-common, cause of keto hair loss can occur when calories dip lower than 1200 for an extended period of time (such as a month). Shedding occurs during hair's resting, non-growth phase, known as the tellogen phase. Known as tellogen effluvium, this type of hair loss is usually temporary; normal hair growth returns in 6 to 18 months of suitable calorie intake.

The Keto Flu

The *keto flu* is one of the most despised keto symptoms. This constellation of symptoms feels a bit like the flu virus, except, instead of being caused by a pathogen, it occurs when your body changes its energy source, often between the third and seventh day. Keto flu symptoms range from headaches and brain fog to perspiration, dizziness, nausea, stomachaches, irritability, diarrhea or constipation, lack of focus, slowed physical and mental response, fitful sleep, sugar cravings, heart palpitations, and muscle aches. The severity of symptoms varies from person to person: Some keto-eaters barely break a sweat, while others are laid up in bed for up to two weeks.

Keto flu is caused by several reactions happening at once: adapting to using fat instead of glycogen for energy, mineral imbalance, dehydration, and lack of micronutrients. There is also the very potent, and often overlooked, factor of carbohydrate withdrawal, a state that is talked about frequently in the keto community. A 2018 study, by University of Michigan researchers, looked at withdrawal symptoms of those who stopped eating refined, processed food (which is high in simple carbohydrates). The study, which was published in the December 2018 issue of *Appetite*, found that withdrawal symptoms among those who had stopped eating processed food were similar to symptoms experienced by those going through drug withdrawal.

The best way to deal with keto flu is to be prepared. Ease into carb restriction, drink one liter or more of water each day, take a multivitamin-mineral supplement, use pink Himalayan salt and bone broth to help balance electrolytes (more on this in chapter 4), eat keto-compliant foods high in the electrolyte potassium (including leafy-green veggies, salmon, nuts, avocados, and mushrooms), and be sure to get enough sleep.

Keto Dangers in the News

Like any popular diet—from veganism to raw food to paleo—ketogenic eating gets its share of bad press. In other words, be prepared to hear negative stories about the ketogenic diet on TV. Common "Don't Try Keto" themes that crop up in the media include:

* Keto-eaters are in danger of developing disordered eating.

* Keto-eaters don't get enough fruits and vegetables.

* The side effects of keto are unattractive.

* You're not meant to stay on the ketogenic diet long term. Just so you know: While many people "do keto" only until they've reached their goal weight, others stay on the diet for life because they like the way they feel when eating keto.

* No one knows what the long-term effects of the diet are.

You may be tempted to ignore media negativity outright, but I actually think the media is doing its readers a service: Keto eating is not a bad thing. It is just not for everyone, especially those who are not willing to put the work in to make sure they are eating in a healthful high-fat, low-carb way. Instead of being scared by news stories, view them as a powerful reminder to take the keto diet seriously so you can stay healthy while reaping the diet's many benefits.

CHAPTER 4

GENERAL GUIDELINES FOR KETO NEWBIES

B y now, you should understand what the keto diet is, how it works, the diet's benefits, and possible challenges to overcome. But if you are still wondering, "How should I do this keto thing?," you are not alone. The diet's complexity may seem overwhelming, but this chapter demystifies the diet by offering helpful snack suggestions and a comprehensive list of food groups and food items to avoid. You'll also discover how some nonfood factors—including sleep, exercise, hydration, and alcohol—can make or break your results.

14 KETO-SAFE SNACKS

There are so many great benefits of eating keto—from fast weight loss to regulating blood sugar to helping heal the nervous system. But there is at least one downside to the plan: finding convenient grab-and-go, keto-safe foods to enjoy when you're away from your own kitchen. Here are 14 of my favorite premade nibbles that you can pick up while you're on the run, toss in your tote to make sure you're covered, or stash in your office desk drawer.

1. Pitted salted manzanilla olives, such as Trader Joe's: Olives boast plenty of glorious, heart-healthy fats, taste amazing, and satisfy any errant salt craving. Pick up a few of these shelf-stable packs for on-the-go snacking. They fit beautifully in a workout bag or backpack. But remember to bring a plastic bag—five olives, or half the package, is a serving size!

SERVING SIZE **5 olives or about half of a 1.05-ounce package: Amount per serving: Calories 25, Total Fat 2.5g, Total Carbohydrate <1g, Dietary Fiber <1g, Total Sugars 0g, Protein 0g**

2. Organic string mozzarella cheese: This is a keto snack staple. Keep a supply of these in your cheese drawer for when hunger strikes.

> SERVING SIZE   1 stick (28g): Amount per serving: Calories 80, Total Fat 5g, Total Carbohydrate 0g, Dietary Fiber 0g, Total Sugars 0g, Protein 8g

3. 100% beef snack sticks, such as those made by the brand Chomps: If any of you secretly (or not so secretly) love Slim Jims, this is the snack for you. Unlike its Jimmy counterpart, Chomps beef snack sticks contain no mystery ingredients. The only ingredients in the snack stick are grass-fed beef, water, sea salt, lactic acid, celery juice, black pepper, red pepper, garlic salt, coriander, and beef casings—that's it.

> SERVING SIZE   1 stick (32g): Amount per serving: Calories 100, Total Fat 6g, Total Carbohydrate 0g, Dietary Fiber 0g, Total Sugars 0g, Protein 9g

4. Oven-baked cheese chips (or bites): Look for brands that contain only cheese. These dairy-heavy snacks are a high-fat keto-eater's dream!

> SERVING SIZE   30g: Amount per serving: Calories 170, Total Fat 12g Total Carbohydrate 0g, Dietary Fiber 0g, Total Sugars 0g, Protein 15g

5. Precooked uncured bacon: Where would a keto snack list be without bacon? Precooked bacon is perfect for snacking and requires no prep work.

> SERVING SIZE   3 (1–ounce) slices for a total of three ounces: Amount per serving: Calories 100, Total Fat 7g, Total Carbohydrate 0g, Dietary Fiber 0g, Total Sugars 0g, Protein 7g

6. Hard-boiled eggs: Don't have time to boil your own eggs? Most delis, grocery stores, and health food markets carry already-boiled (and in many cases, already-peeled) eggs. If you plan to do it yourself, though, check out the recipe in *The Keto Kit Cookbook* (page 2).

> SERVING SIZE   1 egg: Amount per serving: Calories 60, Total Fat 6g, Total Carbohydrate 0g, Dietary Fiber 0g, Total Sugars 0g, Protein 6g

7. Beef jerky: This savory snack is a great portable way to carry your beef with you, allowing you to enjoy it wherever, whenever.

> SERVING SIZE 1 ounce: Amount per serving: Calories 70, Total Fat 8g, Total Carbohydrate 5g, Dietary Fiber 0g, Total Sugars 5g, Protein 11g

8. Turkey jerky: Because you can never have too much jerky!

> SERVING SIZE 1 ounce: Amount per serving: Calories 60, Total Fat 2g, Total Carbohydrate 6g, Dietary Fiber 0g, Total Sugars 5g, Protein 11g

9. Salmon jerky: And yet another great jerky option! Keeping a variety of jerkies in your pantry ensures that you will have endless options.

> SERVING SIZE 1 ounce: Amount per serving: Calories 80, Total Fat 2g, Total Carbohydrate 2g, Dietary Fiber 0g, Total Sugars 1g, Protein 13g

10. Meat bars, such as Epic bar: Meat, fruit, and nut bars, such as Epic bars, are a great choice as a savory high-fat snack. Be aware, however, that nutrition values, such as carbs, vary from bar to bar, so always check the labels.

> SERVING SIZE 1 chicken sriracha Epic bar: Amount per serving: Calories 100, Total Fat 4g, Total Carbohydrate 1g, Dietary Fiber 0g, Total Sugars 0g, Protein 15g

11. Roasted seaweed: Alkalizing and filled with important nutrients, such as vitamin E, vitamin K, calcium, phosphorus, and zinc, seaweed is fantastic for you.

> SERVING SIZE 3.5 ounce package: Amount per serving: Calories 60, Total Fat 4g, Total Carbohydrate 2g, Dietary Fiber 2g, Total Sugars 0g, Protein 2g

12. Seasoned kale chips: Sometimes you just want to crunch, which can be challenging on a keto eating plan. Kale chips, while a bit higher in carbs than many keto snacks, can be a nutritious, superfood choice.

> SERVING SIZE 1 cup: Amount per serving: Calories 150, Total Fat 11g, Total Carbohydrate 8g, Dietary Fiber 3g, Total Sugars 3g, Protein 6g

13. Roasted coconut chips: A bit carb-heavy, these are nonetheless a great, nutritious once-in-a-while way to satisfy a craving for sweets (which contain even greater amounts of carbohydrates!).

SERVING SIZE ¼ cup: Amount per serving: Calories 120, Total Fat 8g, Total Carbohydrate 9g, Dietary Fiber 2.5g, Total Sugars 6g, Protein 1g

14. Single-serving guacamole to-go: Avocados are an essential (and favorite) keto ingredient, rich in healthy fats and other nutrients. And while enjoying a whole avocado is always an option, you may want something a bit more fun and simple to carry. Single-serving, portable guacamole packs are easy to enjoy with a spoon or with your fave low-carb veggie, such as celery.

SERVING SIZE 2-ounce package: Amount per serving: Calories 100, Total Fat 9g, Total Carbohydrate 4g, Dietary Fiber 2g, Total Sugars 1g, Protein 1g

TIP: For a great list of keto foods you should keep in your kitchen, check out "Keto Food Staples" (page 47).

100 FOODS THAT ARE BEST TO AVOID

While I dislike the idea that any food is forbidden, even I must admit that there are many foods out there that just aren't worth their macros. Here is my own "stay away" list for any keto-eater.

NOTE: These are in no particular order. And also note that total carb grams are listed, not net carbs. For a complete nutritional picture, I suggest researching each of these foods and reviewing their total nutritional makeup, including both macronutrients and micronutrients.

	FOOD	SERVING	AVERAGE CARB
	GRAINS AND GRAIN-BASED FOODS		
1.	**WHEAT** (including wheat-related grains and foods, such as spelt, rye, semolina, farina, couscous, pasta, bread, etc.)	1 piece whole-wheat bread	14 grams
2.	**OATS** (including oat-related foods, such oatmeal, granola, etc.)	1 cup cooked oatmeal	26 grams
3.	**RICE** (white, brown, wild, and other varieties)	1 cup white rice	45 grams
4.	**CORN** (including corn-related foods, such as popcorn, tortilla chips, polenta, etc.)	1 ear corn on the cob	25 grams
5.	**MILLET**	1 cup cooked millet	146 grams
6.	**BARLEY**	1 cup cooked barley	135 grams
7.	**TEFF** (including teff-flour foods, such as injera)	½ cup cooked teff	25 grams
8.	**QUINOA**	½ cup cooked quinoa	20 grams
9.	**AMARANTH**	1 cup cooked amaranth	46 grams
10.	**BUCKWHEAT**	½ cup cooked buckwheat groats	20 grams
	BEANS AND OTHER LEGUMES		
11.	**BUTTER BEANS, BROAD BEANS, LIMAS, ETC.**	½ cup cooked lima beans	20 grams
12.	**KIDNEY BEANS, CANNELLINI BEANS, NAVY BEANS, PINK BEANS, PINTO BEANS, BLACK BEANS, BLACK-EYED PEAS, ETC.**	½ cup cooked pinto beans	22 grams
13.	**BROWN LENTILS, RED LENTILS, BLACK LENTILS, FRENCH LENTILS, ETC.**	½ cup cooked brown lentils	20 grams
14.	**GARBANZO BEANS** (also known as chickpeas)	½ cup cooked garbanzo beans	22.5 grams
15.	**MUNG BEANS**	½ cup cooked mung beans	19.3 grams
16.	**SPLIT GREEN** or yellow peas	½ cup cooked green split peas	21 grams

	FOOD	SERVING	AVERAGE CARB
	FRUIT		
17.	**APPLE**	1 medium apple	21 grams
18.	**APRICOT**	1 medium apricot	4 grams
19.	**BANANA**	1 medium banana	24 grams
20.	**CANTALOUPE**	1 cup	12 grams
21.	**CHERRIES**	1 cup	19 grams
22.	**FIGS**	1 medium fig	10 grams
23.	**GRAPES**	1 cup	26 grams
24.	**KIWI**	1 medium kiwi	10 grams
25.	**MANGO**	1 medium mango	35 grams
26.	**PAPAYA**	1 cup	14 grams
27.	**PEAR**	1 medium pear	22 grams
28.	**PEACHES**	1 medium apple	21 grams
29.	**PINEAPPLE**	1 cup	20 grams
30.	**PLUMS**	1 medium plum	8 grams
31.	**WATERMELON**	1 cup	12 grams

NOTE: It is best to avoid all fruit, dried fruit, and fruit juices, other than the ones listed on the Keto Food Staples list (page 48). This is a list of the worst and most popular offenders.

	DRIED FRUITS		
32.	**RAISINS**	¼ cup	33 grams
33.	**PRUNES**	5 prunes	32 grams
34.	**DATES**	5 dates	31 grams
35.	**DRIED FIGS**	5 dried figs	27 grams
	FRUIT JUICE		
36.	**APPLE JUICE**	8 ounces	28 grams
37.	**GRAPE JUICE**	8 ounces	37 grams
38.	**ORANGE JUICE**	8 ounces	27 grams

	FOOD	SERVING	AVERAGE CARB
VEGETABLES			
39.	**RUSSET POTATO** (sometimes known as Irish or baking potato)	1 medium potato	26 grams
40.	**SWEET POTATO**	1 medium-sized baked sweet potato	20 grams
41.	**PARSNIPS**	1 cup	24 grams
42.	**CARROTS**	1 cup	12 grams
43.	**PUMPKIN/WINTER SQUASH**	1 cup	16 grams
44.	**LEEKS**	1 cup	12 grams
45.	**JICAMA**	1 cup	58 grams
46.	**ONIONS**	1 cup	15 grams
47.	**BEETS**	1 cup	13 grams
48.	**GREEN PEAS**	½ cup	21 grams
49.	**CELERIAC**	1 cup	14 grams
50.	**JERUSALEM ARTICHOKE**	1 cup	26 grams
51.	**GARLIC**	1 clove	4 grams

TIP: With so many low-carb veggies to choose from (see page 48), there is no reason to overdo it on these high-carb varieties. If you choose to enjoy the vegetables on this list, enjoy them in moderation.

	FOOD	SERVING	AVERAGE CARB
VEGETABLE JUICE			
52.	**TOMATO JUICE**	8 ounces	10 grams
53.	**BEETROOT JUICE**	8 ounces	22 grams
54.	**VEGETABLE COCKTAIL** (such as V8®)	8 ounces	10 grams

TIP: It's hard to believe something as nutrient-dense as vegetable juice can be high in carbs, but, unfortunately, it is. My suggestion: Stick to the real deal!

	FOOD	SERVING	AVERAGE CARB
	SWEETENERS		
55.	**WHITE TABLE SUGAR** (cane sugar)	1 teaspoon	4 grams
56.	**RAW CANE SUGAR** (turbinado)	1 teaspoon	5 grams
57.	**BROWN SUGAR**	1 teaspoon	4.5 grams
58.	**MOLASSES**	1 tablespoon	15 grams
59.	**HONEY**	1 tablespoon	17 grams
60.	**AGAVE NECTAR**	1 tablespoon	16 grams
61.	**MAPLE SYRUP**	1 tablespoon	14 grams
62.	**CORN SYRUP**	1 tablespoon of light corn syrup	15 grams
63.	**BARLEY MALT SYRUP**	1 tablespoon	14 grams
64.	**BROWN RICE SYRUP**	1 tablespoon	15.5 grams

NOTE: It is best to avoid all sweeteners. Even low-carb sweeteners can increase your body's desire for calories and bring on cravings, making it more difficult to stick to your food plan. If you must use a sweetener, the ones most often used in the keto world are stevia, allulose (a natural chemical found in wheat, figs, and grapes), and erythritol (derived from fermented corn). Each of these sweeteners contains less than 0.5 grams of sugars per teaspoon. Stevia can be found in most supermarkets, allulose and erythritol can be purchased from online retailers and some health food stores.

	FOOD	SERVING	AVERAGE CARB
	CONDIMENTS		
65.	**KETCHUP**	1 tablespoon	5 grams
66.	**HONEY MUSTARD**	1 tablespoon	4 grams
67.	**BREAD AND BUTTER PICKLES**	3 pickle chips	4 grams
68.	**COCKTAIL SAUCE**	2 tablespoons	5.5 grams
69.	**JARRED SALSA**	2 tablespoons	4 grams
70.	**TARTAR SAUCE**	2 tablespoons	4 grams

NOTE: Condiments are often packed with hidden sugars, especially the ones on this list. Make sure you always consult the label or, to be safe, make the condiment yourself.

FOOD	SERVING	AVERAGE CARB
UNHEALTHY OILS AND FATS		
71. **CANOLA OIL**	1 tablespoon	0 grams
72. **SOYBEAN OIL**	1 tablespoon	0 grams
73. **VEGETABLE OIL**	1 tablespoon	0 grams
74. **SAFFLOWER OIL**	1 tablespoon	0 grams
75. **CORN OIL**	1 tablespoon	0 grams
76. **COTTONSEED OIL**	1 tablespoon	0 grams
77. **SUNFLOWER OIL**	1 tablespoon	0 grams
78. **HYDROGENATED VEGETABLE SHORTENING**	1 tablespoon	0 grams
79. **PARTIALLY-HYDROGENATED VEGETABLE SHORTENING**	1 tablespoon	0 grams

NOTE: Because keto eating is all about the fats, it's easy to assume that all fats are good. But that's just not true. I don't include carb counts on these items because these fats have no carbs. That said, these particular fats are thought to harm the heart. Try to avoid cooking with them, or consuming them in any form, if possible.

FOOD	SERVING	AVERAGE CARB
PACKAGED SNACK FOODS		
80. **CHIPS** (potato, corn, tortilla, snack mixes, etc.)	1 ounce	15 grams
81. **POPCORN**	2½ cups	20 grams
82. **COOKIES**	1 chocolate chip cookie	10 grams
83. **BARS** (granola bars, cereal bars, most protein bars)	1 crunchy granola bar	15 grams
84. **CANDY** (chocolate, gummy candies, hard candies, etc.)	1.55-ounce single-size milk chocolate bar	26 grams
85. **CRACKERS**	5 saltine crackers	11 grams

FOOD	SERVING	AVERAGE CARB
PACKAGED BREAKFAST FOODS		
86. **SWEETENED YOGURT**	6-ounce single-size low-fat, berry-flavored yogurt	33 grams
87. **BREAKFAST PASTRIES** (muffins, croissants, doughnuts, Danish, cinnamon rolls, toaster pastries, etc.)	1 old fashioned–style doughnut	29 grams
88. **BAGELS**	1 plain bagel	40 grams
89. **FRUIT SMOOTHIES**	8 ounces homemade smoothie, made with banana and strawberries	50 grams
90. **PACKAGED CEREAL**	1 cup bran and raisin cereal without milk	45 grams

NOTE: Breakfast can be a minefield for anyone who is trying to eat healthfully on the keto diet. The list of Packaged Breakfast Foods should be avoided outright, but if you're including packaged breakfast options in your keto plan, make sure to read labels and make smart choices.

FOOD	SERVING	AVERAGE CARB
PACKAGED CONVENIENCE FOODS		
91. **BOXED RICE OR GRAIN MIXES**	2½ ounces of prepared chicken-flavored rice pilaf	41 grams
92. **FROZEN OR BOXED PASTA SIDE DISHES**	½ of 7.25-ounce box of prepared macaroni and cheese	60 grams
93. **FROZEN DINNERS**	Single-size chicken potpie	420 grams
94. **CANNED SOUPS, STEWS, AND CHILIES**	1 cup of canned minestrone soup	19 grams

NOTE: Packaged convenience foods can make meal prep easier. But they also add large amounts of sodium, chemical ingredients, and carbs to your diet. Although some options might seem keto-friendly, it is best to avoid prepackaged foods, if possible.

	FOOD	SERVING	AVERAGE CARB
		SWEETS	
95.	**ICE CREAM AND FROZEN CONFECTIONS** (including ice cream sandwiches, popsicles, frozen fruit bars, etc.)	1 fudgesicle	19 grams
96.	**PUDDING CUPS**	3.25-ounce single-size chocolate pudding cup	20 grams
97.	**JELLO CUPS**	3.4-ounce single-size cherry-flavored gelatin cup	19 grams
98.	**APPLESAUCE** and other fruit sauce cups	4-ounce single-size unsweetened applesauce cup	13 grams
99.	**SNACK CAKES**	1 Devil Dog	21.5 grams
100.	**BAKED GOODS** (including pies, cakes, cobblers, brownies, cookies, etc.)	2 × 2-inch homemade brownie	35 grams

NOTE: Sugary foods—whether they're sweetened by sugarcane, agave, honey, or something else—are incredibly high in carbohydrates, making them a no-no for keto-eaters. Above are a few sweet foods to steer clear of.

STAYING HYDRATED ON THE KETO DIET

Hydration is a topic of much discussion in keto communities, probably because dehydration is one of the first symptoms you may notice when you go keto. If you've ever tried a low-carb diet before, you may have lost a large amount of weight—basically water weight—in the first week. On the first week of the keto diet, it isn't uncommon to lose up to 10 pounds. You probably also observed how often you were going to the bathroom.

When your body enters ketosis, it stops using glycogen, or stored carbs, for fuel. As a result, your body's carbohydrate stash dwindles as you begin to use fat instead for fuel, and you start to lose large amounts of water weight. That's because each gram of glycogen stored in the body helps the body hold on to 3–4 grams of water. As the glycogen stores diminish, so does the stored water trapped in your body. You can expect most of this excess water to exit the body while you're urinating, but you will also lose it during respiration.

Staying hydrated by drinking at least one liter of water a day helps ensure that you feel good and your body systems work efficiently. As long as you remain in ketosis, this consumed water will not be stored: You'll excrete it along with any other stored water.

With all this excreted water, you might experience a loss of electrolytes. The body needs electrolytes, which travel in our bodily fluids, for daily activity, including functioning of the nervous system and keeping your heart beating. To ensure that your electrolyte balance isn't disrupted on a keto diet, many keto-eaters drink a special electrolyte concoction, or a mixture of sea salt or (my fave) mineral-rich pink Himalayan salt and water (see below and left for a recipe).

Another reason hydration is so important on the ketogenic diet is that, for many people, the switch to a very low-carb diet often means giving up familiar fiber-filled food, such as oatmeal and fruit. With high amounts of fat and protein, and low amounts of fiber, keto-eaters often experience constipation. Drinking water can help make elimination more regular and comfortable.

Keto Electrolyte Drinks

You may be familiar with mainstream electrolyte drinks. Typically available in neon greens, reds, oranges, yellows, and blues—and sold in large plastic bottles—these are filled with a range of minerals that your body needs to replace after heavy sweating (or vomiting). For a keto-eater, these drinks present a problem: They are loaded with carbs. There are special keto-created electrolyte drinks on the market, which you may want to check out, but they are often expensive and difficult to find. Here are a couple of economical and convenient options to make your own electrolyte drink.

Salt Water
MAKES 1 SERVING

> 8 ounces of water
> ½ teaspoon pink Himalayan salt

1. Pour water into a glass and add salt. Stir vigorously until the salt dissolves. Drink.

Electrolyte Sipper

MAKES A LITTLE MORE THAN 1 LITER, TO BE SIPPED THROUGHOUT THE DAY

5 cups water

2 tablespoons lemon or lime juice

½ teaspoon potassium chloride or lite salt (which is a mixture of sodium and potassium chloride)

¼ teaspoon pink Himalayan salt

2 teaspoon powdered magnesium supplement (such as Natural Calm)

Granulated or liquid stevia, to taste (optional)

1. Pour water into a large pitcher or carafe.

2. Stir in the remaining ingredients until well combined. This does not need to be refrigerated if you drink it within an 8-hour period.

What Is an Electrolyte?

Electrolytes are minerals that form ions (molecules with electric charges) in solution; in the case of your body, these solutions are bodily fluids. Electrolytes carry an electric charge, and come in the form of sodium, potassium, magnesium, chloride, calcium, and phosphorus.

Electrolytes are crucial to keeping the body hydrated, as well as for nerve and muscle functioning. Simply put, without electrolytes, your nervous system would not work properly. They also help specific bodily functions to occur—and occur efficiently. Too few electrolytes can lead to a range of health issues, including fatigue, insomnia, numbness, headaches, digestive issues, and—more seriously—irregular hearbeat.

A WORD ABOUT ALCOHOL

Let's be frank: Alcohol is fun. At least I think it is. A glass of red wine with my husband as I sit on the sofa. A beer at a ball game. A glass of sangria at my favorite Spanish restaurant. I like it all. But . . . I am going to be honest: One drink and I am more likely to eat something that is not keto. You may have more willpower than I do, but I guarantee that after downing two or three drinks, you'll be more tempted to mindlessly stuff your face with a stray carb than you would if you had not had those drinks. And just like that, you've thrown yourself out of ketosis. This is one of the unseen dangers of drinking on a keto diet—and it's the reason I tell people to refrain from drinking when they're just starting out on the ketogenic plan.

Plus, it is important to understand the way that a keto-eater metabolizes alcohol. When you're in ketosis, your body uses your stored fat for energy. When you consume alcohol, your liver will default to using the by-products of the metabolized alcohol instead of the fat you want it to burn. This means the body's ability to create ketones slows down until all the alcohol in your system has been processed.

That said, there are a few alcoholic options that are safer than others—as long as you drink no more than one, and limit yourself to no more than one day a week. (So, yes, that's basically one drink a week.) Look for unsweetened liquors that are around 40 percent alcohol (vodka, whiskey, gin, scotch, brandy, rum, and tequila). These generally contain zero carbs and sugars when drunk neat, on the rocks, or mixed with water or seltzer. Any other mixers will add carbs to the drink.

One last thing about drinking while eating keto: You'll get drunk faster. Carbs slow down the metabolization of alcohol, so it takes longer for you to feel the effects of what you drink. Without dietary carbs, however, the effects of alcohol kick in quickly. So be prepared!

A WORD ABOUT CAFFEINE

You'll come across a lot of conflicting views on caffeine and the ketogenic diet. On the one hand, there is evidence that caffeine could disrupt the metabolism of glucose. This could knock you out of ketosis, according to the American Diabetes Association's magazine *Diabetes Care*.

On the other hand, some research suggests that drinking a cup or two of coffee a day (sans flavored syrup, caramel, or chocolate shavings) doesn't change the results of the keto diet. Some evidence holds that caffeine slightly speeds up the metabolism for faster fat burning.

With all this in mind, only you can make the ultimate decision on whether caffeine supports or prevents ketosis for you. Experiment with or without caffeine while on the diet, and if you find it difficult to reach or maintain ketosis, try switching things up in your daily caffeine routine.

SLEEP AND ITS ROLE IN KETO

I have some good news and some bad news: The ketogenic diet can reduce the need for sleep. In fact, you may have heard seasoned keto-eaters boast about how rested they feel on six hours of sleep. They aren't talking through their hat: This really does happen. A 2007 study on the sleep of epileptic children on the keto diet was published by the International League Against Epilepsy. This study found that while the ketogenic diet may decrease total time spent asleep (the average nighttime sleep before the diet was about 600 minutes; after 3 months on the diet, it was 546 minutes; and after 12 months on the diet, it had crept up to 573 minutes), it can improve the quality of one's sleep by increasing the amount of REM sleep you receive. REM stands for Rapid Eye Movement and it is characterized by rapid eye movements and dreaming. REM sleep is thought to be important not only for a healthy nervous system, but for memory and learning. It is during REM sleep that your brain processes the information you've come across during the day. The brain also forms neural connections, creates neurotransmitters, and makes mood-boosting dopamine and serotonin to be used during waking hours during this part of the sleep cycle. The average REM time (not the total sleep time, but the total REM time) before the diet was about 69 minutes; after 3 months on the diet, the total REM time was 97 minutes; and after 12 months on the diet, REM sleep had increased to 116 minutes. It isn't known exactly how or why a high-fat, low-carb diet produces these results, but it is something to look forward to once you reach ketosis.

But here's the bad news: As your body is transitioning from burning glycogen for fuel to burning fat for fuel in the early days of a high-fat, low-carb diet, there is a chance you'll experience insomnia. Carbohydrates promote the secretion of the sleep-enhancing amino acid L-tryptophan. L-tryptophan promotes the production of serotonin, which is a neurotransmitter known for calming the body and contributing to better sleep. Serotonin, in turn, is converted into melatonin, the sleep hormone.

The ketogenic diet, however, doesn't include many carbs, so the amount of L-tryptophan needed to induce rest isn't available, thus leading to lower serotonin and melatonin levels. So you may have trouble falling asleep, experience middle-of-the-night waking, and find yourself rising earlier than usual until your body has reached ketosis.

NOTE: If you've looked at *The Keto Kit Journal*, you'll see a section on tracking your sleep. Skimping on quality sleep can both hinder your ability to reach ketosis and kick you out of ketosis. Do you see the conundrum here? On the one hand, as a keto newcomer, your sleep will almost certainly be disrupted in the early days of keto eating, as your body transitions from burning glucose to burning fat for energy. On the other hand, once you reach ketosis and are "fat-adapted" (this is a fancy way of saying that your body has become accustomed to burning fat, not glucose, as energy, and has settled into a rhythm), your sleep cycles naturally change and you'll sleep slightly less each night (this amount varies depending on the individual), but more deeply. Make no mistake, however: Sleep remains vitally important once you reach ketosis. If you do not have a quality night's sleep, you can slip out of ketosis.

EXERCISE AND HOW IT AFFECTS YOUR RESULTS

When you exercise, your muscles use carbohydrates and glycogen (carbs that have been stored in your body tissue) as energy. Does that mean that you can't safely exercise while you're eating in a low-carb way?

Not exactly. However you now need to be a bit more intentional with both how you exercise, and what you eat before and after your workout. Before you begin to worry, let me break down the best exercise and energy options.

Aerobic or Cardio

These exercises generally last more than 3 minutes and can be high impact, such as running or jumping jacks, or low impact, such as walking, swimming, roller skating, or cycling. Daily low-impact aerobic exercise for as long as feels comfortable is ideal for keto-eaters and usually requires no adjustment in diet. This will differ from individual to individual; I, for example, can walk 2 or more hours comfortably, while some keto-eating friends tire after 20 minutes.

Anaerobic or Strength Training

Exercise that requires bursts of energy, including weight lifting with moderate to heavy weights, wind sprints, interval training, or any stop-and-start type of physical movements are considered anaerobic and promote speed, strength, power, and muscle mass. During anaerobic exercise, muscles rely on carbohydrates for fuel. If you plan to include anaerobic exercises into your workout routine, you can eat 15–25 grams of fast-acting carbs, such as fruit, within 20 minutes before and after your workout. This will give your muscles the carbs they need to perform their tasks, as well as the carbs they need to safely recover. Targeting this small amount of carbs directly before and after the workout allows the carbs to be used by your muscles, without kicking your body out of ketosis.

Flexibility Work

Yoga, general and targeted stretching, and Pilates are examples of movements that stretch muscles to keep them limber and allow you to maintain a healthy range of motion. Flexibility exercise also keeps joints healthy and prevents injuries. These are ideal for keto-eaters and usually require no adjustment in diet.

Stability or Core Work

Keeping your core strong helps your entire body function more efficiently. When you have a strong abdomen, hips, and glutes, you can stand straight without fatigue, providing your inner organs with plenty of room to function. A strong core also ensures that you are not overworking another part of the body: The classic example is someone with a weak core who experiences frequent back problems. Because his core is too weak to rely on, he overrelies on his back muscles to perform tasks like lifting. A strong core also helps prevent hip, back, shoulder, and neck pain, and preserves our balance as we age. Good examples of core exercises are planking, crunches, and push-ups. These are low-intensity exercises and don't require any changes in a keto diet.

STRESS VERSUS KETO

When your body is stressed, your adrenal glands create and distribute cortisol. Known as the fight-or-flight hormone, cortisol stimulates your sympathetic nervous system to release adrenaline and glycogen (that very thing a keto-eater is trying to avoid!). When these hormones are in your bloodstream, they provide your muscles with more energy to run from danger or, if need be, stand and fight whatever scary thing is in front of you. For a keto-eater, this is a particularly bad thing because when glycogen is released, you can be kicked out of ketosis.

We live in a stressful world. Stressed about losing your job? Angry over your commute? Frustrated by your children? Anxious about getting a report in on time? Your body perceives all stressors as physical obstacles, so any of these "everyday" triggers are "read" by your body in the same way as it would read the need to outrun an attacker or fight off a shark. Unfortunately, daily low-level stress means you have a constant stream of glycogen coursing through your bloodstream, making ketosis nearly impossible to reach and maintain.

If you want to reach and maintain ketosis, you must find a way to avoid or manage stress. Practicing meditation or yoga, avoiding toxic people, learning to "let things roll off your back," spending time in nature, exercising regularly, meeting with a therapist—these are just a sampling of stress-relieving tools you can use to maintain the daily calm needed for ketosis.

CHAPTER 5

OUTFITTING YOUR KETO KITCHEN

Most of us don't give much thought to what my grandmother used to call "setting up your kitchen." We have some plates and utensils, and various pots and pans. We buy food we like to eat. If we're trying a new recipe, we may purchase an ingredient we don't usually keep around. And we just keep on going.

But did you know that meal planning can be much easier if you have a foundational plan? It doesn't need to be complicated, but whether you're a keto-eater or not, being strategic about the food you have in your kitchen can make meal prep, lunch making, cooking, snacking—and anything else having to do with food—so much easier, faster, and less exhausting.

KETO FOOD STAPLES

Stocking your keto pantry is not difficult. Really! Just make sure you clean out your fridge and freezer to free up some room because many keto foods require refrigeration. Here's an easy beginner's keto shopping list.

POULTRY

* Chicken thighs
* Chicken breast
* Chicken, whole
* Turkey breast
* Turkey drumsticks
* Turkey, whole
* Other poultry, including duck, goose, grouse, pheasant, quail, etc.
* Eggs

SEAFOOD

* Salmon, steaks and filets
* Tuna, steaks and filets
* Bluefish
* White fishes
* Calamari (not breaded)
* Octopus
* Shrimp
* Shellfish
* Smoked fish (such as salmon, whitefish, and trout)

RED MEAT

* Ground beef, preferably 80% or 85% fat
* Flank steaks
* Sirloin
* Chuck roast
* Pork loin
* Pork chops
* Pork shoulder
* Pork butt
* Prosciutto
* Uncured bacon
* Sausage (Italian, Mexican chorizo, breakfast, kielbasa, bulk)
* Dried, cured sausage (such as Spanish chorizo, pepperoni, salami, etc.)
* Liverwurst
* Lamb chops
* Lamb roast
* Lamb shanks

DAIRY

* Heavy cream (also known as heavy whipping cream)
* Butter, unsalted or salted
* Ghee (A liquid butter from which the milk solids have been removed.)
* Cheese
* Cream cheese
* Whole-milk, unflavored yogurt, traditional or Greek

VEGETABLES (FRESH OR FROZEN)

* Asparagus
* Avocado
* Cabbage
* Cauliflower
* Celery
* Chili peppers, including jalapeño, poblano, and serrano
* Cucumber
* Eggplant
* Lettuce, any variety
* Spinach, baby and regular
* Spaghetti squash
* Summer squash, including crookneck, yellow, and zucchini
* Zucchini

FRUIT (FRESH OR FROZEN)

* Blackberries
* Cranberries
* Raspberries
* Fresh lemons
* Fresh limes

SNACKS

* Oil-cured olives (kalamata, niçoise, etc.)
* Jerky, including beef, venison, elk, bison, salmon, turkey, etc.
* Pork rinds
* Cheese chips

PANTRY STAPLES

* Almond flour
* Coconut flour
* Canned bone broth (chicken, beef, fish)
* Coconut milk (Look at the label and make sure not to buy a product that specified as "light," "lite," "low-calorie," or "reduced-fat." Instead, look for a label that states, "coconut milk", which will give you every drop of the coconut fat.)
* Coconut cream
* Extra-virgin olive oil
* Coconut oil
* Avocado oil
* Tuna packed in oil
* Salmon packed in oil
* Sardines
* Anchovies
* Herring
* Stevia, granulated or liquid
* Unsweetened, flaked coconut
* Coconut butter
* Cacao butter

SPICES

* Garlic powder
* Onion powder
* Spices of your choice
* Dried herbs of your choice
* Pink Himalayan salt

CONDIMENTS

* Hot sauce, such as Tabasco®
* Prepared mustard, such as yellow, brown, and whole-grain mustard (Note: Avoid "flavored" mustards, which have carbs and sugars. These include honey mustard, chipotle mustard, wasabi mustard, horseradish mustard, sriracha mustard, etc.)
* Mayonnaise (avoid reduced-fat mayonnaise)
* Dill pickles
* Capers

CONVENIENCE ITEMS

* Cauliflower rice
* Broccoli rice
* Cauliflower pizza crust
* Cauliflower mash
* Spiralized zucchini

Freezing Foods

A freezer packed with keto-compliant food means I can make a meal quickly. I also freeze uneaten portions of keto meals in individual-size serving containers for fast grab-and-go lunches. If you're unsure about how to freeze foods, here are a few tips:

* All meat, poultry, fish, and some dairy (like cheese), can be frozen. Though there are many ways to prepare food for freezing, I prefer the "double wrap" method: First, wrap individual portions of food in waxed paper or plastic freezer wrap. Then wrap the outer layer in heavy foil. Alternatively, you can place the item in a freezer-proof container and then wrap with an outer layer of foil, just to make sure everything remains airtight and fresh. Then place a piece of tape on the wrapped item and, with a permanent marker, write what is in the package, the date it was frozen, and the "use by" date, or about three months out.

* Most of the cooked meals in *The Keto Kit Cookbook* can be placed in freezer-proof containers and frozen—use your best judgement.

* There are many foods that you might not realize can be frozen. Some include shredded cheese, blocks of cheese, ripe avocado, and small amounts of canned sauce, condiments, coconut milk, whole milk, half-and-half, or whipping cream.

* To thaw previously frozen food, place it your refrigerator. Most items will thaw in 8 to 24 hours.

HOW TO READ A FOOD LABEL

One of the easiest ways to make sure you're eating well on a keto diet is to make your own food from whole ingredients. But, for most of us, that's easier said than done. We often need to opt for prepared foods here and there to augment what we make ourselves. But how can we choose foods that support our way of eating? Fortunately for readers in the United States, the federal Food and Drug Administration (FDA) requires food manufacturers to have a food and nutrition label prominently displayed on prepared foods. These labels list ingredients and also include the food's nutrition information per serving, such as calories, amount of carbohydrates, fat content, protein, fiber, sodium, and sugars.

Food labels are standardized, which means that they are set up according to a government-created template that includes the following data, in this order:

Serving Size: Located at the top of the panel, the serving size tells you how large (or small) a serving of that particular food happens to be. Serving sizes are standardized to make it easier to compare similar foods; they are provided in familiar imperial units, such as cups, ounces, or pieces, followed by the metric units, usually the number of grams.

Number of Servings: Some foods are packaged in single-serving containers. Most foods however, contain several servings per container. **Pay attention to both the serving size and how many servings a package contains. Then ask yourself: "How many servings am I consuming?"** Many of us are guilty of eating a large bag of potato chips or a tub of ice cream (which may contain 6 servings). If this sounds like you, then you have to multiply the calories and other nutrient numbers (including the Percent Daily Values; see below) by 6.

Calories: This refers to a single serving's total calorie count, aka "energy." Below the serving's calories, the label states the calories from fat.

Percent Daily Value: On the right side of the label, beginning above the Total Fat entry, you'll see something called "Percent Daily Value." The DV, as it's also known, gives a very rough (some people would even say "inaccurate") estimate of the nutrients in one serving of the food. For example, if the label lists 15 percent for calcium, it means that one serving provides 15 percent of the calcium you need each day. DVs are based on a 2,000-calorie diet for healthy adults. Keep in mind that, in real life, different individuals have different calorie and nutrient needs, based on their size, activity level, gender, whether they are pregnant or lactating, and other factors.

Total Fat: This is how much fat, in grams, a single serving contains.

Saturated Fat: This is how much of the fat in each single serving is saturated. In science-speak, saturated fat is a type of fat containing a high proportion of fatty acid molecules without double bonds, once considered to be less healthy in the diet than unsaturated fat. Saturated fat is solid at room temperature. Saturated fats have previously been thought in nutrition circles to raise blood cholesterol levels. But views on saturated fat are quickly changing. Recent research shows that saturated fat isn't the heart-hurter it was once accused of being; many diets—including keto—includes natural sources of saturated fat.

Trans Fat: Almost all trans fat found in processed food is chemically created during a process called "partial hydrogenation," in which hydrogen molecules are added to liquid vegetable oil to create a solid or semi-solid fat. Trans fat increases the level of bad cholesterol and decreases the level of good cholesterol in the blood. This, in turn, can increase the risk of developing cardiovascular disease, the leading cause of death in both men and women in the United States. The US Department of Agriculture's "Dietary Guidelines for Americans" recommends keeping the intake of trans fat as low as possible by limiting foods containing partially hydrogenated oils.

Cholesterol: This is a type of fat found in animal products, including dairy products. The measurement tells you how much of the total fat is cholesterol and its measure in milligrams (mg).

Sodium: Measured in milligrams (mg), this is the total salt content in the prepared food.

Total Carbohydrates: Measured in grams (g).

Fiber (sometimes written as "Dietary Fiber"): Measured in grams. Soluble fiber (which swells and forms a gel-like substance when it comes in contact with water, such as oats and legumes) and insoluble fiber (which does not expand in liquid and is found in fruits and vegetables) are not given separate measures. On a food label, fiber is fiber.

Sugars: Measured in grams, this refers to the total amount sugar in a food, including naturally occurring sugars, added sweeteners, and carbohydrates.

Protein: Measured in grams.

Micronutrients: In the United States, only two vitamins (A and C) and two minerals (calcium and iron) are required to be listed on food labels. But, when vitamins or minerals are added to the food, or when a vitamin or mineral claim is made, those nutrients must be listed on the nutrition label. These are listed by their Daily Percentage Value.

Ingredients List: Ingredients are listed in order of predominance by weight. The ingredient that weighs the most is listed first, and the ingredient that weighs the least is listed last.

If you take a look at the ingredients sections of food labels for plain yogurt and flavored, you'll see a difference. One yogurt might contain cultured, pasteurized, organic whole milk and active cultures. The other might also have the milk and active cultures, plus a host of other ingredients, including added sugar, cornstarch, and flavorings. A quick look at the nutrition section of both labels will show that the differences in ingredients translates to differences in the amounts of sugar grams, as well as differences in the amounts of other nutrients. This is why it is important, as a keto-eater, to always look at labels when you are shopping. An item you think is good for you may contain too many carbohydrate grams to work with your eating plan, while a different brand or flavor of that food may work perfectly for you. In general, anywhere there are sweeteners—including honey, molasses, fructose, corn syrup, and everyday cane sugar—there will be carbs.

HOW TO AVOID EATING TOO MUCH

The prospect of eating avocados, bacon, and cream every day can be so tantalizing that we forget that the keto diet is not a food free-for-all. No one—including keto-eaters—should eat until they feel queasy or overburden their digestive tract. Further, because the majority of keto ingredients are so calorie-dense, overeating even a small amount of them can get in the way of weight loss. If you struggle with eating too much of a good thing, these tips may help.

- **Stay hydrated.** Oftentimes, we mistake thirst for hunger.

- **Carry your own keto snacks.** Snacks can be an slippery slope when you are not prepared. Pack a piece or two of salmon jerky or stock up on snack-sized containers and fill them with cubed cheese, salami, slices of cucumber, or other keto-compliant foods.

- **Don't keep trigger foods in your home.** We all have foods that are difficult for us to stop eating. Be it coconut cream, liverwurst, avocados, bacon, jerky, or any other keto ingredient you can't resist, don't keep it in your home. You can consume it when eating out, but keeping it in your kitchen can lead to "extended eating episodes," also known as bingeing.

- **Don't overorder in restaurants.** Go for keto-compliant salads, soups, and appetizers, which are typically more reasonably sized than entrées.

- **Chew well.** This aids digestion and gives your brain time to register that you're full, so you don't overeat. A good rule of thumb is counting to 20 while chewing each bite.

- **Avoid drinking your calories.** True, there are some amazing keto drinks out there. In fact, you'll find several in our accompanying *Keto Kit Cookbook* (chapter 7). But your body is sated more thoroughly when you eat food. Drinking too many calories can lead to stalled weight loss or even weight gain.

- **Eat mindfully.** We often eat mindlessly. We stuff food into our mouths while working on the computer, watching TV, or when we're on the run. Before we even realize what we've done, we've eaten two or three servings of a food and thrown off our macros, or loaded on calories that we did not need. Plus, wolfing down food is not enjoyable. The pleasure of eating lies in slowing down and fully experiencing all the elements of your meal.

KETO EQUIPMENT

Things like mixers and food processors are great for all kitchens, regardless of the diet you follow. However, eating the keto way can be so much easier if you collect these few specific items.

- **Calculator:** If you are terrible at math, as I am, a handy calculator nearby will help you tally up macros easily.

- **Digital scale:** When you're eyeballing ingredients, it's easy to guess wrong. Normally, this isn't such a big deal, but when you're trying to attain ketosis, being an ounce or two off with your ingredients can keep you from reaching or maintaining your goal.

- **Silicone bakeware:** Due to their lack of structure-giving ingredients, keto recipes can sometimes be a bit fragile. Silicone baking mats, muffin cups, and other bakeware ensures that what you make doesn't end up in crumbs.

- **Spiralizer (or a spiralizer attachment for your stand mixer or food processor):** Sure, you can purchase spiralized zucchini at your local market, but it's expensive, and not always fresh. This kitchen essential makes quick veggie noodles and it's fun, too!

- **Slow cooker:** Big cuts of meat are transformed into delicious pulled pork, chicken, and brisket for sandwiches or keto bowls with this must-have appliance. Plus, you'll want to start making your own bone broth with all those bones, right? Toss them in the slow cooker, cover with water, salt generously, set for 10 hours, and go about your life.

- **Aluminum foil:** Lots of aluminum foil. It makes cleanup a breeze when you can line pans with foil.

- **Liquid measuring cup:** Precision is important in keto cooking. A liquid measuring cup allows you to measure fluid ounces, milliliters, and cups.

- **Measuring cups, aka "dry measures" and measuring spoons:** I'll bet you already have these.

Watch Your Plate Size

While you don't have to obsess over calories on the keto diet, you will lose weight faster and experience more efficient digestion if you avoid overeating. If you find it difficult to stop eating when you are full, consider eating from smaller plates and bowls.

Several studies have shown that when people use smaller dishes, they tend to serve themselves less food, and consume fewer calories. Scientists from the Universities of Oxford, Cambridge, Plymouth, and Bristol, in the UK, reviewed data from controlled trials and published their findings in the September 2015 issue of *The Cochrane Database of Systematic Reviews*. Their observations stated that people ate more food and drank more nonalcoholic drinks when offered larger portion sizes, packages, or tableware.

An average dinner plate in the UK, Europe, and the United States, is about 12 inches in diameter, so opt for dinner plates that are a maximum of 8½ to 10½ inches in diameter.

It should be noted, however, that a 2018 study by researchers at the Department of Psychology at Ben-Gurion University of the Negev in Israel, found that smaller plate sizes did not decrease the amount of food consumed when diners had not eaten in three hours or more. The research was published in the September 2018 issue of the nutrition journal *Appetite*. So try smaller plates, but be sure it's not the only thing you do to keep serving sizes in check.

CHAPTER 6

TIPS AND TRICKS TO MAKE KETO LIVING EASY

As a writer, a nutrition educator, and the mother of three boys, I know what it is like to be so busy that you throw up your hands in despair and turn to premade food. And if that is the direction you ultimately take, please don't feel guilty. It's all good. After all, there are more and more keto-meal options on the market today, from supermarket grab-and-go meals to keto convenience foods, to ketogenic delivery services.

But learning how to manage your own keto meal-making is worth attempting for a few reasons. The most obvious is that premade keto food is expensive. With all the coconut, avocado, high-quality oils, beef, salmon, and so on, the ketogenic diet does not come cheap. Making your own low-carb, high-fat meals is an obvious way to save while eating keto.

Further, many of the premade keto options taste awful at worst, bland at best. Making your own food ensures that you are consuming foods you love— and enjoying your meals is emotionally important when upending your diet and diving into something new.

Lastly, the only way you really know exactly what is in food is if you make it yourself. When you cook homemade keto dishes, you know exactly how much of each ingredient you used, and this is vitally important when you are calculating your macros.

While ketogenic cooking has a reputation for being fussy, time-intensive, and difficult, it doesn't have to be. With a bit of know-how, you'll learn how easy it is to make yummy, keto-approved meals that even the busiest among us can find time to put together.

GROCERY SHOPPING MADE EASY

Here are some tips for making shopping easier.

- **Choose a quiet time.** I shop first thing on Sunday mornings because no one in my Manhattan neighborhood seems to shop early on the weekend, meaning the shopping experience is pleasant, the store is easy to navigate, and my trip is very efficient. Pick a time that works with your schedule, but also consider when others might find the time to do their shopping.

- **If grocery shopping seems difficult to fit into your schedule, have the groceries brought to you.** Most local grocery stores offer delivery service and some even list their food items (with prices) online. You can choose what you need and pick a delivery time. It's that simple. You can also use an online grocery service. In the Northeast, PeaPod and FreshDirect are popular. Nationwide, there is AmazonFresh.

- **Order in bulk.** If you choose to use an online service, stock up on fresh meat and poultry, a few flats of eggs, and other animal-based products, such as cream, butter, and cheese. The up-front cost may be high, but when you calculate the per pound cost, it's often cheaper than traditional shopping.

- **Be careful about subscribing to a CSA or a produce box delivery service.** Many of the items CSAs deliver are fruits and roots—items that aren't ideal for keto-eaters. You'll save money, time, and frustration by ordering what you can eat (and want) from an online delivery store.

PUTTING FOOD PREP ON AUTOMATIC

Few of us have much free time to devote to meal-making, which is actually fine because good food doesn't require a lot of time to make. Good food can be made a bit here, a bit there, whenever you have a spare moment. Use the time you have and you'll be just fine. Here are a few of my secrets.

- **Practice component cooking.** *The Keto Kit Cookbook* has several recipes that can be made ahead and used in many recipes or combined with other ingredients for a quick lunch. Check out the

Staples chapter for items such as Big Batch Chicken Thighs (page 3) or Pulled Pork (page 8).

- **Utilize your freezer.** Storing individual portions in the freezer makes for easy prep during busy nights. Plus, this time-saving step also helps you avoid repetitive meals throughout the week, a common downfall of dieting.

- **Cook once, eat twice.** Rely on recipes that have four or more servings, so you can eat now and then again later.

- **Be time-efficient.** If you like to cook, earmark about two hours on the weekend or your days off when you can make large batches of "fatabulous" foods. I personally like to use Saturday mornings for food sourcing and Sunday mornings for cooking. Each Saturday, I shop for the week. On Sunday morning, I prep cauliflower and broccoli rice (to cook later), start a pot of chicken, beef, or pork stock, and prep green salad ingredients.

- **Use snippets of time when they appear.** When I have 10 or 15 unexpected minutes, I will often do some quick meal prep. For me, these include peeling and chopping veggies, defrosting meat or poultry, throwing something in the slow cooker, hopping online to order specialty items, or doing a quick cupboard inventory to see if I am running low on pantry ingredients.

- **Find a shopping partner.** Go halvies with a friend on a membership to a big box store, such as Costco or Sam's Club. Shop together, or take turns doing each other's shopping. Plus, when you have someone to shop with, she holds you more accountable to your keto eating plan!

THE BARE-BONES KETO COOKING EQUIPMENT GUIDE

It's tempting when you start a new diet, to run out and stock your kitchen with a number of new kitchen helpers. You don't need anything new, however, to cook keto. Whether you are a keto-eater, a vegetarian, or a standard American diet lover, a cluttered kitchen looks unappetizing, is hard to keep sanitary, and is difficult (or, in some cases, dangerous) to work in. The following items are generally all you need to easily turn out wonderful meals.

- **The biggies:** An oven with a stovetop, a refrigerator with a freezer, and—if you have room and can afford it—a dishwasher.

- **Knives:** A well-made chef's knife that feels great in your hand, a paring knife, and a serrated knife.

- **Countertop appliances:** Limit yourself to no more than three countertop appliances to avoid clutter. Keto-eaters may be interested in a food processor, a high-powered blender, and a coffeepot. Keep less-used appliances off the counter in a dedicated kitchen cabinet, and pull them out only when you use them.

- **Pots and pans:** Most of us use the same pan and the same few pots frequently, which is why most people really only need a frying/sauté pan, a small or medium pot, and a pot that is large enough to make stock. Keep these heavily used pots and pans on your stovetop and tuck away others in a cupboard.

- **Bakeware:** As with pots, most of us use the same few baking pans. If you're in the market for a few new pieces, I recommended a 12-cup muffin tin, two 9-inch cake pans, two baking sheets, a 9 x 11-inch glass pan, and a 2-quart casserole dish.

- **Cooking utensils:** Let the foods you eat regularly guide your choices. Keep items you use daily within easy reach. For instance, in a large vessel near the knife block, I keep a vegetable peeler, a citrus reamer, a ladle, a large flat spoon, a wooden spoon, and a Danish whisk. Your less-used cooking utensils can remain out of sight in a drawer or cupboard. Keto-eaters may want to keep a box grater and a spiralizer within arm's reach as well.

SAVING MONEY ON KETO

The keto diet can be pricey. But with a bit of advance planning, there are ways to lower your ketogenic grocery bill.

- **Most keto foods freeze well.** When you see a sale on a keto-approved ingredient you love, stock up so you have it on hand. For instance, freeze a discounted organic butter, a few low-priced salmon steaks, or some bulk-bought avocados (I tell you one way to do this in Chapter 5, but I also like this quick method: peel and pit first, rub with oil, then cover with freezer wrap).

- **Look into online bulk buying.** You'll find everything online, from different cuts of beef like chops, steaks, and roasts to fresh-caught salmon to cases of coconut cream. The possibilities are endless.

- **Hit the frozen aisle.** Frozen veggies often cost 50–75 percent less than their fresh counterparts. And get this: Frozen veggies are flash-frozen when picked so they usually have higher nutrition counts.

- **Shop at stores that have "manager's specials."** If you can find a grocery store that sells soon-to-be expired meat, poultry, produce, and other items, you can nab huge discounts. One of my favorite meat-buying coups was when I bought $85 worth of ground beef that was four days away from its expiration date for $9.97. Just be sure to use this meat immediately or wrap it in food wrap and stash it in the freezer the moment you come home with it.

- **Consider alternative meat cuts, such as organ meats, and eggs.** Organ meats are much cheaper than traditional cuts of meat and poultry. Plus, eggs are a good source of protein for a very low cost.

- **Shop at more than one store.** Sometimes one store will consistently have great sales on meat and paper products, but be off-the-charts expensive when it comes to produce. The store that has great prices on fish may be disappointing when it comes to cheese, cream, and coconut products. Buying groceries wherever they are cheapest might seem like a hassle, but will save you overall.

THE IMPORTANCE OF PACKING YOUR FOOD

Planning for office, school, and other away-from-home meals will allow you to succeed on the keto diet. For many of us, the meals we eat away from home are the ones where we are most likely to make bad choices. Set yourself up for keto success by making your own away-from-home meals. Here are some suggestions.

- Stock up on one-cup (8-ounce), single-serve, freezer-safe food containers (get at least seven).

- Purchase a heat-insulated container (I like the 12-ounce and 16-ounce sizes). I also recommend buying a sealable drink cup.

- Collect a few mini containers for sauce and condiments.

- Invest in reusable flatware you can keep at your desk.

- Find a few large, freezer-proof containers for big-batch cooking.

- Don't forget the food wrap!

- If you want a lunch box or food pack to carry your meal, don't hesitate to buy what you need.

- If you have keto-eating friends or coworkers, meal prep together. Suggest that everyone double or triple their recipes, and then divide them into single-serve containers and share. This kind of cooking co-op saves huge amounts of time and is a fun way to ensure that you all stick to your eating plan.

- When packing a takeaway keto meal, make sure to stash a keto drink, or a decadent fat bomb, in your lunch bag. Everyone deserves a treat.

Don't Forget the Fun!

Humans are hardwired for fun. If we enjoy something, we stick with it. If something is drudgery, we eventually drop it for other pursuits (and then feel guilty for not being "strong enough" to stick with it).

Hands down, the most important ingredient when it comes to keto cooking is fun. Experiment with recipes, ingredients, and parts of your routine, such as the best time to be in the kitchen, until you hit a groove. Invite your roommate, partner, family members, or friends into the kitchen with you. Share meals with coworkers and friends. Eat foods you enjoy. Life is too short to waste on being miserable.

KETO MENUS AND MEAL PLANS

There is a plethora of keto information available to you, especially in this kit. Having access to a lot of information is a wonderful thing, but it can also be overwhelming, even intimidating, to wade through. This chapter is narrowly focused on one thing: one month of menus, meal plans, and lists that serve as game plans for food prep or grocery shopping to set you up for success.

SAMPLE MEAL PLAN

Planning ahead is a terrific way to have a successful keto week. The first week in this plan is structured as a day-by-day plan of menus, shopping lists, and prep tips. For the following weeks, I hope the first week's structure will inspire you to apply the planning and cooking tips moving forward. I believe that beginners should start out on the higher end of allowed carbs to help reduce possible "keto flu" and other transitioning symptoms (see page 27). The first week's worth of daily menus takes this into consideration.

How to Alter the Carb and Fat Counts in the Sample Meal Plan

This diet plan is calculated based on the needs of a middle-aged, moderately active woman with between 30 and 35 percent body fat. (I talk more about body fat percentages—including how to figure out yours—in chapter 2.) This menu hovers around 20–26 grams of net carbs, 100–130 grams of fat, and 80–90 grams of protein. The menus for some days have a bit more of certain macros, some a bit less. But this is a good, solid, and safe place to start your keto journey. These proportions won't overwhelm you with transitioning symptoms (such as headaches, dehydration, or constipation, as discussed in chapter 3). After about a month or two, you may want to adjust your macros, increasing your fat, or decreasing your carbs. My opinion: Go ahead! The menu is flexible and, with simple calculations, you can easily add an extra *fat bomb*, remove a snack, or substitute meals with macros more in line with where you are in your keto journey.

What Do I Count?

Keto-eaters "do" keto in several ways. A large proportion of ketogenic aficionados do not believe in counting calories, concentrating instead on net carbs, fat, and protein. Others add calorie counting to the mix. I am going to be frank here: Counting calories (plus fat, net carbs, and protein) on a keto diet is difficult and not strictly necessary. I personally found it easy to lose weight by concentrating on my macros (fat, net carbs, and protein), so that's what I supply in this chapter's plans. If, in the future, you do decide to count calories, feel free! You can find terrific calorie counters online, or in book form at your local bookstore or library. There are even calorie-counting apps for your phone.

EATING KETO AWAY FROM HOME

Staying true to your ketogenic commitment is easiest when you're eating at home: Everything you need is within reach, you have your favorite keto-compliant foods readily available, and you won't encounter diet-wrecking surprises. However, there may be times when you will need to travel, leaving you to navigate the nonketogenic world. Here are my best strategies when I must eat away from home.

- **Approach the experience calmly and confidently.** A healthy journey always begins with a healthy attitude. Having a clear and collected approach will help open your eyes to the keto-compliant food possibilities.

- **Carry a few portable staples or snacks.** What you can bring will obviously depend on where you are going. A quick road trip? Pack two or three coolers with snacks and staples, including cooked animal proteins, butter, avocados, yogurt, cheese, bone broth, riced cauliflower, a thermos of beef stew, some fat bombs, a can or two of coconut cream, and as many snacks as you want. And, if possible, book stays in suite-style inns that feature kitchenettes. Taking a plane? Stash enough packaged snacks for your entire trip in your suitcase, plus a few in your carry-on. It's hard to justify a tempting trip to a vending machine when you have a package of jerky in your bag!

- **Take a multivitamin and mineral supplement.** This preemptively takes care of any nutritional gaps you may face while traveling.

- **Review restaurant and room service options beforehand.** Whether traveling for business or pleasure, it's important to identify ketogenic-compliant meals before you arrive at your destination. This is easy with the internet. If you're in a hotel, start with the on-site café or restaurants. Menus are usually listed on the hotel website. Is there anything keto-compliant? Or is there anything that can be tweaked to become ketogenic? (For instance, ask for the steak without the sauce and swap out the potato for a side of sautéed zucchini.) Go a step further and find some nearby restaurants where you might want to have a meal. Visit their websites, check out their menus, and make note of any appropriate dishes well before you arrive.

- **Be the first one to order.** If you've checked out a restaurant menu online or perused it in person, you will know what you can make work. However, listening to your dining partners order exciting-sounding dishes can be enough to sway you toward an intriguing-sounding nonketo item. Keep that from happening by being the first one to place your order.

- **Find one or two breakfasts that work for you and have them every day.** Putting the first meal of the day on automatic allows you to resist temptation and leaves no room for cheating.

Great options include eggs (made any way) and ham or bacon, or a cup of full-fat, unsweetened yogurt.

- **Commit to avoiding alcohol.** New surroundings often lure us to indulge. Deciding to forgo alcohol makes it more likely that you will stick to your keto standards and avoid being kicked out of ketosis.

- **Tell your friends or colleagues what you need.** If your friends, colleagues, or traveling partners would be interested in hearing more about your way of eating and would offer emotional support, consider sharing what you know about the keto diet. If, however, you are with someone who may try to sabotage your eating plans, it might be best to say nothing.

- **Make sure there is food in your kitchen to come home to.** Stocking your kitchen in anticipation of your return is a good way to make sure you don't fall off your keto wagon. Travelers often neglect to stock their kitchen and then they return home ravenous. This is a vulnerable situation for a keto-eater, one where it is easy to give in to tempting diet-sabatoging foods.

How Strict Do I Need to Be with Myself?

Ketogenic eaters are known to be an exacting bunch. When you consider all the recording and calculations and planning required to reach and maintain ketosis, I suppose that makes sense. But going nuts over a gram of carbs or fats (or anything else, for that matter) is not healthy. Follow these menus for 30 days and move forward one meal at a time. As you live the keto life for a while, you will change things up, based on your personal preferences. My best advice? Follow the plan, but not so rigidly that keto eating feels like a crazy dietary punishment.

HOW TO PLAN MEALS

All keto-eaters have their own way of planning meals. Some start with their favorites and add side dishes and extra ingredients until their daily macro quotient has been met. Others review store specials for on-sale keto-compliant ingredients and build their menus from there. There are even keto-eaters—usually the hard-core, longtime keto-eaters who are trying to nudge their bodies off a weight loss plateau—who create a single day's menu with the precise macros they feel will help them meet their goal. And they eat that menu each and every day, stocking up on all the needed ingredients beforehand.

I encourage you to sit down for an hour at the end of week 1 with your *Keto Kit Journal* and review what worked for you, what did not work for you, and what premade food you have on hand and can use for the next week's meals. Review if you ran into a snag and strategize how to tackle it again in the future. Reflect on your meal prep strategy: Do you prefer morning or evening prep time? Think ahead to any special occasions or food challenges in the upcoming week and plan ahead. Review future meal plans (page 86) or thumb through *The Keto Kit Cookbook* for dishes you are interested in trying. Not each food has to be high in fats, low in carbs, and moderate in protein. As long as what you eat adds up to high fat, low in net carbs, and moderate in protein, you are fine.

Take It Slow

For the first two or three weeks, you should try to make keto eating an easy, doable habit. Don't go crazy counting micronutrients or calories. Aim for a range of fat, net carb, and protein grams each day (like the one I've used for week 1, starting on page 72). Your body will transition to burning fat. In time, you'll hit your first plateau. That is the time to tighten up, jump onto a macro counter, and see what macro you need to increase or decrease to reach your next goal. Right now, however, ease into the keto diet. Enjoy this time of learning.

GET-STARTED, BEGINNING KETO SHOPPING LIST

Isn't it maddening when you get ready to dive into a recipe and you realize you're missing a key ingredient? This shopping list will help ensure that you have everything you need to make all the items on the the first week's worth of menus.

Though I encourage you to follow the menus as written, keep in mind that you're free to change things up from the get-go. Just remember that if you decide to sub another recipe for one suggested in the menu, you'll need to add its ingredients to your shopping list.

Lastly, I've listed items such as salt and pepper that you may have in your kitchen and thus do not need. Yes, the list looks gargantuan, but this is the only time you'll need to purchase some key items for keto eating. As you move forward, you only have to replace the ingredients that you've used up during the week.

PANTRY ITEMS

* 5 (13- to 15-ounce) cans coconut cream
* 5 (13- to 15-ounce) cans coconut milk
* 1 (8- to 16-ounce) jar almond butter, or other nut butter
* 4 ounces chopped pecans
* 1 pound almond meal
* 8 ounces dry red wine
* 32 ounces chicken bone broth
* 1 can oil-packed salmon
* 1 (32-ounce) can tomato sauce (with no sweetener added)
* 1 (28-ounce) can whole tomatoes in juice
* 1 (4-ounce) jar of sun-dried tomatoes, packed in oil
* 1 (6-ounce) jar of high-quality mustard (such as Dijon)
* 1 (15- to 30-ounce) jar of Mayonnaise
* 1 (5- to 12-ounce) bottle of soy sauce or coconut aminos
* 1 (16- to 24-ounce) jar dill pickles
* 2 pints oil-cured Kalamata olives
* Optional: Liquid or granulated stevia

MEAT

* 2 pounds bacon
* 4 pounds ground beef
* 1 pound ground lamb
* 1 pound Italian sausage (sweet or hot)
* 3 pounds pork shoulder or butt (sometimes called "picnic roast")
* 8 ounces liverwurst

POULTRY

* 5-pound boneless skinless chicken thighs

FISH

* 4 salmon filets

PRODUCE

* 4 lemons
* 2 large heads cauliflower
* 2 (16-ounce) bags riced cauliflower or 2 additional heads of cauliflower
* 1 (16-ounce) bag broccoli rice
* 2 large zucchini squash or 2 (8-ounce) packages of spiralized zucchini noodles
* 1 medium head cabbage
* 3 bunches radishes
* 2 turnips
* 2 kohlrabi bulbs
* 2 small red onions
* 1 yellow or Spanish onion
* 1 head garlic
* 3 red bell pepper
* 2 seedless English cucumber
* 1 (1 pound) box baby spinach
* 1 (1 pound) box spring mix salad
* 2 plum tomatoes
* 1 head romaine lettuce
* 1 bunch scallions
* 2 or 3 fresh jalapeños
* 1 (4-inch) piece fresh ginger
* 1 small bunch celery
* 2 portobello mushrooms
* 4 Hass avocados
* 1 pound fresh or frozen watermelon chunks

DAIRY

* 6 (3-ounce) packages cream cheese
  1 quart heavy cream, aka "whipping cream"
* 1 quart whole milk
* 4 single-service cartons whole-milk, unsweetened yogurt (or Greek-style yogurt)
* 1 (32-ounce) carton whole-milk, unsweetened yogurt (for recipes)
* 1 dozen large eggs
* 3 ounces feta cheese
* 16 ounces cheddar cheese
* 8 ounces parmesan cheese
* 8 ounces provolone cheese

FATS

* Extra-virgin olive oil
* Coconut oil
* Avocado oil
* Butter

SEASONINGS

* Salt
* Pepper
* Garlic powder
* Paprika
* Chili powder
* Cumin
* Ground allspice
* Celery salt
* Dried oregano
* Dried basil
* Dried rosemary
* Ground cloves
* Mustard powder
* Madras curry powder
* Ground cinnamon
* Cream of tartar
* Apple cider vinegar
* Red wine vinegar

A WEEK'S WORTH OF SAMPLE MENUS

Here are some easy, day-by-day, meal-by-meal plans for the first week of keto meals. Along with strategic menus for the first seven days, I have offered my advice for meal prepping in the morning and evening to ensure success. I suggest using this approach as a blueprint for the remaining meal plans for day 8 through day 30, starting on page 86.

Before you dive in, I would like to offer one piece of advice: Keep food easy. The easier the food is—whether it's to find, to make, to serve, or to eat—the more likely it is that you'll stick to the diet plan. The keto diet can be challenging at first, so while a more complicated recipe might be keto-compliant, I suggest going for the quick and easy recipes on this plan and offered in *The Keto Kit Cookbook*.

DAY 0

Pre-Week Prep Activities

- Organize and wash your food storage containers. If you need any, pick some up while shopping. (*about 10 minutes*)

- Review the shopping list (see pages 68–70). Scan your pantry, refrigerator, and freezer for ingredients you might already have. Cross them off your shopping list. (*about 10 minutes*)

- Go shopping. (*about 30 minutes*)

- Put your groceries away. (*about 10 minutes*)

- Make Simple Nut Butter Fudge (kit cookbook, page 114) and wrap tightly. Store in the fridge. You'll be using pieces of this fudge as fat bombs throughout the week. (*about 10 minutes*)

- Make Pizza Bombs (kit cookbook, page 107). Place in a tightly covered container. Store in the fridge. You'll be enjoying Pizza Bombs several times throughout the week. (*about 10 minutes*)

- Hard-boil two eggs for later in the week. Store in the fridge. (*about 20 minutes*)

- Assemble Keto Greek Salad (kit cookbook, page 68). Make the salad without dressing and store it in a food-service container. Prepare the dressing according to recipe directions and store in a small container. Place both containers in a lunch bag with a napkin, a water bottle, and utensils. (*about 10 minutes*)

- Place yogurt in the lunch bag. (*about 1 minute*)

- Count 20 olives and add to a small plastic food bag or container. Place in the lunch bag. (*about 2 minutes*)

- Place lunch bag in the fridge so you can grab lunch as you walk out the door tomorrow morning. (*about 1 minute*)

DAY 1

Morning Food Prep

- Review the Roasted Low-Carb Roots recipe (kit cookbook, page 26). Prepare the veggies as specified by the recipe. Place in a large food storage container and toss with the olive oil and seasonings. Put the lid on the container and store in the lower part of the fridge or in a veggie drawer. You will roast these tomorrow before dinner. *(about 10 minutes)*

- Turn to Big Batch Chicken Thighs (kit cookbook, page 3). In a large food container or a glass baking dish, whisk together oil, soy sauce, and seasonings. Add the chicken and turn to coat. Place the lid on the container, or cover the baking dish with foil, and place in the fridge. *(about 10 minutes)*

- Prepare an Egg Cup (kit cookbook, page 34). *(about 5 minutes)*

- Make Keto Coffee Latte (kit cookbook, page 170) and place it in a portable drink container. *(about 5 minutes)*

BREAKFAST: **23.6g fat, 2.4g net carbs, 21.9g protein**
* 8-ounce glass of water
* Egg Cup (kit cookbook, page 34)

SNACK: **34.4g fat, 12g net carbs, 9g protein**
* 8-ounce glass of water
* 1 (8-ounce) carton unsweetened, full-fat, traditional-style yogurt
* Keto Coffee Latte (kit cookbook, page 170)

LUNCH: **26g fat, 1.3g net carbs, 7.9g protein**
* 8-ounce glass of water
* Keto Greek Salad (kit cookbook, page 68)

SNACK: 20g fat, 6.2g net carbs, 1.6g protein

* 8-ounce glass of water
* 20 oil-packed olives, any type

Evening Food Prep

- Preheat oven to 425°F. (*about 2 minutes*)

- Remove prepared chicken thighs and root vegetables from the fridge. (*about 2 minutes*) Distribute the vegetables on 1 or 2 baking pans in a single layer and place in the oven. (*about 2 minutes*)

- Place the baking dish of chicken thighs in the oven as well. (*about 2 minutes*)

- Set a timer for 20 minutes as a reminder to check the veggies, and then the chicken, per recipe instructions. (*about 1 minute*) Remove items from the oven and plate for dinner. Pack cooled leftovers in food storage containers. Place the containers in the fridge. (*about 5 minutes*)

- After dinner, make Signature Tomato Soup (kit cookbook, page 59) for days 3 and 4. When soup is cool, place in single-serve containers and place the containers in fridge. (*about 10 minutes*)

DINNER: 23.7g fat, 19.8g net carbs, 45.3 protein

* 8-ounce glass of water
* Big Batch Chicken Thighs (kit cookbook, page 3)
* Roasted Low-Carb Roots (kit cookbook, page 26)

What If I Cheat?

Most of us have started a diet only to "cheat" at some point. Cheating on the ketogenic diet will slow down the time it takes you to enter ketosis, but it's not the end of the world. Just get back on the ketogenic plan with your next meal. In other words, don't let what you wish you hadn't eaten influence the next thing you eat.

DAY 2

Morning Food Prep

■ Chop 1½ cups of chicken meat from your day 1 dinner and mix with mayonnaise and any spices you would like. Pack in a small food container. Put 3 cups of baby spinach in another food container. Rub a drop of oil on the cut surface of ¼ of an avocado to keep it from browning. Wrap tightly in food wrap. Place all three items in a lunch bag. *(about 10 minutes)*

■ Wrap a piece of Simple Nut Butter Fudge and a Pizza Bomb in food wrap or place in mini food storage containers. Add the fat bombs to your lunch bag. *(about 5 minutes)*

■ Prepare breakfast. *(about 10 minutes)*

BREAKFAST: 28.5g fat, 2.5g net carbs, 11.7g protein
* 8-ounce glass of water
* Baked Avocado (kit cookbook, page 37)

SNACK: 20.1g fat, 8.8g net carbs, 2.1g protein
* 8-ounce glass of water
* Green Keto Lemonade (kit cookbook, page 178)
* 20 oil-packed olives (any type)

LUNCH: 45.2g fat, 6g net carbs, 27.3g protein
* 8-ounce glass of water
* 1 cup chicken salad, made with 1½ cups of chopped chicken thigh meat from last night's dinner and 2 tablespoons of mayonnaise
* 3 cups baby spinach
* ¼ small avocado

SNACK: 7.1g fat, 0.8g net carbs, 2.9g protein
* 8-ounce glass of water
* Pizza Bomb (kit cookbook, page 107)

DINNER: 24.4g fat, 6.4g net carbs, 43.4g protein

* 8-ounce glass of water
* Stuffed Salmon (kit cookbook, page 162)
* Spiralized Zucchini Noodles (kit cookbook, page 139)

Evening Meal Prep

■ Make Stuffed Salmon for dinner. (*about 20 minutes*)

■ While salmon is baking, prepare Spiralized Zucchini Noodles. (*about 10 minutes*)

■ Pack away leftovers in food storage containers. (*about 5 minutes*)

■ Put together the Keto Italiano Stuffed Peppers (kit cookbook, page 130) for tomorrow's lunch, and place in the oven to bake. When cool, pack a single serving in a food container. Save the other stuffed pepper for dinner on day 4. (*about 25 minutes*)

> TIP: As you study these weekly meal plans, you'll notice that certain foods show up on several days, often in slightly different guises. That is intentional. Efficient keto cooks create meals with keto-compliant building blocks. Using elements from one meal for future meals is smart, time-saving, easy on your wallet, and less wasteful.

DAY 3

TOTAL MACROS
126.1g fat, 24.5g net carbs, 89.2g protein

Morning Food Prep

- Wrap a Pizza Bomb in food wrap or place in mini food storage containers. Add the fat bombs to your lunch bag. *(about 5 minutes)*

- Remove containers of Signature Tomato Soup and Keto Italiano Stuffed Peppers and place in your lunch bag. *(about 5 minutes)*

- Place ingredients for Pulled Pork (kit cookbook, page 8) in your slow cooker. Turn to high and set timer for 6 hours. *(about 10 minutes)*

BREAKFAST: 9.6g fat, 0.7g net carbs, 12.6g protein
* 8-ounce glass of water
* 2 hard-boiled eggs (kit cookbook, page 2)

SNACK: 7.1g fat, 0.8g net carbs, 2.9g protein
* 8-ounce glass of water
* Pizza Bomb (kit cookbook, page 107)

LUNCH: 30.2g fat, 8.5g net carbs, 29.8g protein
* 8-ounce glass of water
* Keto Italiano Stuffed Peppers (kit cookbook, page 130)
* Serving of Signature Tomato Soup (kit cookbook, page 59)

SNACK: 22.4g fat, 10.3g net carbs, 14.5g protein
* 8-ounce glass of water
* 10 raw, unsalted almonds
* 1 (8-ounce) carton unsweetened, full-fat, traditional-style yogurt

DINNER: 56.7g fat, 4.2g net carbs, 29.4g protein
* 8-ounce glass of water
* Pulled Pork (kit cookbook, page 8)
* Cauliflower Mash (kit cookbook, page 140), topped with 1½ tablespoons of melted butter

Evening Meal Prep

- Make Cauliflower Mash to serve with Pulled Pork. (*about 10 minutes*)

- After dinner, place leftover food in single-serving containers and place in the fridge. (*about 5 minutes*)

- Prepare Bacon-Liverwurst Balls (kit cookbook, page 101). Package balls in mini single-serve food containers. (*about 15 minutes*)

- Prepare the meat and salad dressing for Cheeseburger Salad (kit cookbook, page 71), storing each component in separate food storage containers in the fridge. Shred the lettuce and prep the veggies and store those in separate food storage containers in the fridge. (*about 10 minutes*)

Using Leftovers Wisely

If you want to be a successful keto-eater, get used to doubling small-size recipes and packing away the extras for future meals. Leftovers are the secret to easy keto eating. As you'll find in our *Keto Kit Cookbook*, the majority of recipes make two to eight servings, giving you ample opportunity to cook once, and eat twice (or more!). I also suggest investing in freezer-safe food storage containers, so you can assemble future meals as you pack away leftovers. Having frozen grab-and-go meals on hand makes keto living a cinch.

DAY 4

Morning Food Prep

- Make Watermelon Cooler (kit cookbook, page 179) and place in a travel-proof shaker cup. Place in your lunch bag. (*about 5 minutes*)

- Prepare breakfast. (*about 10 minutes*)

- Store leftover hash in single-service food containers in the fridge. (*about 5 minutes*)

- Assemble Cheeseburger Salad (kit cookbook, page 71) in a food container. Place in your lunch bag. (*about 5 minutes*)

- Place Bacon Liverwurst Ball in your food bag. (*about 2 minutes*)

BREAKFAST: 43.5g fat, 4.3g net carbs, 28.3g protein
* 8-ounce glass of water
* Tex-Mex Keto Hash (kit cookbook, page 42)

SNACK: 0.3g fat, 5g net carbs, 0.9g protein
* 8-ounce glass of water
* Watermelon Cooler (kit cookbook, page 179)

LUNCH: 22.7g fat, 5g net carbs, 14.2g protein
* 8-ounce glass of water
* Cheeseburger Salad (kit cookbook, page 71)

SNACK: 16.9g fat, 1.3g net carbs, 9g protein
* 8-ounce glass of water
* Bacon Liverwurst Ball (kit cookbook, page 101)

DINNER: 40g fat, 9.4g net carbs, 31.8g protein
* 8-ounce glass of water
* Keto Italiano Stuffed Peppers (kit cookbook, page 130)
* Serving of Signature Tomato Soup (kit cookbook, page 59)
* ¼ avocado, diced and used as garnish for the soup

Evening Meal Prep

- Prepare Keto Shepherd's Pie (kit cookbook, page 145) for tomorrow's lunch. While it is baking, warm up Keto Italiano Stuffed Pepper and Signature Tomato Soup for dinner. *(about 15 minutes)*

- After dinner, if you're making Cauliflower Rice (kit cookbook, page 138) from scratch, prep a head of cauliflower. Store riced cauliflower in single-serve food containers in the fridge. You can cook the rice at the moment or tomorrow. If you're preparing the rice, store in single-serving food storage containers. *(about 5 minutes)*

- Make Keto Indi Curry (kit cookbook, page 143) for tomorrow's dinner. *(about 15 minutes)*

- Portion single-servings of Keto Shepherd's Pie and Keto Indi Curry into food storage containers. *(about 10 minutes)*

DAY 5

TOTAL MACROS
125.8g fat, 25.6g net carbs, 80.9g protein

Morning Food Prep

- Place the ingredients for Fatty Chai Latte (kit cookbook, page 174) in a travel-proof shaker cup. Place in your lunch bag. (*about 5 minutes*)

- Add a Pizza Bomb and a container of Keto Shepherd's Pie to your lunch bag with a napkin and utensils. Place lunch bag where you won't forget it. (*about 5 minutes*)

- Prepare the Cauliflower Rice, if not done during Day 4 p.m. prep. (*about 5 minutes*)

BREAKFAST: 8g fat, 8g net carbs, 8.5g protein
* 8-ounce glass of water
* 1 (8-ounce) carton unsweetened, full-fat, traditional-style yogurt

SNACK: 33.1g fat, 4.5g net carbs, 2.8g protein
* 8-ounce glass of water
* Fatty Chai Latte (kit cookbook, page 174)

LUNCH: 30.4g fat, 3g net carbs, 32.1g protein
* 8-ounce glass of water
* Keto Shepherd's Pie (kit cookbook, page 145)

SNACK: 15.9g fat, 5.8g net carbs, 5.9g protein
* 8-ounce glass of water
* Pizza Bomb (kit cookbook, page 107)

DINNER: 38.4g fat, 4.3g net carbs, 31.6g protein
* 8-ounce glass of water
* Keto Indi Curry (kit cookbook, page 143)
* Cauliflower Rice (kit cookbook, page 138)

Evening Meal Prep

- Make Portobello Buns (kit cookbook, page 81) for tomorrow's Pulled Pork Sandwich. Wrap tightly in food wrap and store in the fridge. *(about 10 minutes)*

- Make the meat filling for Keto Soft Tacos (kit cookbook, page 86). When cool, package in a food storage container and keep in the fridge. *(about 10 minutes)*

- Make the Nutty 3-Ingredient Crackers (kit cookbook, page 120). Portion in individual mini storage containers and keep in a cupboard, drawer, or in the fridge. *(about 15 minutes)*

DAY 6

TOTAL MACROS
126.8g fat, 28g net carbs, 88.4g protein

Morning Food Prep

- Make Keto Breakfast Cakes (kit cookbook, page 39). Package any leftovers in food wrap and store in the freezer. *(about 10 minutes)*

- Make the Watermelon Cooler (kit cookbook, page 179) and pour into a travel-proof shaker cup. Place in lunch bag. *(about 5 minutes)*

- Place Nutty 3-Ingredient Crackers, Portobello Buns, and single-serve container of Pulled Pork in your lunch bag, and place somewhere where you won't forget it. *(about 5 minutes)*

BREAKFAST: 19g fat, 5g net carbs, 17g protein
* 8-ounce glass of water
* Keto Breakfast Cakes, eaten with no topping (kit cookbook, page 39)

SNACK: 19.5g fat, 4g net carbs, 9.5g protein
* 8-ounce glass of water
* Nutty 3-Ingredient Crackers (kit cookbook, page 120)

LUNCH: 50.9g fat, 8.4g net carbs, 32.8g protein
* Pulled Pork Sandwich, made with ½ cup leftover pulled pork from past dinner
* Portobello Buns made from 2 portobello mushroom caps (kit cookbook, page 81)

SNACK: 0.3g fat, 5g net carbs, 0.9g protein
* 8-ounce glass of water
* Watermelon Cooler (kit cookbook, page 179)

DINNER: 37.1g fat, 5.6g net carbs, 28.2g protein
* 8-ounce glass of water
* Keto Shepherd's Pie (kit cookbook, page 145)
* 1½ cup mixed baby salad greens dressed with 1 tablespoon of Keto Salad Dressing (kit cookbook, page 16)

Evening Meal Prep

- Warm up Shepherd's Pie. Dress salad for dinner. *(about 2 minutes)*

- Make Salmon Dairy Blobs (kit cookbook, page 104) for tomorrow's snack and portion into mini food storage containers. Store in the fridge. *(about 10 minutes)*

- Make Stuffed Cabbage Rolls (kit cookbook, page 148). When cool, portion rolls into single serve food containers and store in the fridge. *(about 20 minutes)*

- Prepare Bacon-Guacamole Soup (kit cookbook, page 55; remember the cooked bacon slices you prepared on day 2). Package into single-serve food storage containers and place in the fridge. *(about 10 minutes)*

DAY 7

TOTAL MACROS
117.7g fat, 21.7g net carbs, 81.2g protein

Morning Food Prep

- Prepare Baked Avocado (kit cookbook, page 37). *(about 10 minutes)*

- While Baked Avocado is baking, assemble Keto Coffee Latte and pour into a travel-proof shaker cup. Place in your lunch bag. *(about 5 minutes)*

- Make the egg white tortillas for the Keto Soft Tacos (kit cookbook, page 86). *(about 10 minutes)*

- Package the Keto Soft Tacos (I like to keep the "tortillas" and meat filling separate and put them together the moment I eat them) and place in your lunch bag. Add a container of Bacon-Guacamole Soup and a Salmon Dairy Blob. *(about 5 minutes)*

BREAKFAST: 28.5g fat, 9.2g net carbs, 11.7g protein
* 8-ounce glass of water
* Baked Avocado (kit cookbook, page 37)

SNACK: 26.4g fat, 4g net carbs, 0.5g protein
* 8-ounce glass of water
* Keto Coffee Latte (kit cookbook, page 170)

LUNCH: 38.9g fat, 2.6g net carbs, 35.9g protein
* 8-ounce glass of water
* Keto Soft Tacos (kit cookbook, page 86)
* Bacon-Guacamole Soup (kit cookbook, page 55)

SNACK: 14.9g fat, 0.8g net carbs, 6.4g protein
* 8-ounce glass of water
* Salmon Dairy Blobs (kit cookbook, page 104)

DINNER: 9g fat, 5.1g net carbs, 26.7g protein
* 8-ounce glass of water
* Stuffed Cabbage Rolls (kit cookbook, page 148)

Evening Meal Prep

- Reheat a serving of Stuffed Cabbage Rolls. (*about 10 minutes*)

- After dinner review the contents of your fridge. What do you have that needs to be incorporated into the next day's lunch or frozen for future use? What should you replenish when you go food shopping? (*about 10 minutes*)

MEAL PLANS FOR DAY 8 THROUGH DAY 30

Follow these meal plans for 30 days of keto eating. As with week 1, these menus have been calculated to include 20–26 grams of net carbs, 100–130 grams of fat, and 80–90 grams of protein. As you progress on the diet, adjust the menus as needed, adding more protein or fat or reducing your carbs.

As in every aspect of the keto plan, these eating plans should be specific to you. While these menus set you up for success, you can also achieve great results if you personalize the plan. Whether you are swapping out a recipe, need to grab something quick between meetings, or going out to a restaurant with friends or family, it is okay to deviate from the plan. Just make sure to plan accordingly and stick to your keto-eating dos and don'ts as best you can.

DAY 8

TOTAL MACROS
117.3g fat, 24g net carbs, 87.2g protein

BREAKFAST: 23.6g fat, 2.4g net carbs, 21.9g protein
* 8-ounce glass of water
* Egg Cup (kit cookbook, page 34)

SNACK: 13g fat, 8.7g net carbs, 9g protein
* 8-ounce glass of water
* 1 (8-ounce) carton unsweetened, full-fat, traditional-style yogurt
* 1 tablespoon of coconut cream, stirred into yogurt

LUNCH: 37g fat, 4.3g net carbs, 9.4g protein
* 8-ounce glass of water
* Keto Greek Salad (kit cookbook, page 68)
* Half a medium avocado, sliced or cubed

SNACK: 20g fat, 6.2g net carbs, 1.6g protein
* 8-ounce glass of water
* 20 oil-packed olives (any type)

DINNER: 23.7g fat, 1.9g net carbs, 45.3g protein
* 8-ounce glass of water
* Big Batch Chicken Thighs (kit cookbook, page 3)
* Roasted Low-Carb Roots (kit cookbook, page 26)

DAY 9

TOTAL MACROS
130.5g fat, 21.5g net carbs, 91.7g protein

BREAKFAST: 41.8g fat, 1.8g net carbs, 28.4g protein
* 8-ounce glass of water
* BLT Stack (kit cookbook, page 38)

SNACK: 8g fat, 8g net carbs, 8.5g protein
* 8-ounce glass of water
* 1 (8-ounce) carton unsweetened, full-fat, traditional-style yogurt

LUNCH: 40g fat, 5g net carbs, 26g protein
* 8-ounce glass of water
* 1 cup of chicken salad, made with 1½ cups of chopped chicken thigh meat from last night's dinner and 1 tablespoon of mayonnaise
* 3 cups baby spinach

SNACK: 7.1g fat, 0.8g net carbs, 2.9g protein
* 8-ounce glass of water
* Pizza Bomb (kit cookbook, page 107)

DINNER: 33.6g fat, 5.9g net carbs, 25.9g protein
* 8-ounce glass of water
* Beef Stroganoff Stew (kit cookbook, page 52)
* 3 medium celery stalks

DAY 10

BREAKFAST: 9.6g fat, 0.7g net carbs, 12.6g protein
* 8-ounce glass of water
* Two hard-boiled eggs (kit cookbook, page 2)

SNACK: 30.2g fat, 3.1g net carbs, 5.5g protein
* 8-ounce glass of water
* Simple Nut Butter Fudge (kit cookbook, page 114)

LUNCH: 37.8g fat, 3.1g net carbs, 29.8g protein
* 8-ounce glass of water
* Meaty Fried "Rice" (kit cookbook, page 134)
* 3 celery stalks

SNACK: 13g fat, 9.5g net carbs, 9g protein
* 8-ounce glass of water
* 1 (8-ounce) carton unsweetened, full-fat, traditional-style yogurt
* 1 tablespoon unsweetened shredded coconut
* 1 tablespoon coconut cream

DINNER: 40.2g fat, 4.2g net carbs, 29.4g protein
* 8-ounce glass of water
* Pulled Pork (kit cookbook, page 8)
* Cauliflower Mash (kit cookbook, page 140)

DAY 11

BREAKFAST: 43.5g fat, 4.3g net carbs, 28.3g protein
* 8-ounce glass of water
* Tex-Mex Keto Hash (kit cookbook, page 42)

SNACK: 4.8g fat, 0.4g net carbs, 6.3g protein
* 8-ounce glass of water
* 1 hard-boiled egg (kit cookbook, page 2)

LUNCH: 22.7g fat, 5g net carbs, 14.2g protein
* 8-ounce glass of water
* Cheeseburger Salad (kit cookbook, page 71)

SNACK: 16.9g fat, 1.3g net carbs, 9g protein
* 8-ounce glass of water
* Bacon-Liverwurst Ball (kit cookbook, page 101)

DINNER: 40g fat, 9.4g net carbs, 31.8g protein
* 8-ounce glass of water
* Keto Italiano Stuffed Peppers (kit cookbook, page 130)
* Serving of Signature Tomato Soup (kit cookbook, page 59)
* ¼ avocado, diced and used as garnish for the soup

DAY 12

BREAKFAST: 8g fat, 8g net carbs, 8.5g protein

* 8-ounce glass of water
* 1 (8-ounce) carton unsweetened, full-fat, traditional-style yogurt

SNACK: 4.8g fat, 0.4g net carbs, 6.3g protein

* 8-ounce glass of water
* 1 hard-boiled egg (kit cookbook, page 2)

LUNCH: 41.4g fat, 5.2g net carbs, 33.5g protein

* 8-ounce glass of water
* Keto Italiano Lasagna (kit cookbook, page 160)

SNACK: 15.9g fat, 5.8g net carbs, 5.9g protein

* 8-ounce glass of water
* Pizza Bomb (kit cookbook, page 107)

DINNER: 56.8g fat, 6.3g net carbs, 34.4g protein

* 8-ounce glass of water
* Keto Meatballs (kit cookbook, page 7)
* Spiralized Zucchini Noodles (kit cookbook, page 139)

DAY 13

BREAKFAST: 30.1g fat, 5.8g net carbs, 17.6g protein

* 8-ounce glass of water
* Keto Breakfast Cakes, eaten with no topping (kit cookbook, page 39)
* 2 tablespoons heavy cream, whipped (with no sweetener)

SNACK: 19.5g fat, 4g net carbs, 9.5g protein

* 8-ounce glass of water
* Nutty 3-Ingredient Crackers (kit cookbook, page 120)

LUNCH: 50.9g fat, 3.4g net carbs, 47.1g protein

* Chard Leaf Meatball Hoagie Wrap (kit cookbook, page 94)

SNACK: 0.3g fat, 5g net carbs, 0.9g protein

* 8-ounce glass of water
* Watermelon Cooler (kit cookbook, page 179)

DINNER: 22.3g fat, 2.8g net carbs, 14.1g protein

* 8-ounce glass of water
* Keto Quiche (kit cookbook, page 23)
* ¼ avocado, cubed

DAY 14

TOTAL MACROS
128.5g fat, 22.7g net carbs, 85.5g protein

BREAKFAST: 28.5g fat, 2.5g net carbs, 11.7g protein
* 8-ounce glass of water
* Baked Avocado (kit cookbook, page 37)

SNACK: 4.8 fat, 2.6g net carbs, 4.3g protein
* 8-ounce glass of water
* Chia-Berry Fresca (kit cookbook, page 181)

LUNCH: 33.5g fat, 6.6g net carbs, 25.9g protein
* Beef Stroganoff Stew (kit cookbook, page 52)
* 3 celery stalks

SNACK: 17g fat, 3.9g net carbs, 9.5g protein
* 8-ounce glass of water
* Bacon-Liverwurst Ball (kit cookbook, page 101)
* Green Keto Lemonade (kit cookbook, page 178)

DINNER: 45.2g fat, 8.1g net carbs, 34.1g protein
* 8-ounce glass of water
* Keto Italiano Lasagna (kit cookbook, page 160)
* Radish Slaw (kit cookbook, page 27)

DAY 15

TOTAL MACROS
130.6g fat, 26g net carbs, 87.2g protein

BREAKFAST: 12.8g fat, 8.4g net carbs, 14.8g protein
* 8-ounce glass of water
* 1 (8-ounce) carton unsweetened, full-fat, traditional-style yogurt
* 1 hard-boiled egg (kit cookbook, page 2)

SNACK: 33.1g fat, 4.5g net carbs, 2.8g protein
* 8-ounce glass of water
* Fatty Chai Latte (kit cookbook, page 174)

LUNCH: 30.4g fat, 3g net carbs, 32.1g protein
* 8-ounce glass of water
* Keto Shepherd's Pie (kit cookbook, page 145)

SNACK: 15.9g fat, 5.8g net carbs, 5.9g protein
* 8-ounce glass of water
* Pizza Bomb (kit cookbook, page 107)

DINNER: 38.4g fat, 4.3g net carbs, 31.6g protein
* 8-ounce glass of water
* Keto Indi Curry (kit cookbook, page 143)
* Cauliflower Rice (kit cookbook, page 138)

DAY 16

TOTAL MACROS
127.7g fat, 23.8g net carbs, 85.7g protein

BREAKFAST: 23.6g fat, 2.4g net carbs, 21.9g protein
* 8-ounce glass of water
* Egg Cup (kit cookbook, page 34)

SNACK: 34.4g fat, 12g net carbs, 9g protein
* 8-ounce glass of water
* 1 (8-ounce) carton unsweetened, full-fat, traditional-style yogurt
* Keto Coffee Latte (kit cookbook, page 170)

LUNCH: 26g fat, 1.3g net carbs, 7.9g protein
* 8-ounce glass of water
* Keto Greek Salad (kit cookbook, page 68)

SNACK: 20g fat, 6.2g net carbs, 1.6g protein
* 8-ounce glass of water
* 20 oil-packed olives (any type)

DINNER: 23.7g fat, 1.9g net carbs, 45.3g protein
* 8-ounce glass of water
* Big Batch Chicken Thighs (kit cookbook, page 3)
* Roasted Low-Carb Roots (kit cookbook, page 26)

DAY 17

TOTAL MACROS:
26.3g fat, 25.1g net carbs, 91.9g protein

BREAKFAST: 41.8g fat, 1.8g net carbs, 28.4g protein
* 8-ounce glass of water
* BLT Stack (kit cookbook, page 38)

SNACK: 8g fat, 8g net carbs, 8.5g protein
* 8-ounce glass of water
* 1 (8-ounce) carton unsweetened, full-fat, traditional-style yogurt

LUNCH: 45.2g fat, 6g net carbs, 27.3g protein
* 8-ounce glass of water
* 1 cup chicken salad, made with 1½ cups of chopped chicken thigh meat from last night's dinner and two tablespoons of mayonnaise
* 3 cups baby spinach
* ¼ small avocado

SNACK: 8.8g fat, 5.5g net carbs, 0.9g protein
* 8-ounce glass of water
* Orange-Scented Chocolates (kit cookbook, page 118)

DINNER: 22.5g fat, 3.8g net carbs, 26.8g protein
* 8-ounce glass of water
* Keto Bowl Blueprint (kit cookbook, page 150)

DAY 18

TOTAL MACROS
132.2g fat, 21.1g net carbs, 88.3g protein

BREAKFAST: 19g fat, 5g net carbs, 17g protein

* 8-ounce glass of water
* Keto Breakfast Cakes, eaten with no topping (kit cookbook, page 39)

SNACK: 37.7g fat, 3.2g net carbs, 2.5g protein

* 8-ounce glass of water
* Coconut Coffee Shake (kit cookbook, page 171)

LUNCH: 18.9g fat, 3.3g net carbs, 31.1g protein

* Cilantro-Lime Shrimp Scampi with Zucchini Noodles (kit cookbook, page 132)
* ¼ avocado, cubed

SNACK: 19.5g fat, 4g net carbs, 9.5g protein

* 8-ounce glass of water
* Nutty 3-Ingredient Crackers (kit cookbook, page 120)

DINNER: 37.1g fat, 5.6g net carbs, 28.2g protein

* 8-ounce glass of water
* Keto Shepherd's Pie (kit cookbook, page 145)

DAY 19

TOTAL MACROS
125.7g fat, 21.6g net carbs, 85.7g protein

BREAKFAST: 9.6g fat, 0.7g net carbs, 12.6g protein

* 8-ounce glass of water
* 2 hard-boiled eggs (kit cookbook, page 2)

SNACK: 30.2g fat, 3.1g net carbs, 5.5g protein

* 8-ounce glass of water
* Simple Nut Butter Fudge (kit cookbook, page 114)

LUNCH: 37.7g fat, 5.6g net carbs, 29.7g protein

* 8-ounce glass of water
* Meaty Fried "Rice" (kit cookbook, page 134)
* 3 medium celery stalks

SNACK: 8g fat, 8g net carbs, 8.5g protein

* 8-ounce glass of water
* 1 (8-ounce) carton unsweetened, full-fat, traditional-style yogurt

DINNER: 40.2g fat, 4.2g net carbs, 29.4g protein

* 8-ounce glass of water
* Pulled Pork (kit cookbook, page 8)
* Cauliflower Mash (kit cookbook, page 140)

DAY 20

BREAKFAST: 43.5g fat, 4.3g net carbs, 28.3g protein

* 8-ounce glass of water
* Tex-Mex Keto Hash (kit cookbook, page 42)

SNACK: 4.8g fat, 5g net carbs, 0.5g protein

* 8-ounce glass of water
* Green Keto Lemonade (kit cookbook, page 178)

LUNCH: 26.8g fat, 4.2g net carbs, 22.8g protein

* Deli Counter Lettuce Sub (kit cookbook, page 84)
* ¼ avocado, sliced
* Radish Slaw (kit cookbook, page 27)

SNACK: 8.8g fat, 5.5g net carbs, 0.9g protein

* 8-ounce glass of water
* Orange-Scented Chocolates (kit cookbook, page 118)

DINNER: 36.7g fat, 3.5g net carbs, 36.3g protein

* 8-ounce glass of water
* Cream of Turkey Soup with Bacon (kit cookbook, page 62)

DAY 21

BREAKFAST: 12.8g fat, 8.4g net carbs, 14.8g protein

* 8-ounce glass of water
* 1 (8-ounce) carton unsweetened, full-fat, traditional-style yogurt
* 1 hard-boiled egg (kit cookbook, page 2)

SNACK: 41.2 fat, 5.9g net carbs, 4.6g protein

* 8-ounce glass of water
* Fatty Chai Latte (kit cookbook, page 174)
* 3 medium celery stalks with ½ tablespoon natural peanut butter

LUNCH: 30.4g fat, 3g net carbs, 32.1g protein

* 8-ounce glass of water
* Keto Shepherd's Pie (kit cookbook, page 145)

SNACK: 7.1g fat, 0.9g net carbs, 2.9g protein

* 8-ounce glass of water
* Pizza Bomb (kit cookbook, page 107)

DINNER: 38.4g fat, 4.3g net carbs, 31.6g protein

* 8-ounce glass of water
* Keto Indi Curry (kit cookbook, page 143)
* Cauliflower Rice (kit cookbook, page 138)

DAY 22

BREAKFAST: 28.5g fat, 2.5g net carbs, 11.7g protein
* 8-ounce glass of water
* Baked Avocado (kit cookbook, page 37)

SNACK: 29.2g fat, 5.9g net carbs, 9.5g protein
* 8-ounce glass of water
* Nutty 3-Ingredient Crackers (kit cookbook, page 120)
* ¼ cup Keto Hummus (kit cookbook, page 14)

LUNCH: 12.7g fat, 6.2g net carbs, 12.7g protein
* Serving of Signature Tomato Soup (kit cookbook, page 59)
* 1 hard-boiled egg (kit cookbook, page 2)
* Three medium stalks celery

SNACK: 13.1g fat, 5.8g net carbs, 12g protein
* 8-ounce glass of water
* Orange-Scented Chocolate (kit cookbook, page 118)
* ⅓ cup whole milk cottage cheese (large curd)

DINNER: 47.7g fat, 2.6g net carbs, 43.8g protein
* 8-ounce glass of water
* Inside-Out Avocado Burger Pockets (kit cookbook, page 85)

DAY 23

BREAKFAST: 4.8g fat, 0.4g net carbs, 6.3g protein
* 8-ounce glass of water
* 1 hard-boiled egg (kit cookbook, page 2)

SNACK: 19.4g fat, 0.4g net carbs, 1.6g protein
* 8-ounce glass of water
* Iced Keto Coffee (kit cookbook, page 171)

LUNCH: 52g fat, 5.6g net carbs, 22g protein
* Italian Sausage Bowl (kit cookbook, page 156)

SNACK: 16.4g fat, 12.4g net carbs, 12.9g protein
* 8-ounce glass of water
* 1 (8-ounce) carton unsweetened, full-fat, traditional-style yogurt
* 1 tablespoon natural peanut butter, stirred into the yogurt
* 3 medium celery sticks

DINNER: 38.4g fat, 3.4g net carbs, 44g protein
* 8-ounce glass of water
* Stuffed Salmon (kit cookbook, page 162)
* Cauliflower Keto Steak (kit cookbook, page 166)

DAY 24

BREAKFAST: 30.1g fat, 5.8g net carbs, 17.6g protein

* 8-ounce glass of water
* Keto Breakfast Cakes, eaten with no topping (kit cookbook, page 39)
* 2 tablespoons heavy cream, whipped (with no sweetener)

SNACK: 7.2g fat, 2.6g net carbs, 9.3g protein

* 8-ounce glass of water
* 1-ounce serving beef jerky

LUNCH: 32.2g fat, 4.9g net carbs, 1.7g protein

* Cauliflower-Tabbouleh Salad (kit cookbook, page 69)
* ¼ avocado, cubed

SNACK: 5.6g fat, 1.6g net carbs, 2.8g protein

* 8-ounce glass of water
* 2-tablespoon serving of Keto Cheese Dip (kit cookbook, page 122)
* 5 celery sticks

DINNER: 54.5g fat, 4.2g net carbs, 48.1g protein

* 8-ounce glass of water
* Fish Baked in Coconut Milk (kit cookbook, page 11)
* Keto Broccoli Rabe Sauté (kit cookbook, page 24)

DAY 25

BREAKFAST: 43.5g fat, 4.3g net carbs, 28.3g protein

* 8-ounce glass of water
* Tex-Mex Keto Hash (kit cookbook, page 42)

SNACK: 4.8g fat, 0.4g net carbs, 6.3g protein

* 8-ounce glass of water
* 1 hard-boiled egg (kit cookbook, page 2)

LUNCH: 22.7g fat, 5g net carbs, 14.2g protein

* 8-ounce glass of water
* Cheeseburger Salad (kit cookbook, page 71)

SNACK: 16.9g fat, 1.3g net carbs, 9g protein

* 8-ounce glass of water
* Bacon-Liverwurst Ball (kit cookbook, page 101)

DINNER: 40g fat, 9.4g net carbs, 31.8g protein

* 8-ounce glass of water
* Keto Italiano Stuffed Peppers (kit cookbook, page 130)
* Serving of Signature Tomato Soup (kit cookbook, page 59)
* ¼ avocado, diced and used as garnish for the soup

DAY 26

BREAKFAST: 8g fat, 8g net carbs, 8.5g protein
* 8-ounce glass of water
* 1 (8-ounce) carton unsweetened, full-fat, traditional-style yogurt

SNACK: 10g fat, 3.1g net carbs, 1.6g protein
* 8-ounce glass of water
* 10 oil-packed olives (any type)

LUNCH: 64.4g fat, 5g net carbs, 47.1g protein
* 8-ounce glass of water
* Keto Cobb Salad (kit cookbook, page 73)

SNACK: 0.1g fat, 2.6g net carbs, 0.5g protein
* 8-ounce glass of water
* Green Keto Lemonade (kit cookbook, page 178)

DINNER: 40g fat, 9.4g net carbs, 31.8g protein
* 8-ounce glass of water
* Keto Italiano Stuffed Peppers (kit cookbook, page 130)
* Serving of Signature Tomato Soup (kit cookbook, page 59)
* ¼ avocado, diced and used as garnish for the soup

DAY 27

BREAKFAST: 9.6g fat, 0.7g net carbs, 12.6g protein
* 8-ounce glass of water
* 2 hard-boiled eggs (kit cookbook, page 2)

SNACK: 30.2g fat, 3.1g net carbs, 5.5g protein
* 8-ounce glass of water
* Simple Nut Butter Fudge (kit cookbook, page 114)

LUNCH: 37.8g fat, 5.8g net carbs, 29.8g protein
* 8-ounce glass of water
* Meaty Fried "Rice" (kit cookbook, page 134)
* 3 medium celery stalks

SNACK: 8g fat, 8g net carbs, 8.5g protein
* 8-ounce glass of water
* 1 (8-ounce) carton unsweetened, full-fat, traditional-style yogurt

DINNER: 40.2g fat, 4.2g net carbs, 29.4g protein
* 8-ounce glass of water
* Pulled Pork (kit cookbook, page 8)
* Cauliflower Mash (kit cookbook, page 140)

DAY 28

TOTAL MACROS
128.8g fat, 24.7g net carbs, 88.6g protein

BREAKFAST: 23.6g fat, 2.4g net carbs, 21.9g protein
* 8-ounce glass of water
* Egg Cup (kit cookbook, page 34)

SNACK: 24g fat, 12.4g net carbs, 10.1g protein
* 8-ounce glass of water
* 1 (8-ounce) carton unsweetened, full-fat, traditional-style yogurt
* 2 tablespoon unsweetened shredded coconut
* 2 tablespoons coconut cream

LUNCH: 37.5g fat, 2.8g net carbs, 9.4g protein
* 8-ounce glass of water
* Keto Greek Salad (kit cookbook, page 68)
* ½ medium avocado

SNACK: 20g fat, 6.2g net carbs, 1.6g protein
* 8-ounce glass of water
* 20 oil-packed olives (any type)

DINNER: 23.7g fat, 1.9g net carbs, 45.3g protein
* 8-ounce glass of water
* Big Batch Chicken Thighs (kit cookbook, page 3)
* Roasted Low-Carb Roots (kit cookbook, page 26)

DAY 29

TOTAL MACROS
124.7g fat, 28.1g net carbs, 85.4 g protein

BREAKFAST: 29.9g fat, 5.8g net carbs, 17.9g protein
* 8-ounce glass of water
* Keto Breakfast Cakes (kit cookbook, page 39)
* Two tablespoons of heavy cream, whipped or poured over breakfast cakes unwhipped

SNACK: 29.5g fat, 5g net carbs, 11.5g protein
* 8-ounce glass of water
* Nutty 3-Ingredient Crackers (kit cookbook, page 120)
* 2 tablespoons cream cheese

LUNCH: 32.6g fat, 13.5g net carbs, 37.9g protein
* Cauliflower-Leek Bisque (kit cookbook, page 49)
* Keto Poke-Ish Bowl (kit cookbook, page 155)

SNACK: 16.2g fat, 1.9g net carbs, 5g protein
* 8-ounce glass of water
* Bacon Avocado Plop (kit cookbook, page 105)

DINNER: 16.5g fat, 1.9g net carbs, 13.1g protein
* 8-ounce glass of water
* Keto Quiche (kit cookbook, page 23)

DAY 30

TOTAL MACROS
127.3g fat, 24.1g net carbs, 91.6g protein

BREAKFAST: 41.8g fat, 1.8g net carbs, 28.4g protein
* 8-ounce glass of water
* BLT Stack (kit cookbook, page 38)

SNACK: 18.4g fat, 9.5g net carbs, 9.6g protein
* 8-ounce glass of water
* 1 (8-ounce) carton unsweetened, full-fat, traditional-style yogurt
* 2 tablespoons coconut cream

LUNCH: 45.2g fat, 6g net carbs, 27.3g protein
* 8-ounce glass of water
* 1 cup chicken salad, made with 1½ cups of chopped chicken thigh meat from last night's dinner and 2 tablespoons of mayonnaise
* 3 cups baby spinach
* ¼ small avocado

SNACK: 7.1g fat, 0.8g net carbs, 2.9g protein
* 8-ounce glass of water
* Pizza Bomb (kit cookbook, page 107)

DINNER: 14.8g fat, 6g net carbs, 23.4g protein
* 8-ounce glass of water
* Thai Coconut Soup (kit cookbook, page 60)

RESOURCES

The Complete Book of Food Counts, 9th Edition: The Book That Counts It All by Corinne T. Netzer. In this day of online searching, do you really need a book of food counts? Maybe not, but having a book that you can quickly open and find the macros (and micros, too, if you'd like) of any ingredient, is helpful.

https://ketohc.com Keto Health Care sells fat calipers, digital scales, breath meters, and various supplements.

https://www.kissmyketo.com Kiss My Keto is an online keto store that sells keto urine test strips. There is also an informative blog with first person guest posts from a variety of keto experts.

https://www.ketogenic-diet-resource.com/ This comprehensive website not only talks about how the keto diet works, but takes a look at the various health conditions that may be helped by the diet. There is also a list of resources.

https://www.verywellfit.com/recipe-nutrition-analyzer-4157076 VeryWellFit's recipe nutrition analyzer is a brilliant tool to help calculate the macros in your favorite recipes. Just plug in the ingredients and the number of servings a recipe makes, and you'll have a custom-generated list of macros.

https://www.ruled.me/start-here/ Ruled.Me is a popular website that offers a soup-to-nuts lineup of keto-oriented topics, from how to begin to the "keto calculator" that helps you come up with the number of macros you may want to eat each day to meet your goals.

https://charliefoundation.org Charlie Abraham saw a disappearance of epilepsy symptoms when he tried a keto diet. His website dives deep into the large number of health conditions that have been shown by research to be improved by a keto diet.

https://www.nutritionadvance.com/ An easy-to-navigate site with a wide range of helpful articles on low-carb diets.

BIBLIOGRAPHY

Abbas E. Kitabchi. "Hyperglycemic Crises in Adult Patients With Diabetes." Diabetes Care, July 2009. http://care.diabetesjournals.org/content /32/7/1335

America Heart Association. "What Is Metabolic Syndrome?" 2015. https: //www.heart.org/-/media/data-import/downloadables/pe-abh-what-is -metabolic-syndrome-ucm_300322.pdf

Benjamin, Emelia J., Michael J. Blaha, Stephanie E. Chiuve, Mary Cushman, Sandeep R. Das, Rajat Deo, Sarah D. de Ferranti et al. "Heart Disease and Stroke Statistics—2017 Update: A Report From the American Heart Association." Circulation 135, no. 10 (January 25, 2017): https://doi .org/10.1161/CIR.0000000000000485.

Desilver, Drew. "What's on Your Table? How America's Diet Has Changed Over the Decades." Pew Research, December 16, 2013. http://pewrsr .ch/2htxtkX.

Epilepsy Ontario. "Ketogenic Diet for Epilepsy." July 2015. http: //epilepsytoronto.org/wp-content/uploads/2016/05/KetogenicDiet1.pdf.

Gibas, Madeline K., Kelly J. Gibas. "Induced and Controlled Dietary Ketosis as a Regulator of Obesity and Metabolic Syndrome Pathologies." Supplement, *Diabetes & Metabolic Syndrome: Clinical Research & Reviews* 11, S1 (November 11, 2017): https://doi.org/10.1016/j.dsx.2017.03.022.

Hallböök, Tove, Johan Lundgren, and Ingmar Rosén. "Ketogenic Diet Improves Sleep Quality in Children with Therapy-resistant Epilepsy." *Epilepsia* 48, no. 1 (January 2007): https://doi.org/10.1111/j.1528 -1167.2006.00834.x

Hollands Gareth J., Ian Shemilt, Theresa M. Marteau, Susan A. Jebb, Hannah B. Lewis, Yinghui Wei, Julian P. T. Higgins, and David Ogilvie. "Portion, Package or Tableware Size for Changing Selection and Consumption of Food, Alcohol and Tobacco." *The Cochrane Database of Systematic Reviews*, no. 9 (September 14, 2015): https://doi.10.1002 /14651858.CD011045.pub2.

LaBerge, Ann F. "How the Ideology of Low Fat Conquered America." *Journal of the History of Medicine and Allied Sciences* 63, no. 2 (April 1, 2008): https://doi.org/10.1093/jhmas/jrn001.

Lane, James D., Christina E. Barkauskas, Richard S. Surwit, and Mark N. Feinglos. "Caffeine Impairs Glucose Metabolism in Type 2 Diabetes." *Diabetes Care* 27, no. 8 (August 2004): https://doi.org/10.2337/diacare.27.8.2047.

Nordmann, Alain J., Abigail Nordmann, Matthias Briel, Ulrich Keller, William S. Yancy Jr, Bonnie J. Brehm, Heiner C. Bucher. "Effects of Low-Carbohydrate vs Low-Fat Diets on Weight Loss and Cardiovascular Risk Factors: A Meta-analysis of Randomized Controlled Trials." *Archives of Internal Medicine* 166, no. 3 (February 13, 2006): https//doi.10.1001/archinte.166.3.285.

"One-Year Study of Atkins Diet Shows Surprising Results, Penn Researchers Report." Penn Medicine News, May 1, 2003. https://www.pennmedicine.org/news/news-releases/2003/may/oneyear-study-of-atkins-diet-s.

Pennington, Alfred W. "A Reorientation on Obesity." *New England Journal of Medicine* (June 4, 1953): https://www.nejm.org/doi/pdf/10.1056/NEJM195306042482301.

Schulte, Erica M., Julia K. Smeal, Jessi Lewis, and Ashley N. Gearhardt. "Development of the Highly Processed Food Withdrawal Scale," *Appetite*, 131 (December 1, 2018): https://doi.org/10.1016/j.appet.2018.09.013

Smiley, Dawn, Prakash Chandra, and Guillermo E. Umpierrez. "Update on Diagnosis, Pathogenesis and Management of Ketosis-prone Type 2 Diabetes Mellitus." *Diabetes Management* 1, no. 6 (November 1, 2011): https://www.ncbi.nlm.nih.gov/pmc/articles/PMC3351851/.

Strofman, Carl E and Jong M. Rho. "The Ketogenic Diet as a Treatment Paradigm for Diverse Neurological Disorders." *Frontiers in Pharmacology* 3, no. 59 (April 9, 2012): https://doi.org/10.3389/fphar.2012.00059.

U.S. Food and Drug Administration. "Labeling and Nutrition." December 2018. https://www.fda.gov/food/labelingnutrition/default.htm

Wheless, James W. "History of the Ketogenic Diet." *Epilepsia* (November 2008): https://doi.org/10.1111/j.1528-1167.2008.01821.x.

"Women Spend Six Years of Their Lives on a Diet, According to New Research." Forza Industries, April 29, 2016. http://forzaindustries.com/press-office/2016/4/29/women-spend-six-years-of-their-lives-on-a-diet-according-to-new-research

Zitron-Emanuel, Noa, Tzvi Ganel. "Food Deprivation Reduces the Susceptibility to Size-contrast Illusions." *Appetite* 128 (September 1, 2018): https://doi.org/10.1016/j.appet.2018.06.006

INDEX

THE KETO KIT
JOURNAL

STERLING
New York

STERLING
New York

An Imprint of Sterling Publishing Co., Inc.
1166 Avenue of the Americas
New York, NY 10036

This publication is intended for informational purposes only and is not intended to provide or replace conventional medical advice, treatment, or diagnosis or be a substitute to consulting with licensed medical or healthcare providers. The publisher does not claim or guarantee any benefits, healing, cure, or any results in any respect and shall not be liable or responsible for any use or application of any content in this publication in any respect including without limitation any adverse effects, consequence, loss, or damage of any type resulting or arising from, directly or indirectly, any use or application of any content herein. Any trademarks are the property of their respective owners, are used for editorial purposes only, and the publisher makes no claim of ownership and shall acquire no right, title, or interest in such trademarks by virtue of this publication.

This publication is a component of the *The Keto Kit*
(ISBN: 978-1-4549-3507-0) and is not to be sold separately.

ISBN 978-1-4549-3510-0

For information about custom editions, special sales, and premium
and corporate purchases, please contact Sterling Special Sales
at 800-805-5489 or specialsales@sterlingpublishing.com.

Manufactured in Canada

2 4 6 8 10 9 7 5 3 1

sterlingpublishing.com

Cover design by David Ter-Avanesyan
Interior design by Christine Heun
Icons: Victor/iStock

CONTENTS

INTRODUCTION

One of the things that makes *The Keto Kit* so special—and such an effective support for new keto-eaters—is this journal.

Really.

Of course *The Keto Kit Diet* is essential in guiding you through keto's ins and outs, as well as providing you with the knowledge you'll need to be successful. *The Keto Kit Cookbook* will ensure that you always have delicious easy-to-make, keto-compliant food to enjoy (a common downfall of keto newbies is they don't know what to eat). But the Keto Kit Journal. . . . Well, this deceptively simple log-style workbook is the secret to your success.

As you thumb through *The Keto Kit Journal*, you'll see inspirational quotes, dedicated space to record your intentions and reflections, and daily calendar entries to record your food intake, water intake, hours slept, stress levels, and exercise. Reaching and maintaining ketosis has a lot to do with your food choices. But there are other factors that help you attain and stay in ketosis, including your water intake, proper sleep, stress management, and physical movement. You'll learn more about all of these when you read *The Keto Kit Diet* book.

I cannot force you to use this journal. But I believe that you'll lose weight so much faster, and reach ketosis so much more quickly—and find the entire diet so much easier—if you do. Studies show that people who record what they eat, are more likely to lose weight.

In a study published in the September 2012 issue of *Journal of the Academy of Nutrition and Dietetics*, researchers from Cancer Education and Career Development Program Institute for Health Research and Policy University of Illinois at Chicago studied 123 post-menopausal women with an average age of 58 and a BMI of 31.1 (which is considered obese) for an entire year. Subjects were encouraged to increase fruit and vegetable intake, exercise regularly, decrease sugar and alcohol consumption, and keep a daily food journal. At the end of the year, participants lost an average of 10.7 percent of their overall bodyweight. But here's why I am sharing this study: Women at the 75th percentile of number of food journals submitted had a 3.7 percent greater weight loss than those at the 25th percentile. In plain English, women who used their food journals the most, had higher weight loss.

Several similar studies have found the same thing: Writing down what you eat helps you lose weight. Recording what you eat makes you mindful of what you are putting in your mouth and helps you remember what you've already consumed, so you don't end up over-eating at the end of the day.

Furthermore, recording your food intake—and the amount of water you drank, how many hours you slept, how stressed you felt during the day, and your daily exercise routine—keeps you focused on self-care. Paying attention to how you care for yourself is enlightening and motivates you to keep up the good work. This attention to self-care is an easy support system that can help form new, healthy habits—habits that will put your keto eating on autopilot.

But how do you use *The Keto Kit Journal?* When you first dive into keto-eating, keep this journal nearby—I like to keep it in my handbag—so you can record a meal or a snack the moment you consume it. When I am waiting for a slow computer to load, or I'm in transit on public transportation, I pull it out and fill in the sleep, stress, and exercise sections. You can also keep it by your bedside to use right before you turn in. Or, you can photocopy pages and post them at your desk, in your kitchen, or some other spot you'll be sure to see them. Truly, the best way to use *The Keto Kit Journal* is consistently. So find a method that works for you and stick to it. If, for some reason, you keep forgetting to use *The Keto Kit Journal*, course-correct and use the workbook in a different way. It may take a bit of experimenting to make recording your healthy actions a daily habit, but don't give up.

—Stephanie Pedersen

You don't have to see the WHOLE staircase, just take the FIRST STEP.

—*Martin Luther King, Jr.*

PERSONAL GOALS

Having a goal will keep you focused and writing it down here will keep you accountable. Here are some tips to consider when setting a goal.

CONSIDER WHAT'S IMPORTANT TO YOU: Your goal is personal. Think of why you decided to start *The Keto Kit* journey. Whatever the reason, it is a good one.

BE SPECIFIC BUT REALISTIC: Make your goal measurable. Instead of "to lose weight," a better goal is "to lose 10 pounds in the next month." Set goals that can be attained so you will not be discouraged.

USE "I WILL" RATHER THAN "I WANT": This phrase will set you up for success. Affirmative statements have been proven to have subtle positive effects.

SET A DEADLINE: An end date makes your goal more of a challenge. This journal is 7 weeks so consider that your deadline.

MY GOAL

....

....

....

....

I will achieve this because . . .

....

....

....

I will achieve this by . . .

....

....

....

WEEK 1

This week I want to accomplish . . .

This week I want to overcome . . .

My inspiration this week is . . .

FOOD LOG

DATE _____

	MON	TUE	WED	THUR	FRI	SAT	SUN

BREAKFAST

	AMOUNT	CAL.	FAT	CARBS	FIBER	NET CARB	PROTEIN
TOTAL							

LUNCH

	AMOUNT	CAL.	FAT	CARBS	FIBER	NET CARB	PROTEIN
TOTAL							

SNACKS

	AMOUNT	CAL.	FAT	CARBS	FIBER	NET CARB	PROTEIN
TOTAL							

DINNER

	AMOUNT	CAL.	FAT	CARBS	FIBER	NET CARB	PROTEIN
TOTAL							

SUPPLEMENTS

WATER

EXERCISE

ACTIVITY	MINUTES	CAL. BURNED

SLEEP

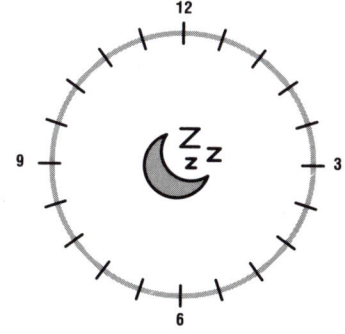

DAILY REFLECTION

HOW WAS YOUR DAY?

 1   2   3   4   5   6   7   8   9   10

FOOD LOG

DATE _____

	MON	TUE	WED	THUR	FRI	SAT	SUN

BREAKFAST

	AMOUNT	CAL.	FAT	CARBS	FIBER	NET CARB	PROTEIN
TOTAL							

LUNCH

	AMOUNT	CAL.	FAT	CARBS	FIBER	NET CARB	PROTEIN
TOTAL							

SNACKS

	AMOUNT	CAL.	FAT	CARBS	FIBER	NET CARB	PROTEIN
TOTAL							

DINNER

	AMOUNT	CAL.	FAT	CARBS	FIBER	NET CARB	PROTEIN
TOTAL							

SUPPLEMENTS

WATER

EXERCISE

ACTIVITY	MINUTES	CAL. BURNED

SLEEP

DAILY REFLECTION

HOW WAS YOUR DAY?

| 1 | 2 | 3 | 4 | 5 | 6 | 7 | 8 | 9 | 10 |

FOOD LOG

DATE _____

		MON	TUE	WED	THUR	FRI	SAT	SUN

BREAKFAST

	AMOUNT	CAL.	FAT	CARBS	FIBER	NET CARB	PROTEIN
TOTAL							

LUNCH

	AMOUNT	CAL.	FAT	CARBS	FIBER	NET CARB	PROTEIN
TOTAL							

SNACKS

	AMOUNT	CAL.	FAT	CARBS	FIBER	NET CARB	PROTEIN
TOTAL							

DINNER

	AMOUNT	CAL.	FAT	CARBS	FIBER	NET CARB	PROTEIN
TOTAL							

SUPPLEMENTS

WATER

EXERCISE

	ACTIVITY	MINUTES	CAL. BURNED
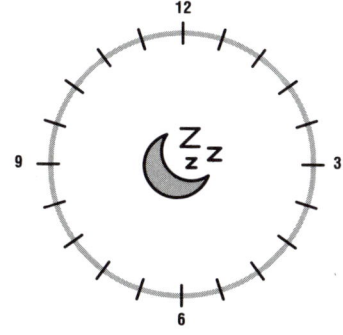			

SLEEP

DAILY REFLECTION

HOW WAS YOUR DAY?

1   2   3   4   5   6   7   8   9   10

FOOD LOG

DATE _____

	MON	TUE	WED	THUR	FRI	SAT	SUN
BREAKFAST	AMOUNT	CAL.	FAT	CARBS	FIBER	NET CARB	PROTEIN
TOTAL							
LUNCH	AMOUNT	CAL.	FAT	CARBS	FIBER	NET CARB	PROTEIN
TOTAL							
SNACKS	AMOUNT	CAL.	FAT	CARBS	FIBER	NET CARB	PROTEIN
TOTAL							
DINNER	AMOUNT	CAL.	FAT	CARBS	FIBER	NET CARB	PROTEIN
TOTAL							

SUPPLEMENTS

WATER

EXERCISE

	ACTIVITY	MINUTES	CAL. BURNED
🏃🏋️			
🏃🏋️			
🏃🏋️			
🏃🏋️			
🏃🏋️			
🏃🏋️			
🏃🏋️			

SLEEP

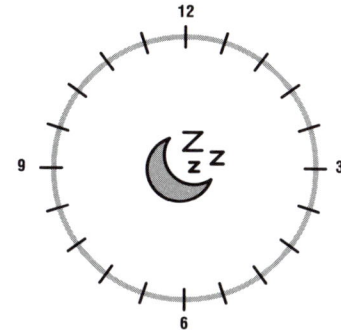

DAILY REFLECTION

 HOW WAS YOUR DAY?

1   2   3   4   5   6   7   8   9   10

FOOD LOG

DATE _____

	MON	TUE	WED	THUR	FRI	SAT	SUN

BREAKFAST

	AMOUNT	CAL.	FAT	CARBS	FIBER	NET CARB	PROTEIN
TOTAL							

LUNCH

	AMOUNT	CAL.	FAT	CARBS	FIBER	NET CARB	PROTEIN
TOTAL							

SNACKS

	AMOUNT	CAL.	FAT	CARBS	FIBER	NET CARB	PROTEIN
TOTAL							

DINNER

	AMOUNT	CAL.	FAT	CARBS	FIBER	NET CARB	PROTEIN
TOTAL							

SUPPLEMENTS

WATER

EXERCISE

	ACTIVITY	MINUTES	CAL. BURNED

SLEEP

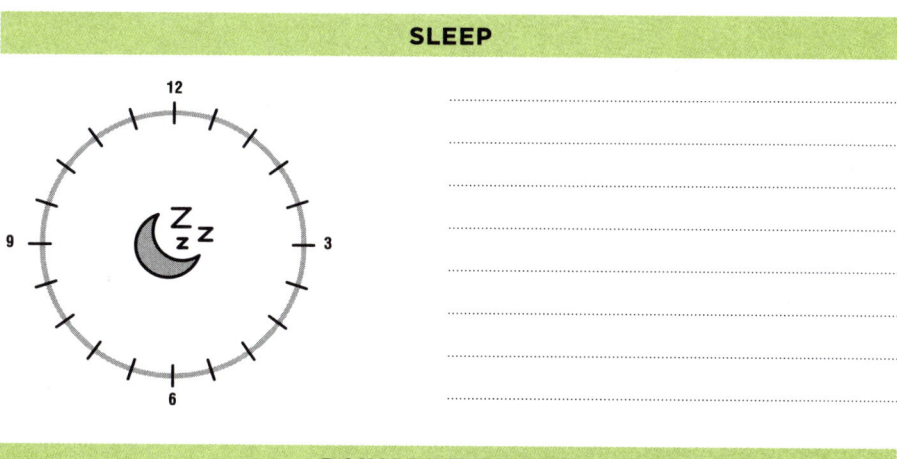

DAILY REFLECTION

HOW WAS YOUR DAY?

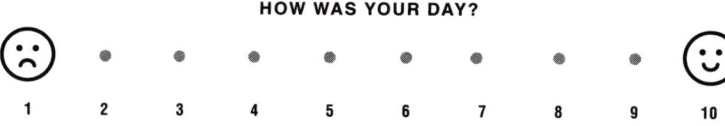

1   2   3   4   5   6   7   8   9   10

FOOD LOG

DATE _____

	MON	TUE	WED	THUR	FRI	SAT	SUN
BREAKFAST	AMOUNT	CAL.	FAT	CARBS	FIBER	NET CARB	PROTEIN
TOTAL							
LUNCH	AMOUNT	CAL.	FAT	CARBS	FIBER	NET CARB	PROTEIN
TOTAL							
SNACKS	AMOUNT	CAL.	FAT	CARBS	FIBER	NET CARB	PROTEIN
TOTAL							
DINNER	AMOUNT	CAL.	FAT	CARBS	FIBER	NET CARB	PROTEIN
TOTAL							

SUPPLEMENTS

WATER

EXERCISE

	ACTIVITY	MINUTES	CAL. BURNED

SLEEP

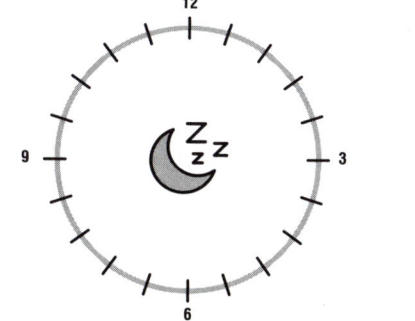

DAILY REFLECTION

HOW WAS YOUR DAY?

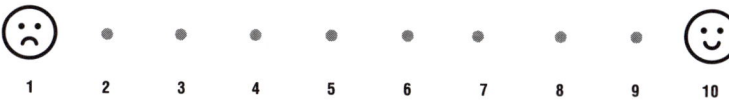

1   2   3   4   5   6   7   8   9   10

FOOD LOG

DATE _____

	MON	TUE	WED	THUR	FRI	SAT	SUN
BREAKFAST	AMOUNT	CAL.	FAT	CARBS	FIBER	NET CARB	PROTEIN
TOTAL							
LUNCH	AMOUNT	CAL.	FAT	CARBS	FIBER	NET CARB	PROTEIN
TOTAL							
SNACKS	AMOUNT	CAL.	FAT	CARBS	FIBER	NET CARB	PROTEIN
TOTAL							
DINNER	AMOUNT	CAL.	FAT	CARBS	FIBER	NET CARB	PROTEIN
TOTAL							

SUPPLEMENTS

WATER

EXERCISE

	ACTIVITY	MINUTES	CAL. BURNED

SLEEP

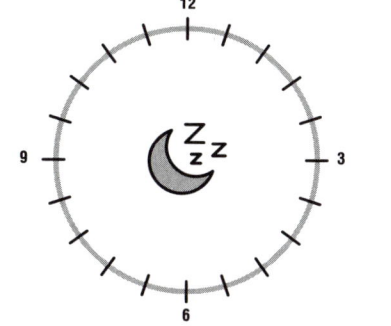

DAILY REFLECTION

HOW WAS YOUR DAY?

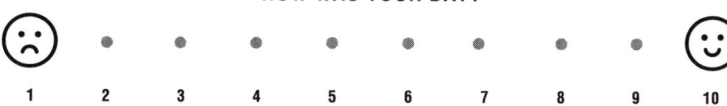

1   2   3   4   5   6   7   8   9   10

I am not WHAT HAS HAPPENED to me. I am what I CHOOSE to become.

—Carl Jung

WEEKLY REFLECTIONS

This week I accomplished . . .

This week I overcame . . .

My goals next week are . . .

WEEK 2

This week I want to accomplish . . .

This week I want to overcome . . .

My inspiration this week is . . .

FOOD LOG

DATE _____

		MON	TUE	WED	THUR	FRI	SAT	SUN

BREAKFAST

	AMOUNT	CAL.	FAT	CARBS	FIBER	NET CARB	PROTEIN
TOTAL							

LUNCH

	AMOUNT	CAL.	FAT	CARBS	FIBER	NET CARB	PROTEIN
TOTAL							

SNACKS

	AMOUNT	CAL.	FAT	CARBS	FIBER	NET CARB	PROTEIN
TOTAL							

DINNER

	AMOUNT	CAL.	FAT	CARBS	FIBER	NET CARB	PROTEIN
TOTAL							

SUPPLEMENTS

WATER

EXERCISE

ACTIVITY	MINUTES	CAL. BURNED

SLEEP

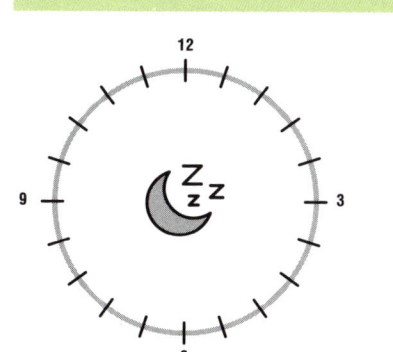

DAILY REFLECTION

HOW WAS YOUR DAY?

1   2   3   4   5   6   7   8   9   10

FOOD LOG

DATE _____	MON	TUE	WED	THUR	FRI	SAT	SUN
BREAKFAST	AMOUNT	CAL.	FAT	CARBS	FIBER	NET CARB	PROTEIN
TOTAL							
LUNCH	AMOUNT	CAL.	FAT	CARBS	FIBER	NET CARB	PROTEIN
TOTAL							
SNACKS	AMOUNT	CAL.	FAT	CARBS	FIBER	NET CARB	PROTEIN
TOTAL							
DINNER	AMOUNT	CAL.	FAT	CARBS	FIBER	NET CARB	PROTEIN
TOTAL							

SUPPLEMENTS

WATER

EXERCISE

ACTIVITY	MINUTES	CAL. BURNED

SLEEP

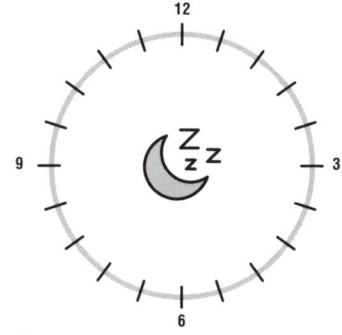

DAILY REFLECTION

HOW WAS YOUR DAY?

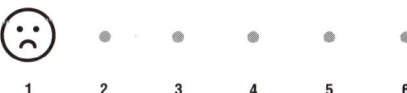

1   2   3   4   5   6   7   8   9   10

FOOD LOG

DATE _____

		MON	TUE	WED	THUR	FRI	SAT	SUN

BREAKFAST

	AMOUNT	CAL.	FAT	CARBS	FIBER	NET CARB	PROTEIN
TOTAL							

LUNCH

	AMOUNT	CAL.	FAT	CARBS	FIBER	NET CARB	PROTEIN
TOTAL							

SNACKS

	AMOUNT	CAL.	FAT	CARBS	FIBER	NET CARB	PROTEIN
TOTAL							

DINNER

	AMOUNT	CAL.	FAT	CARBS	FIBER	NET CARB	PROTEIN
TOTAL							

SUPPLEMENTS

WATER

EXERCISE

	ACTIVITY	MINUTES	CAL. BURNED

SLEEP

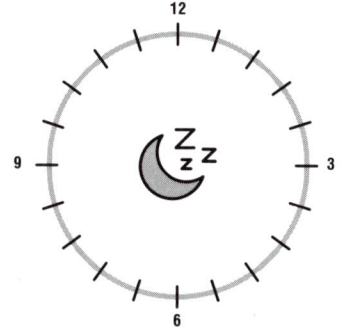

DAILY REFLECTION

HOW WAS YOUR DAY?

 1    2   3    4   5   6   7   8   9   10

FOOD LOG

DATE _____

	MON	TUE	WED	THUR	FRI	SAT	SUN

BREAKFAST

	AMOUNT	CAL.	FAT	CARBS	FIBER	NET CARB	PROTEIN
TOTAL							

LUNCH

	AMOUNT	CAL.	FAT	CARBS	FIBER	NET CARB	PROTEIN
TOTAL							

SNACKS

	AMOUNT	CAL.	FAT	CARBS	FIBER	NET CARB	PROTEIN
TOTAL							

DINNER

	AMOUNT	CAL.	FAT	CARBS	FIBER	NET CARB	PROTEIN
TOTAL							

SUPPLEMENTS

WATER

EXERCISE

	ACTIVITY	MINUTES	CAL. BURNED
🏃 🏋			
🏃 🏋			
🏃 🏋			
🏃 🏋			
🏃 🏋			
🏃 🏋			
🏃 🏋			

SLEEP

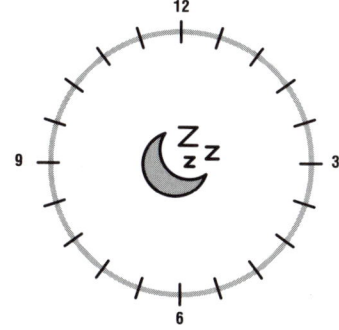

DAILY REFLECTION

HOW WAS YOUR DAY?

1 2 3 4 5 6 7 8 9 10

FOOD LOG

DATE _____

	MON	TUE	WED	THUR	FRI	SAT	SUN

BREAKFAST

	AMOUNT	CAL.	FAT	CARBS	FIBER	NET CARB	PROTEIN
TOTAL							

LUNCH

	AMOUNT	CAL.	FAT	CARBS	FIBER	NET CARB	PROTEIN
TOTAL							

SNACKS

	AMOUNT	CAL.	FAT	CARBS	FIBER	NET CARB	PROTEIN
TOTAL							

DINNER

	AMOUNT	CAL.	FAT	CARBS	FIBER	NET CARB	PROTEIN
TOTAL							

SUPPLEMENTS

WATER

EXERCISE

	ACTIVITY	MINUTES	CAL. BURNED
🏃 🏋			
🏃 🏋			
🏃 🏋			
🏃 🏋			
🏃 🏋			
🏃 🏋			
🏃 🏋			

SLEEP

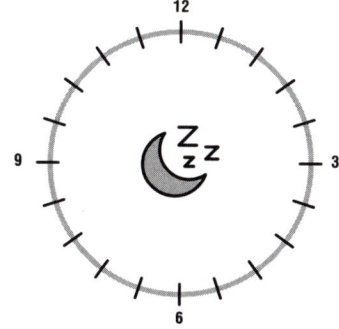

DAILY REFLECTION

HOW WAS YOUR DAY?

1   2   3   4   5   6   7   8   9   10

FOOD LOG

DATE _____

	MON	TUE	WED	THUR	FRI	SAT	SUN

BREAKFAST

	AMOUNT	CAL.	FAT	CARBS	FIBER	NET CARB	PROTEIN
TOTAL							

LUNCH

	AMOUNT	CAL.	FAT	CARBS	FIBER	NET CARB	PROTEIN
TOTAL							

SNACKS

	AMOUNT	CAL.	FAT	CARBS	FIBER	NET CARB	PROTEIN
TOTAL							

DINNER

	AMOUNT	CAL.	FAT	CARBS	FIBER	NET CARB	PROTEIN
TOTAL							

SUPPLEMENTS

WATER

EXERCISE

ACTIVITY		MINUTES	CAL. BURNED

SLEEP

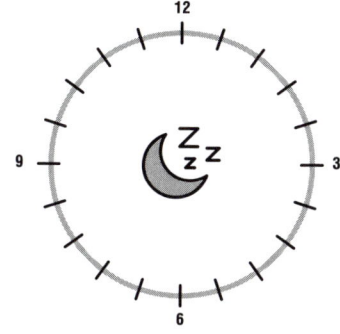

DAILY REFLECTION

HOW WAS YOUR DAY?

1   2   3   4   5   6   7   8   9   10

FOOD LOG

DATE _____

	MON	TUE	WED	THUR	FRI	SAT	SUN

BREAKFAST

	AMOUNT	CAL.	FAT	CARBS	FIBER	NET CARB	PROTEIN
TOTAL							

LUNCH

	AMOUNT	CAL.	FAT	CARBS	FIBER	NET CARB	PROTEIN
TOTAL							

SNACKS

	AMOUNT	CAL.	FAT	CARBS	FIBER	NET CARB	PROTEIN
TOTAL							

DINNER

	AMOUNT	CAL.	FAT	CARBS	FIBER	NET CARB	PROTEIN
TOTAL							

SUPPLEMENTS

WATER

EXERCISE

ACTIVITY		MINUTES	CAL. BURNED
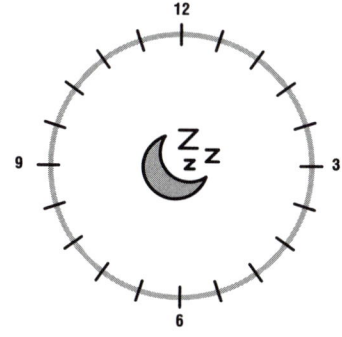			

SLEEP

DAILY REFLECTION

HOW WAS YOUR DAY?

1   2   3   4   5   6   7   8   9   10

If it doesn't CHALLENGE you, it won't CHANGE you.

—*Zig Ziglar*

WEEKLY REFLECTIONS

This week I accomplished . . .

This week I overcame . . .

My goals next week are . . .

WEEK 3

WEEKLY INTENTIONS

This week I want to accomplish . . .

This week I want to overcome . . .

My inspiration this week is . . .

FOOD LOG

DATE _____

	MON	TUE	WED	THUR	FRI	SAT	SUN
BREAKFAST	AMOUNT	CAL.	FAT	CARBS	FIBER	NET CARB	PROTEIN
TOTAL							
LUNCH	AMOUNT	CAL.	FAT	CARBS	FIBER	NET CARB	PROTEIN
TOTAL							
SNACKS	AMOUNT	CAL.	FAT	CARBS	FIBER	NET CARB	PROTEIN
TOTAL							
DINNER	AMOUNT	CAL.	FAT	CARBS	FIBER	NET CARB	PROTEIN
TOTAL							

SUPPLEMENTS

WATER

EXERCISE

ACTIVITY	MINUTES	CAL. BURNED
🏃 🏋		
🏃 🏋		
🏃 🏋		
🏃 🏋		
🏃 🏋		
🏃 🏋		
🏃 🏋		

SLEEP

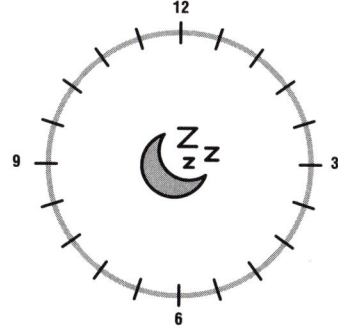

DAILY REFLECTION

HOW WAS YOUR DAY?

1   2   3   4   5   6   7   8   9   10

FOOD LOG

DATE _____

	MON	TUE	WED	THUR	FRI	SAT	SUN

BREAKFAST

	AMOUNT	CAL.	FAT	CARBS	FIBER	NET CARB	PROTEIN
TOTAL							

LUNCH

	AMOUNT	CAL.	FAT	CARBS	FIBER	NET CARB	PROTEIN
TOTAL							

SNACKS

	AMOUNT	CAL.	FAT	CARBS	FIBER	NET CARB	PROTEIN
TOTAL							

DINNER

	AMOUNT	CAL.	FAT	CARBS	FIBER	NET CARB	PROTEIN
TOTAL							

SUPPLEMENTS

WATER

EXERCISE

	ACTIVITY	MINUTES	CAL. BURNED

SLEEP

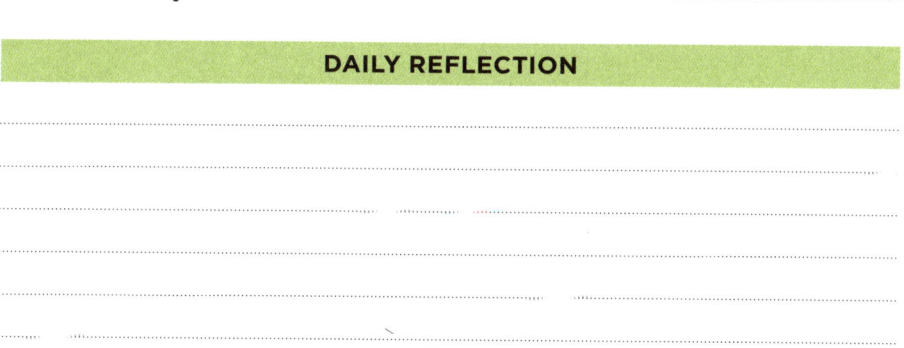

DAILY REFLECTION

HOW WAS YOUR DAY?

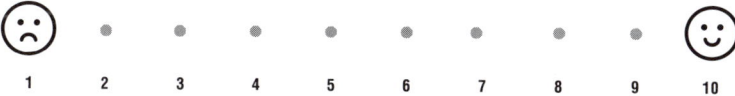

1   2   3   4   5   6   7   8   9   10

FOOD LOG

DATE _____

	MON	TUE	WED	THUR	FRI	SAT	SUN

BREAKFAST

	AMOUNT	CAL.	FAT	CARBS	FIBER	NET CARB	PROTEIN
TOTAL							

LUNCH

	AMOUNT	CAL.	FAT	CARBS	FIBER	NET CARB	PROTEIN
TOTAL							

SNACKS

	AMOUNT	CAL.	FAT	CARBS	FIBER	NET CARB	PROTEIN
TOTAL							

DINNER

	AMOUNT	CAL.	FAT	CARBS	FIBER	NET CARB	PROTEIN
TOTAL							

SUPPLEMENTS

WATER

EXERCISE

ACTIVITY	MINUTES	CAL. BURNED

SLEEP

DAILY REFLECTION

HOW WAS YOUR DAY?

1 2 3 4 5 6 7 8 9 10

FOOD LOG

DATE _____

	MON	TUE	WED	THUR	FRI	SAT	SUN

BREAKFAST

	AMOUNT	CAL.	FAT	CARBS	FIBER	NET CARB	PROTEIN
TOTAL							

LUNCH

	AMOUNT	CAL.	FAT	CARBS	FIBER	NET CARB	PROTEIN
TOTAL							

SNACKS

	AMOUNT	CAL.	FAT	CARBS	FIBER	NET CARB	PROTEIN
TOTAL							

DINNER

	AMOUNT	CAL.	FAT	CARBS	FIBER	NET CARB	PROTEIN
TOTAL							

SUPPLEMENTS

WATER

EXERCISE

ACTIVITY	MINUTES	CAL. BURNED

SLEEP

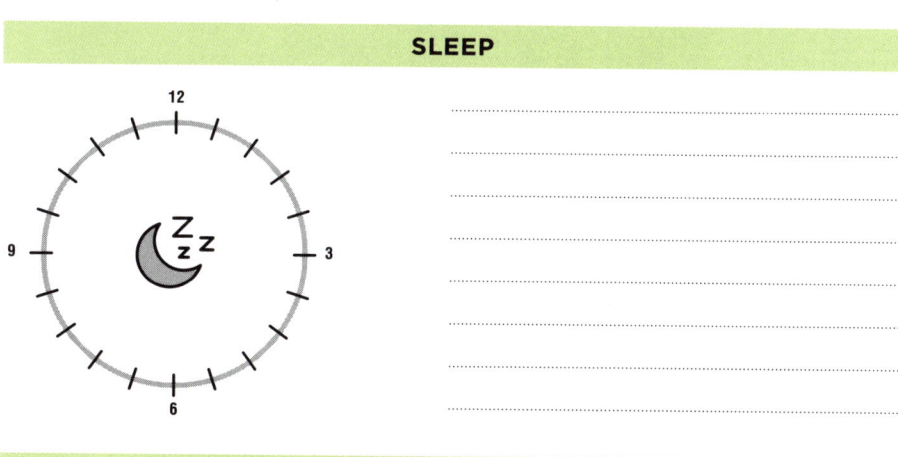

DAILY REFLECTION

HOW WAS YOUR DAY?

1   2   3   4   5   6   7   8   9   10

FOOD LOG

DATE _____

	MON	TUE	WED	THUR	FRI	SAT	SUN
BREAKFAST	AMOUNT	CAL.	FAT	CARBS	FIBER	NET CARB	PROTEIN
TOTAL							
LUNCH	AMOUNT	CAL.	FAT	CARBS	FIBER	NET CARB	PROTEIN
TOTAL							
SNACKS	AMOUNT	CAL.	FAT	CARBS	FIBER	NET CARB	PROTEIN
TOTAL							
DINNER	AMOUNT	CAL.	FAT	CARBS	FIBER	NET CARB	PROTEIN
TOTAL							

SUPPLEMENTS

WATER

EXERCISE

	ACTIVITY	MINUTES	CAL. BURNED

SLEEP

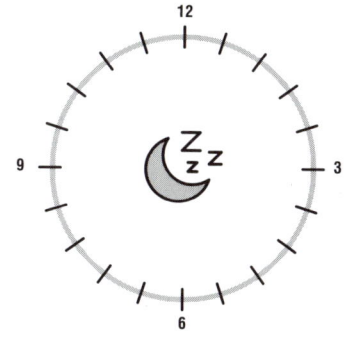

DAILY REFLECTION

HOW WAS YOUR DAY?

1   2   3   4   5   6   7   8   9   10

FOOD LOG

DATE _____

	MON	TUE	WED	THUR	FRI	SAT	SUN

BREAKFAST

	AMOUNT	CAL.	FAT	CARBS	FIBER	NET CARB	PROTEIN
TOTAL							

LUNCH

	AMOUNT	CAL.	FAT	CARBS	FIBER	NET CARB	PROTEIN
TOTAL							

SNACKS

	AMOUNT	CAL.	FAT	CARBS	FIBER	NET CARB	PROTEIN
TOTAL							

DINNER

	AMOUNT	CAL.	FAT	CARBS	FIBER	NET CARB	PROTEIN
TOTAL							

SUPPLEMENTS

WATER

EXERCISE

ACTIVITY		MINUTES	CAL. BURNED
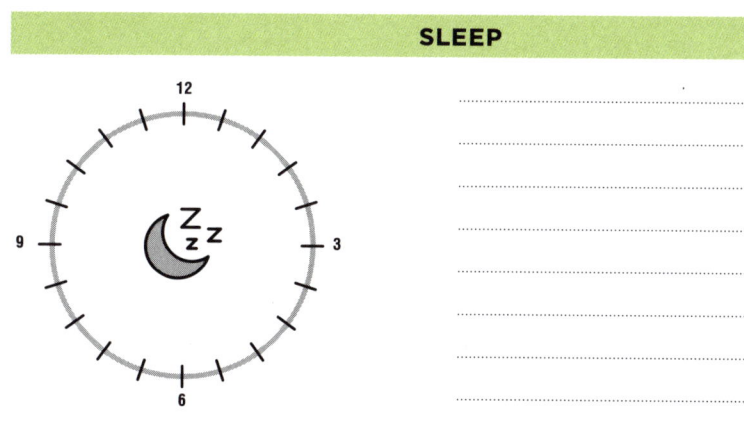			

SLEEP

DAILY REFLECTION

HOW WAS YOUR DAY?

1 2 3 4 5 6 7 8 9 10

FOOD LOG

DATE _____

	MON	TUE	WED	THUR	FRI	SAT	SUN
BREAKFAST	AMOUNT	CAL.	FAT	CARBS	FIBER	NET CARB	PROTEIN
TOTAL							
LUNCH	AMOUNT	CAL.	FAT	CARBS	FIBER	NET CARB	PROTEIN
TOTAL							
SNACKS	AMOUNT	CAL.	FAT	CARBS	FIBER	NET CARB	PROTEIN
TOTAL							
DINNER	AMOUNT	CAL.	FAT	CARBS	FIBER	NET CARB	PROTEIN
TOTAL							

SUPPLEMENTS

WATER

EXERCISE

ACTIVITY	MINUTES	CAL. BURNED

SLEEP

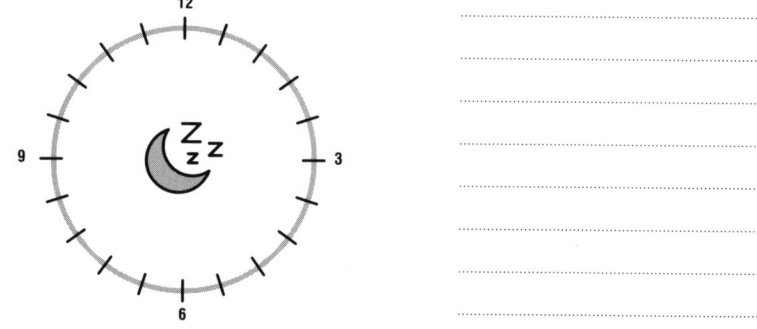

DAILY REFLECTION

HOW WAS YOUR DAY?

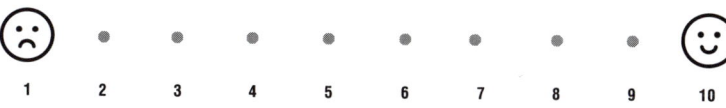

1   2   3   4   5   6   7   8   9   10

The future
DEPENDS
ON WHAT
YOU DO
today.

—*Mahatma Gandhi*

This week I accomplished . . .

This week I overcame . . .

My goals next week are . . .

WEEK 4

This week I want to accomplish . . .

This week I want to overcome . . .

My inspiration this week is . . .

DATE _____

	MON	TUE	WED	THUR	FRI	SAT	SUN
BREAKFAST	AMOUNT	CAL.	FAT	CARBS	FIBER	NET CARB	PROTEIN
TOTAL							
LUNCH	AMOUNT	CAL.	FAT	CARBS	FIBER	NET CARB	PROTEIN
TOTAL							
SNACKS	AMOUNT	CAL.	FAT	CARBS	FIBER	NET CARB	PROTEIN
TOTAL							
DINNER	AMOUNT	CAL.	FAT	CARBS	FIBER	NET CARB	PROTEIN
TOTAL							

SUPPLEMENTS

WATER

EXERCISE

ACTIVITY		MINUTES	CAL. BURNED

SLEEP

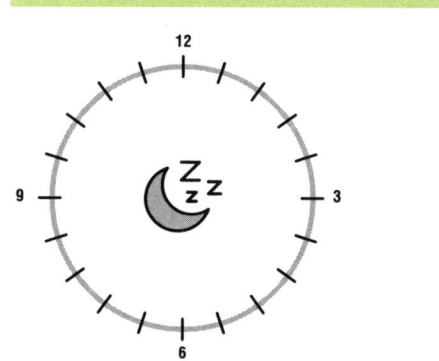

DAILY REFLECTION

FOOD LOG

DATE _____

	MON	TUE	WED	THUR	FRI	SAT	SUN
BREAKFAST	AMOUNT	CAL.	FAT	CARBS	FIBER	NET CARB	PROTEIN
TOTAL							
LUNCH	AMOUNT	CAL.	FAT	CARBS	FIBER	NET CARB	PROTEIN
TOTAL							
SNACKS	AMOUNT	CAL.	FAT	CARBS	FIBER	NET CARB	PROTEIN
TOTAL							
DINNER	AMOUNT	CAL.	FAT	CARBS	FIBER	NET CARB	PROTEIN
TOTAL							

SUPPLEMENTS

WATER

EXERCISE

	ACTIVITY	MINUTES	CAL. BURNED

SLEEP

DAILY REFLECTION

HOW WAS YOUR DAY?

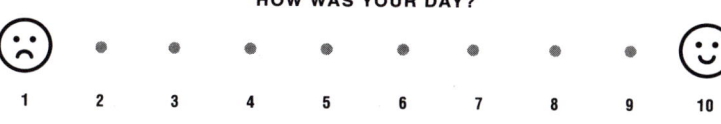

1 2 3 4 5 6 7 8 9 10

FOOD LOG

DATE _____

	MON	TUE	WED	THUR	FRI	SAT	SUN

BREAKFAST

	AMOUNT	CAL.	FAT	CARBS	FIBER	NET CARB	PROTEIN
TOTAL							

LUNCH

	AMOUNT	CAL.	FAT	CARBS	FIBER	NET CARB	PROTEIN
TOTAL							

SNACKS

	AMOUNT	CAL.	FAT	CARBS	FIBER	NET CARB	PROTEIN
TOTAL							

DINNER

	AMOUNT	CAL.	FAT	CARBS	FIBER	NET CARB	PROTEIN
TOTAL							

SUPPLEMENTS

WATER

EXERCISE

ACTIVITY	MINUTES	CAL. BURNED

SLEEP

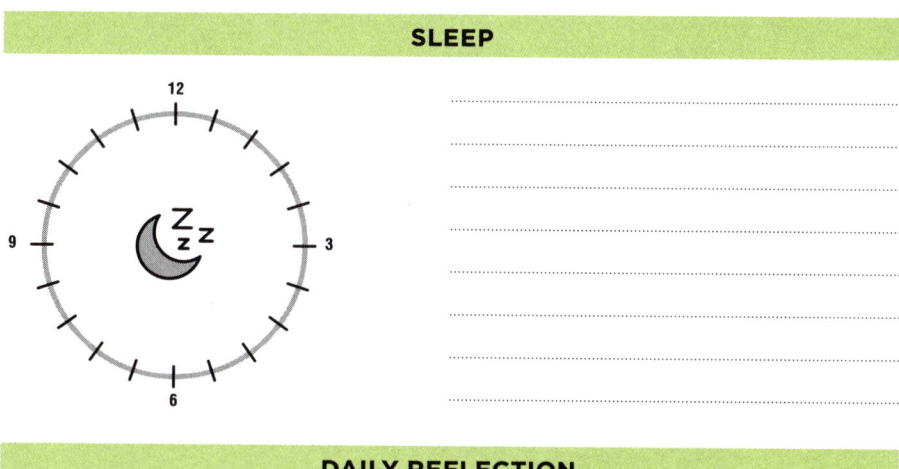

DAILY REFLECTION

HOW WAS YOUR DAY?

1   2   3   4   5   6   7   8   9   10

FOOD LOG

DATE _____

	MON	TUE	WED	THUR	FRI	SAT	SUN

BREAKFAST

	AMOUNT	CAL.	FAT	CARBS	FIBER	NET CARB	PROTEIN
TOTAL							

LUNCH

	AMOUNT	CAL.	FAT	CARBS	FIBER	NET CARB	PROTEIN
TOTAL							

SNACKS

	AMOUNT	CAL.	FAT	CARBS	FIBER	NET CARB	PROTEIN
TOTAL							

DINNER

	AMOUNT	CAL.	FAT	CARBS	FIBER	NET CARB	PROTEIN
TOTAL							

SUPPLEMENTS

WATER

EXERCISE

	ACTIVITY	MINUTES	CAL. BURNED

SLEEP

DAILY REFLECTION

HOW WAS YOUR DAY?

1   2   3   4   5   6   7   8   9   10

FOOD LOG

DATE _____

	MON	TUE	WED	THUR	FRI	SAT	SUN
BREAKFAST	AMOUNT	CAL.	FAT	CARBS	FIBER	NET CARB	PROTEIN
TOTAL							
LUNCH	AMOUNT	CAL.	FAT	CARBS	FIBER	NET CARB	PROTEIN
TOTAL							
SNACKS	AMOUNT	CAL.	FAT	CARBS	FIBER	NET CARB	PROTEIN
TOTAL							
DINNER	AMOUNT	CAL.	FAT	CARBS	FIBER	NET CARB	PROTEIN
TOTAL							

SUPPLEMENTS

WATER

EXERCISE

	ACTIVITY	MINUTES	CAL. BURNED

SLEEP

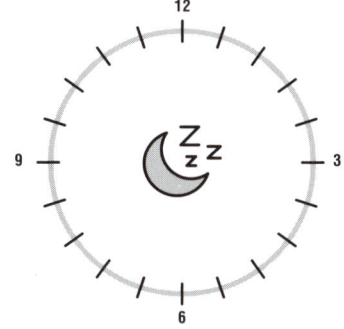

DAILY REFLECTION

HOW WAS YOUR DAY?

1 2 3 4 5 6 7 8 9 10

FOOD LOG

DATE _____

		MON	TUE	WED	THUR	FRI	SAT	SUN
BREAKFAST		AMOUNT	CAL.	FAT	CARBS	FIBER	NET CARB	PROTEIN
	TOTAL							
LUNCH		AMOUNT	CAL.	FAT	CARBS	FIBER	NET CARB	PROTEIN
	TOTAL							
SNACKS		AMOUNT	CAL.	FAT	CARBS	FIBER	NET CARB	PROTEIN
	TOTAL							
DINNER		AMOUNT	CAL.	FAT	CARBS	FIBER	NET CARB	PROTEIN
	TOTAL							

SUPPLEMENTS

WATER

EXERCISE

ACTIVITY	MINUTES	CAL. BURNED

SLEEP

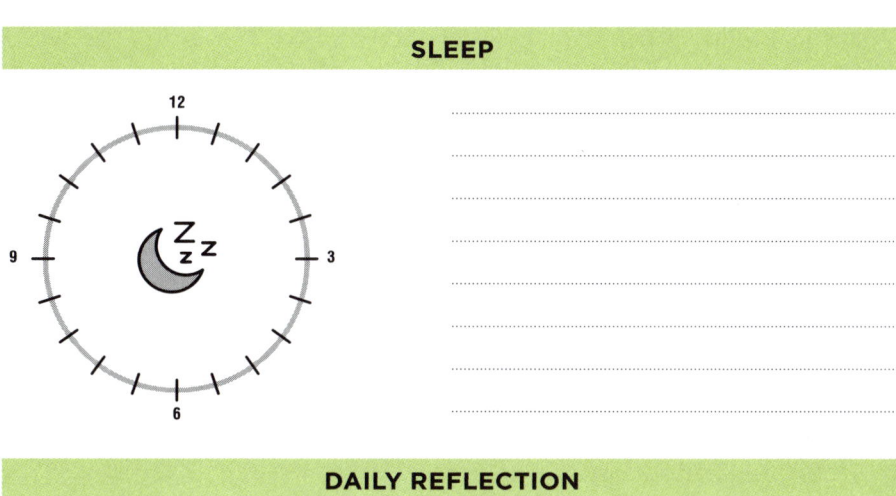

DAILY REFLECTION

FOOD LOG

DATE _____

	MON	TUE	WED	THUR	FRI	SAT	SUN
BREAKFAST	AMOUNT	CAL.	FAT	CARBS	FIBER	NET CARB	PROTEIN
TOTAL							
LUNCH	AMOUNT	CAL.	FAT	CARBS	FIBER	NET CARB	PROTEIN
TOTAL							
SNACKS	AMOUNT	CAL.	FAT	CARBS	FIBER	NET CARB	PROTEIN
TOTAL							
DINNER	AMOUNT	CAL.	FAT	CARBS	FIBER	NET CARB	PROTEIN
TOTAL							

SUPPLEMENTS

WATER

EXERCISE

ACTIVITY	MINUTES	CAL. BURNED

SLEEP

DAILY REFLECTION

If there is NO STRUGGLE, there is NO PROGRESS.

—Frederick Douglass

WEEKLY REFLECTIONS

This week I accomplished . . .

This week I overcame . . .

My goals next week are . . .

WEEK 5

This week I want to accomplish . . .

....

....

....

....

....

....

....

....

This week I want to overcome . . .

....

....

....

....

....

....

....

My inspiration this week is . . .

....

....

....

....

....

....

....

....

FOOD LOG

DATE _____	MON	TUE	WED	THUR	FRI	SAT	SUN

BREAKFAST

	AMOUNT	CAL.	FAT	CARBS	FIBER	NET CARB	PROTEIN
TOTAL							

LUNCH

	AMOUNT	CAL.	FAT	CARBS	FIBER	NET CARB	PROTEIN
TOTAL							

SNACKS

	AMOUNT	CAL.	FAT	CARBS	FIBER	NET CARB	PROTEIN
TOTAL							

DINNER

	AMOUNT	CAL.	FAT	CARBS	FIBER	NET CARB	PROTEIN
TOTAL							

SUPPLEMENTS

WATER

EXERCISE

	ACTIVITY	MINUTES	CAL. BURNED
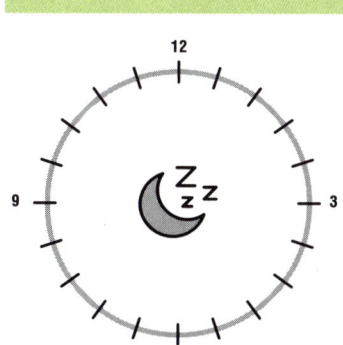			

SLEEP

DAILY REFLECTION

HOW WAS YOUR DAY?

1   2   3   4   5   6   7   8   9   10

FOOD LOG

DATE _____

	MON	TUE	WED	THUR	FRI	SAT	SUN
BREAKFAST	AMOUNT	CAL.	FAT	CARBS	FIBER	NET CARB	PROTEIN
TOTAL							
LUNCH	AMOUNT	CAL.	FAT	CARBS	FIBER	NET CARB	PROTEIN
TOTAL							
SNACKS	AMOUNT	CAL.	FAT	CARBS	FIBER	NET CARB	PROTEIN
TOTAL							
DINNER	AMOUNT	CAL.	FAT	CARBS	FIBER	NET CARB	PROTEIN
TOTAL							

SUPPLEMENTS

WATER

EXERCISE

ACTIVITY		MINUTES	CAL. BURNED

SLEEP

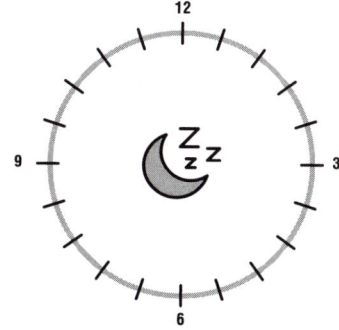

DAILY REFLECTION

HOW WAS YOUR DAY?

| 1 | 2 | 3 | 4 | 5 | 6 | 7 | 8 | 9 | 10 |

FOOD LOG

DATE _____

	MON	TUE	WED	THUR	FRI	SAT	SUN
BREAKFAST	AMOUNT	CAL.	FAT	CARBS	FIBER	NET CARB	PROTEIN
TOTAL							
LUNCH	AMOUNT	CAL.	FAT	CARBS	FIBER	NET CARB	PROTEIN
TOTAL							
SNACKS	AMOUNT	CAL.	FAT	CARBS	FIBER	NET CARB	PROTEIN
TOTAL							
DINNER	AMOUNT	CAL.	FAT	CARBS	FIBER	NET CARB	PROTEIN
TOTAL							

SUPPLEMENTS

WATER

EXERCISE

ACTIVITY		MINUTES	CAL. BURNED

SLEEP

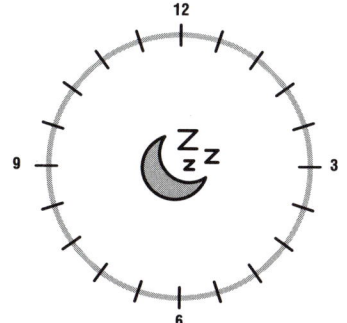

DAILY REFLECTION

HOW WAS YOUR DAY?

 1   2   3   4   5   6   7   8   9   10

FOOD LOG

DATE _____

	MON	TUE	WED	THUR	FRI	SAT	SUN

BREAKFAST

BREAKFAST	AMOUNT	CAL.	FAT	CARBS	FIBER	NET CARB	PROTEIN
TOTAL							

LUNCH

LUNCH	AMOUNT	CAL.	FAT	CARBS	FIBER	NET CARB	PROTEIN
TOTAL							

SNACKS

SNACKS	AMOUNT	CAL.	FAT	CARBS	FIBER	NET CARB	PROTEIN
TOTAL							

DINNER

DINNER	AMOUNT	CAL.	FAT	CARBS	FIBER	NET CARB	PROTEIN
TOTAL							

SUPPLEMENTS

WATER

EXERCISE

ACTIVITY		MINUTES	CAL. BURNED

SLEEP

DAILY REFLECTION

HOW WAS YOUR DAY?

1 2 3 4 5 6 7 8 9 10

DATE _____ | MON | TUE | WED | THUR | FRI | SAT | SUN

BREAKFAST	AMOUNT	CAL.	FAT	CARBS	FIBER	NET CARB	PROTEIN
TOTAL							

LUNCH	AMOUNT	CAL.	FAT	CARBS	FIBER	NET CARB	PROTEIN
TOTAL							

SNACKS	AMOUNT	CAL.	FAT	CARBS	FIBER	NET CARB	PROTEIN
TOTAL							

DINNER	AMOUNT	CAL.	FAT	CARBS	FIBER	NET CARB	PROTEIN
TOTAL							

SUPPLEMENTS

WATER

EXERCISE

	ACTIVITY	MINUTES	CAL. BURNED
🏃 🏋️			
🏃 🏋️			
🏃 🏋️			
🏃 🏋️			
🏃 🏋️			
🏃 🏋️			
🏃 🏋️			

SLEEP

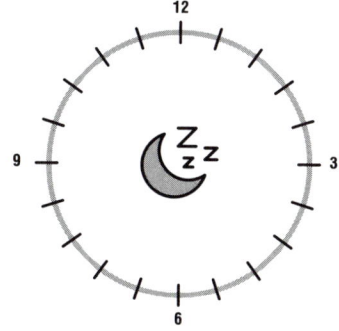

DAILY REFLECTION

HOW WAS YOUR DAY?

1   2   3   4   5   6   7   8   9   10

FOOD LOG

DATE _____

	MON	TUE	WED	THUR	FRI	SAT	SUN

BREAKFAST

	AMOUNT	CAL.	FAT	CARBS	FIBER	NET CARB	PROTEIN
TOTAL							

LUNCH

	AMOUNT	CAL.	FAT	CARBS	FIBER	NET CARB	PROTEIN
TOTAL							

SNACKS

	AMOUNT	CAL.	FAT	CARBS	FIBER	NET CARB	PROTEIN
TOTAL							

DINNER

	AMOUNT	CAL.	FAT	CARBS	FIBER	NET CARB	PROTEIN
TOTAL							

SUPPLEMENTS

WATER

EXERCISE

ACTIVITY	MINUTES	CAL. BURNED

SLEEP

DAILY REFLECTION

HOW WAS YOUR DAY?

1 2 3 4 5 6 7 8 9 10

FOOD LOG

DATE _____

	MON	TUE	WED	THUR	FRI	SAT	SUN
BREAKFAST	AMOUNT	CAL.	FAT	CARBS	FIBER	NET CARB	PROTEIN
TOTAL							
LUNCH	AMOUNT	CAL.	FAT	CARBS	FIBER	NET CARB	PROTEIN
TOTAL							
SNACKS	AMOUNT	CAL.	FAT	CARBS	FIBER	NET CARB	PROTEIN
TOTAL							
DINNER	AMOUNT	CAL.	FAT	CARBS	FIBER	NET CARB	PROTEIN
TOTAL							

SUPPLEMENTS

WATER

EXERCISE

ACTIVITY	MINUTES	CAL. BURNED

SLEEP

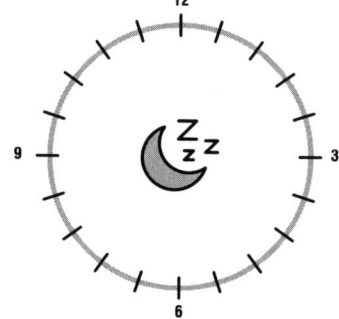

DAILY REFLECTION

HOW WAS YOUR DAY?

1   2   3   4   5   6   7   8   9   10

Nothing is IMPOSSIBLE, the word itself says, 'I'M POSSIBLE!'

—Audrey Hepburn

WEEKLY REFLECTIONS

This week I accomplished . . .

This week I overcame . . .

My goals next week are . . .

WEEK 6

WEEKLY INTENTIONS

This week I want to accomplish . . .

_____

_____

_____

_____

_____

_____

_____

This week I want to overcome . . .

_____

_____

_____

_____

_____

_____

_____

My inspiration this week is . . .

_____

_____

_____

_____

_____

_____

_____

_____

FOOD LOG

DATE _____

	MON	TUE	WED	THUR	FRI	SAT	SUN

BREAKFAST

	AMOUNT	CAL.	FAT	CARBS	FIBER	NET CARB	PROTEIN
TOTAL							

LUNCH

	AMOUNT	CAL.	FAT	CARBS	FIBER	NET CARB	PROTEIN
TOTAL							

SNACKS

	AMOUNT	CAL.	FAT	CARBS	FIBER	NET CARB	PROTEIN
TOTAL							

DINNER

	AMOUNT	CAL.	FAT	CARBS	FIBER	NET CARB	PROTEIN
TOTAL							

SUPPLEMENTS

WATER

EXERCISE

	ACTIVITY	MINUTES	CAL. BURNED

SLEEP

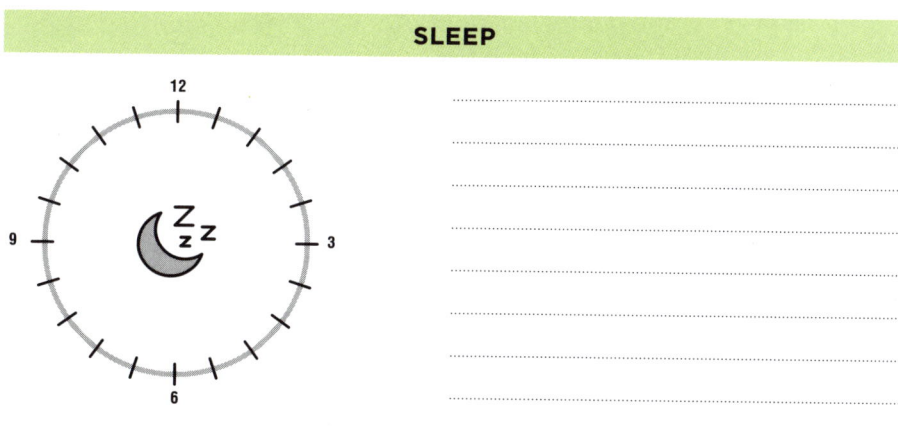

DAILY REFLECTION

HOW WAS YOUR DAY?

1 2 3 4 5 6 7 8 9 10

FOOD LOG

DATE _____

	MON	TUE	WED	THUR	FRI	SAT	SUN

BREAKFAST

	AMOUNT	CAL.	FAT	CARBS	FIBER	NET CARB	PROTEIN
TOTAL							

LUNCH

	AMOUNT	CAL.	FAT	CARBS	FIBER	NET CARB	PROTEIN
TOTAL							

SNACKS

	AMOUNT	CAL.	FAT	CARBS	FIBER	NET CARB	PROTEIN
TOTAL							

DINNER

	AMOUNT	CAL.	FAT	CARBS	FIBER	NET CARB	PROTEIN
TOTAL							

SUPPLEMENTS

WATER

EXERCISE

ACTIVITY	MINUTES	CAL. BURNED

SLEEP

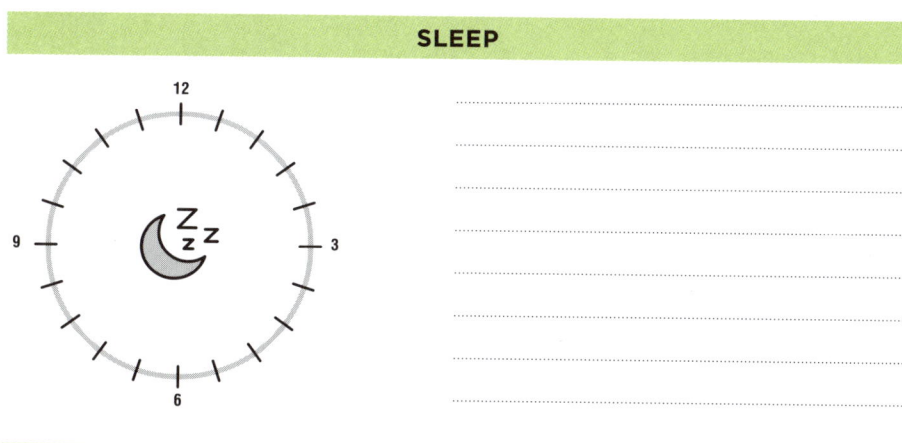

DAILY REFLECTION

HOW WAS YOUR DAY?

1   2   3   4   5   6   7   8   9   10

FOOD LOG

DATE _____

	MON	TUE	WED	THUR	FRI	SAT	SUN

BREAKFAST

	AMOUNT	CAL.	FAT	CARBS	FIBER	NET CARB	PROTEIN
TOTAL							

LUNCH

	AMOUNT	CAL.	FAT	CARBS	FIBER	NET CARB	PROTEIN
TOTAL							

SNACKS

	AMOUNT	CAL.	FAT	CARBS	FIBER	NET CARB	PROTEIN
TOTAL							

DINNER

	AMOUNT	CAL.	FAT	CARBS	FIBER	NET CARB	PROTEIN
TOTAL							

SUPPLEMENTS

WATER

EXERCISE

	ACTIVITY	MINUTES	CAL. BURNED

SLEEP

DAILY REFLECTION

HOW WAS YOUR DAY?

1 2 3 4 5 6 7 8 9 10

FOOD LOG

DATE _____

	MON	TUE	WED	THUR	FRI	SAT	SUN
BREAKFAST	AMOUNT	CAL.	FAT	CARBS	FIBER	NET CARB	PROTEIN
TOTAL							
LUNCH	AMOUNT	CAL.	FAT	CARBS	FIBER	NET CARB	PROTEIN
TOTAL							
SNACKS	AMOUNT	CAL.	FAT	CARBS	FIBER	NET CARB	PROTEIN
TOTAL							
DINNER	AMOUNT	CAL.	FAT	CARBS	FIBER	NET CARB	PROTEIN
TOTAL							

SUPPLEMENTS

WATER

EXERCISE

	ACTIVITY	MINUTES	CAL. BURNED
🏃🏋️			
🏃🏋️			
🏃🏋️			
🏃🏋️			
🏃🏋️			
🏃🏋️			
🏃🏋️			

SLEEP

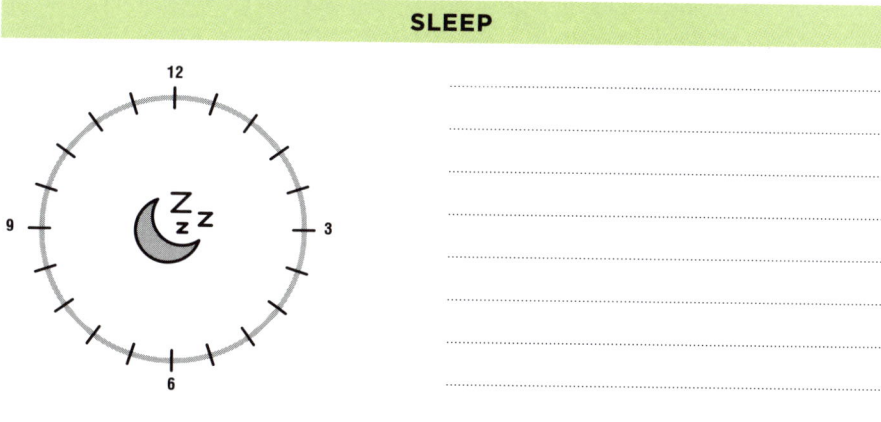

DAILY REFLECTION

HOW WAS YOUR DAY?

| 1 | 2 | 3 | 4 | 5 | 6 | 7 | 8 | 9 | 10 |

FOOD LOG

DATE _____

	MON	TUE	WED	THUR	FRI	SAT	SUN

BREAKFAST

	AMOUNT	CAL.	FAT	CARBS	FIBER	NET CARB	PROTEIN
TOTAL							

LUNCH

	AMOUNT	CAL.	FAT	CARBS	FIBER	NET CARB	PROTEIN
TOTAL							

SNACKS

	AMOUNT	CAL.	FAT	CARBS	FIBER	NET CARB	PROTEIN
TOTAL							

DINNER

	AMOUNT	CAL.	FAT	CARBS	FIBER	NET CARB	PROTEIN
TOTAL							

SUPPLEMENTS

WATER

EXERCISE

	ACTIVITY	MINUTES	CAL. BURNED

SLEEP

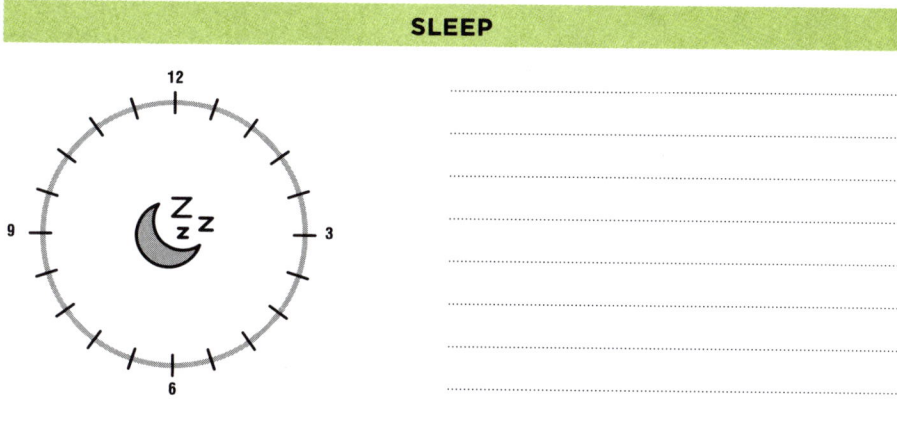

DAILY REFLECTION

HOW WAS YOUR DAY?

:(• • • • • • • • :)

1   2   3   4   5   6   7   8   9   10

FOOD LOG

DATE _____

	MON	TUE	WED	THUR	FRI	SAT	SUN

BREAKFAST

AMOUNT	CAL.	FAT	CARBS	FIBER	NET CARB	PROTEIN

TOTAL

LUNCH

AMOUNT	CAL.	FAT	CARBS	FIBER	NET CARB	PROTEIN

TOTAL

SNACKS

AMOUNT	CAL.	FAT	CARBS	FIBER	NET CARB	PROTEIN

TOTAL

DINNER

AMOUNT	CAL.	FAT	CARBS	FIBER	NET CARB	PROTEIN

TOTAL

SUPPLEMENTS

WATER

EXERCISE

ACTIVITY	MINUTES	CAL. BURNED

SLEEP

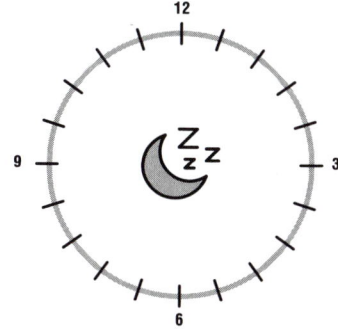

DAILY REFLECTION

HOW WAS YOUR DAY?

   1   2   3   4   5   6   7   8   9   10

FOOD LOG

DATE _____

	MON	TUE	WED	THUR	FRI	SAT	SUN

BREAKFAST

	AMOUNT	CAL.	FAT	CARBS	FIBER	NET CARB	PROTEIN
TOTAL							

LUNCH

	AMOUNT	CAL.	FAT	CARBS	FIBER	NET CARB	PROTEIN
TOTAL							

SNACKS

	AMOUNT	CAL.	FAT	CARBS	FIBER	NET CARB	PROTEIN
TOTAL							

DINNER

	AMOUNT	CAL.	FAT	CARBS	FIBER	NET CARB	PROTEIN
TOTAL							

SUPPLEMENTS

WATER

104　　KETO JOURNAL

EXERCISE

	ACTIVITY	MINUTES	CAL. BURNED

SLEEP

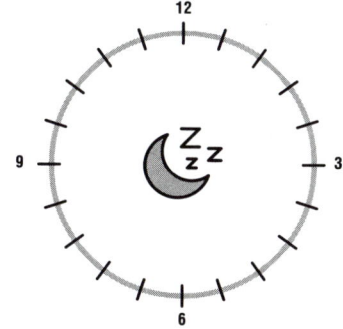

DAILY REFLECTION

A goal should SCARE you a little and EXCITE you a lot.

—Joe Vitale

WEEKLY REFLECTIONS

This week I accomplished . . .

This week I overcame . . .

My goals next week are . . .

WEEK 7

WEEKLY INTENTIONS

This week I want to accomplish . . .

This week I want to overcome . . .

My inspiration this week is . . .

FOOD LOG

DATE _____

	MON	TUE	WED	THUR	FRI	SAT	SUN

BREAKFAST

	AMOUNT	CAL.	FAT	CARBS	FIBER	NET CARB	PROTEIN
TOTAL							

LUNCH

	AMOUNT	CAL.	FAT	CARBS	FIBER	NET CARB	PROTEIN
TOTAL							

SNACKS

	AMOUNT	CAL.	FAT	CARBS	FIBER	NET CARB	PROTEIN
TOTAL							

DINNER

	AMOUNT	CAL.	FAT	CARBS	FIBER	NET CARB	PROTEIN
TOTAL							

SUPPLEMENTS

WATER

EXERCISE

	ACTIVITY	MINUTES	CAL. BURNED

SLEEP

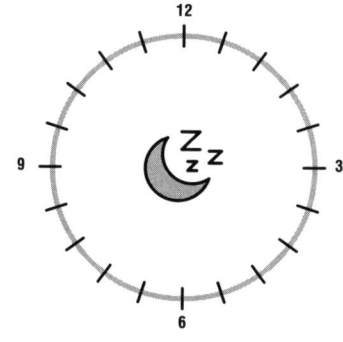

DAILY REFLECTION

HOW WAS YOUR DAY?

1   2   3   4   5   6   7   8   9   10

DATE _____

	MON	TUE	WED	THUR	FRI	SAT	SUN
BREAKFAST	AMOUNT	CAL.	FAT	CARBS	FIBER	NET CARB	PROTEIN
TOTAL							
LUNCH	AMOUNT	CAL.	FAT	CARBS	FIBER	NET CARB	PROTEIN
TOTAL							
SNACKS	AMOUNT	CAL.	FAT	CARBS	FIBER	NET CARB	PROTEIN
TOTAL							
DINNER	AMOUNT	CAL.	FAT	CARBS	FIBER	NET CARB	PROTEIN
TOTAL							

SUPPLEMENTS

WATER

EXERCISE

	ACTIVITY	MINUTES	CAL. BURNED

SLEEP

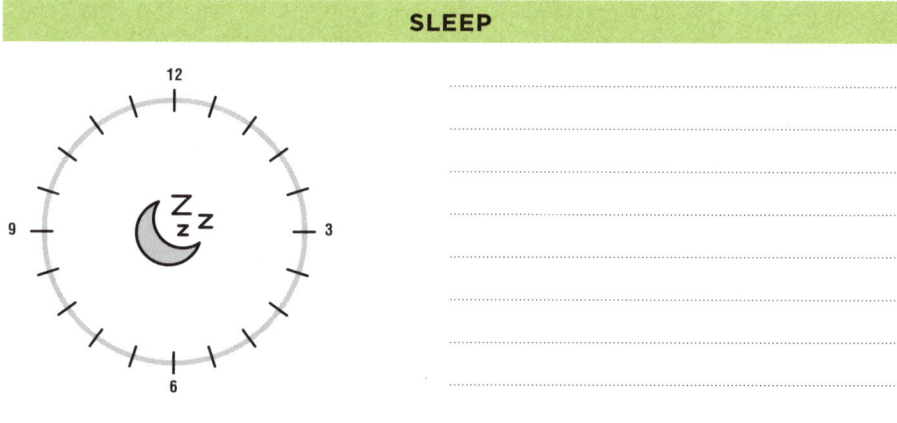

DAILY REFLECTION

HOW WAS YOUR DAY?

1   2   3   4   5   6   7   8   9   10

FOOD LOG

DATE _____

	MON	TUE	WED	THUR	FRI	SAT	SUN
BREAKFAST	AMOUNT	CAL.	FAT	CARBS	FIBER	NET CARB	PROTEIN
TOTAL							
LUNCH	AMOUNT	CAL.	FAT	CARBS	FIBER	NET CARB	PROTEIN
TOTAL							
SNACKS	AMOUNT	CAL.	FAT	CARBS	FIBER	NET CARB	PROTEIN
TOTAL							
DINNER	AMOUNT	CAL.	FAT	CARBS	FIBER	NET CARB	PROTEIN
TOTAL							

SUPPLEMENTS

WATER

EXERCISE

ACTIVITY	MINUTES	CAL. BURNED

SLEEP

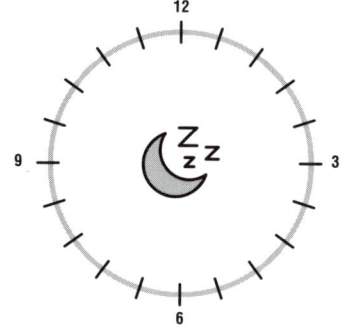

DAILY REFLECTION

HOW WAS YOUR DAY?

1   2   3   4   5   6   7   8   9   10

FOOD LOG

DATE _____

		MON	TUE	WED	THUR	FRI	SAT	SUN

BREAKFAST

	AMOUNT	CAL.	FAT	CARBS	FIBER	NET CARB	PROTEIN
TOTAL							

LUNCH

	AMOUNT	CAL.	FAT	CARBS	FIBER	NET CARB	PROTEIN
TOTAL							

SNACKS

	AMOUNT	CAL.	FAT	CARBS	FIBER	NET CARB	PROTEIN
TOTAL							

DINNER

	AMOUNT	CAL.	FAT	CARBS	FIBER	NET CARB	PROTEIN
TOTAL							

SUPPLEMENTS

WATER

EXERCISE

ACTIVITY	MINUTES	CAL. BURNED

SLEEP

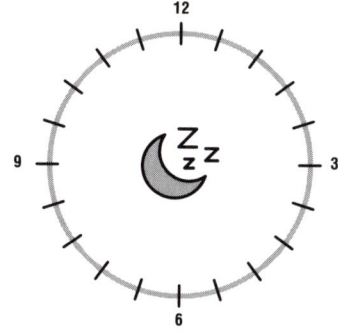

DAILY REFLECTION

FOOD LOG

DATE _____

	MON	TUE	WED	THUR	FRI	SAT	SUN
BREAKFAST	AMOUNT	CAL.	FAT	CARBS	FIBER	NET CARB	PROTEIN
TOTAL							
LUNCH	AMOUNT	CAL.	FAT	CARBS	FIBER	NET CARB	PROTEIN
TOTAL							
SNACKS	AMOUNT	CAL.	FAT	CARBS	FIBER	NET CARB	PROTEIN
TOTAL							
DINNER	AMOUNT	CAL.	FAT	CARBS	FIBER	NET CARB	PROTEIN
TOTAL							

SUPPLEMENTS

WATER

EXERCISE

	ACTIVITY	MINUTES	CAL. BURNED

SLEEP

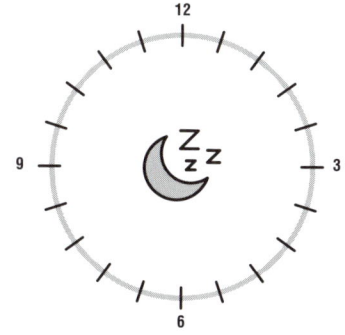

DAILY REFLECTION

HOW WAS YOUR DAY?

1   2   3   4   5   6   7   8   9   10

FOOD LOG

DATE _____

	MON	TUE	WED	THUR	FRI	SAT	SUN
BREAKFAST	AMOUNT	CAL.	FAT	CARBS	FIBER	NET CARB	PROTEIN
TOTAL							
LUNCH	AMOUNT	CAL.	FAT	CARBS	FIBER	NET CARB	PROTEIN
TOTAL							
SNACKS	AMOUNT	CAL.	FAT	CARBS	FIBER	NET CARB	PROTEIN
TOTAL							
DINNER	AMOUNT	CAL.	FAT	CARBS	FIBER	NET CARB	PROTEIN
TOTAL							

SUPPLEMENTS

WATER

EXERCISE

ACTIVITY	MINUTES	CAL. BURNED

SLEEP

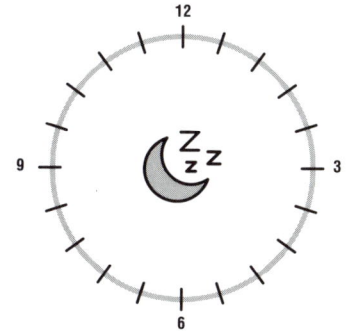

DAILY REFLECTION

HOW WAS YOUR DAY?

 1 2 3 4 5 6 7 8 9 10

FOOD LOG

DATE _____

	MON	TUE	WED	THUR	FRI	SAT	SUN

BREAKFAST

	AMOUNT	CAL.	FAT	CARBS	FIBER	NET CARB	PROTEIN
TOTAL							

LUNCH

	AMOUNT	CAL.	FAT	CARBS	FIBER	NET CARB	PROTEIN
TOTAL							

SNACKS

	AMOUNT	CAL.	FAT	CARBS	FIBER	NET CARB	PROTEIN
TOTAL							

DINNER

	AMOUNT	CAL.	FAT	CARBS	FIBER	NET CARB	PROTEIN
TOTAL							

SUPPLEMENTS

WATER

EXERCISE

ACTIVITY		MINUTES	CAL. BURNED

SLEEP

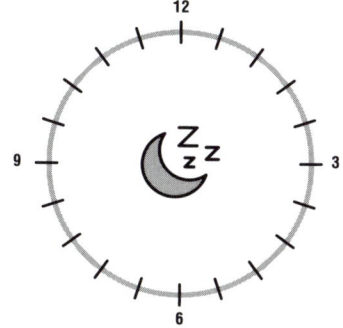

DAILY REFLECTION

HOW WAS YOUR DAY?

1   2   3   4   5   6   7   8   9   10

Don't judge each day by THE HARVEST YOU REAP but by the SEEDS THAT YOU PLANT.

—Robert Louis Stevenson

WEEKLY REFLECTIONS

This week I accomplished . . .

....

....

....

....

....

....

....

....

This week I overcame . . .

....

....

....

....

....

....

....

My goals next week are . . .

....

....

....

....

....

....

....

....

PROGRESS CHARTS

As they say, a picture is worth a thousand words! The following graphs allow you to track your weekly progress visually. Take any statistics such as your weight or body measurements and plot them on the graph below. You can even use the same graph to plot two different groups of data, as our sample dieter did in the graph below, for easy comparison.

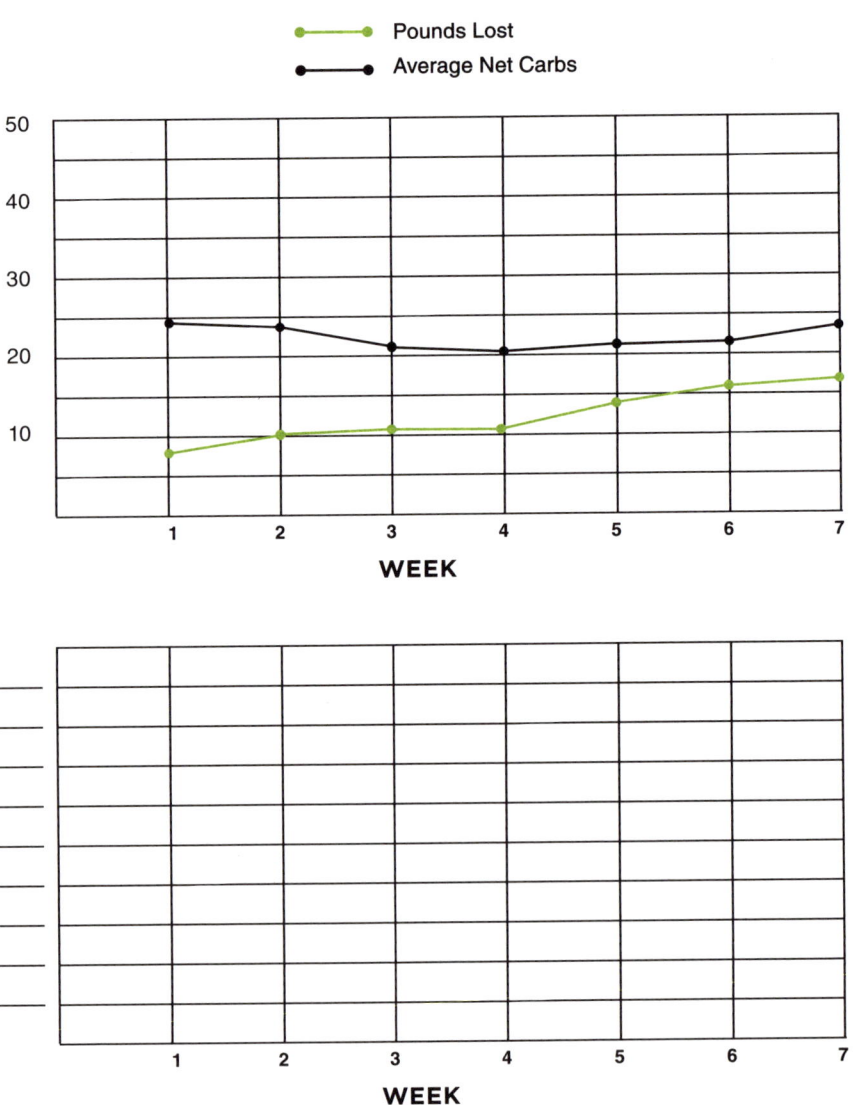

We are WHAT WE REPEATEDLY DO. Excellence, then, is not an act, but a HABIT.

—Aristotle

BEFORE AND AFTER

PHOTO BEFORE

[front]   [side]

PHOTO AFTER

[front]   [side]

MEASUREMENTS BEFORE

WEIGHT

NECK

UPPER ARMS

CHEST

WAIST

HIPS

THIGHS

CALVES

BLOOD PRESSURE

CHOLESTEROL

MEASUREMENTS AFTER

WEIGHT

NECK

UPPER ARMS

CHEST

WAIST

HIPS

THIGHS

CALVES

BLOOD PRESSURE

CHOLESTEROL

EXERCISE CHART

Estimated calories burned per hour based on body weight.

ACTIVITY	130 lbs.	155 lbs.	190 lbs.
aerobics, general	354	422	518
aerobics, high impact	413	493	604
aerobics, low impact	295	352	431
basketball, game	472	563	690
basketball, non-game, general	354	422	518
basketball, officiating	413	493	604
basketball, shooting baskets	266	317	388
basketball, wheelchair	384	457	561
bicycling, < 10 mph, leisure	236	281	345
bicycling, > 20 mph, racing	944	1,126	1,380
bicycling, 10-11.9 mph, light effort	354	422	518
bicycling, 12-13.9 mph, moderate effort	472	563	690
bicycling, 14-15.9 mph, vigorous effort	590	704	863
bicycling, 16-19 mph, very fast, racing	708	844	1035
bicycling, bmx or mountain	502	598	733
bicycling, stationary, light effort	325	387	474
bicycling, stationary, moderate effort	413	493	604
bicycling, stationary, very light effort	177	211	259
bicycling, stationary, very vigorous effort	738	880	1,078
bicycling, stationary, vigorous effort	620	739	906
boxing, in ring, general	708	844	1,035
boxing, punching bag	354	422	518

boxing, sparring	531	633	776
calisthenics (push-ups, sit-ups), vigorous effort	472	563	690
calisthenics, light/moderate effort	266	317	388
carrying heavy loads, such as bricks	472	563	690
circuit training, general	472	563	690
dancing, aerobic, ballet or modern, twist	354	422	518
dancing, ballroom, fast	325	387	474
dancing, ballroom, slow	177	211	259
dancing, general	266	317	388
football or baseball, playing catch	148	176	216
football, competitive	531	633	776
football, touch, flag, general	472	563	690
hiking, cross country	354	422	518
jogging, general	413	493	604
judo, karate, kick boxing, tae kwan do	590	704	863
race walking	384	457	561
rope jumping, fast	708	844	1,035
rope jumping, moderate, general	590	704	863
rope jumping, slow	472	563	690
rowing, stationary, light effort	561	669	819
rowing, stationary, moderate effort	413	493	604
rowing, stationary, very vigorous effort	708	844	1035
rowing, stationary, vigorous effort	502	598	733
running, 10 mph (6-min. mile)	944	1,126	1,380

Activity	130 lbs.	155 lbs.	190 lbs.
running, 10.9 mph (5.5-min. mile)	1,062	1,267	1,553
running, 5 mph (12-min. mile)	472	563	690
running, 5.2 mph (11.5-min. mile)	531	633	776
running, 6 mph (10-min. mile)	590	704	863
running, 6.7 mph (9-min. mile)	649	774	949
running, 7 mph (8.5-min. mile)	679	809	992
running, 7.5 mph (8-min. mile)	738	880	1,078
running, 8 mph (7.5-min. mile)	797	950	1,165
running, 8.6 mph (7-min. mile)	826	985	1,208
running, 9 mph (6.5-min. mile)	885	1,056	1,294
running, cross country	531	633	776
running, general	472	563	690
running, in place	472	563	690
running, on a track, team practice	590	704	863
running, stairs, up	885	1,056	1,294
running, training, pushing wheelchair	472	563	690
running, wheeling, general	177	211	259
soccer, casual, general	413	493	604
soccer, competitive	590	704	863
softball or baseball, fast or slow pitch	295	352	431
stair-treadmill ergometer, general	354	422	518
stretching, hatha yoga	236	281	345
swimming laps, freestyle, fast, vigorous effort	590	704	863

swimming laps, freestyle, light/moderate effort	472	563	690
swimming, backstroke, general	472	563	690
swimming, breaststroke, general	590	704	863
swimming, butterfly, general	649	774	949
swimming, leisurely, general	354	422	518
swimming, sidestroke, general	472	563	690
swimming, synchronized	472	563	690
swimming, treading water, fast/vigorous	590	704	863
swimming, treading water, moderate effort	236	281	345
tai chi	236	281	345
walking, 2 mph, slow pace	148	176	216
walking, 3 mph, moderate pace, walking dog	207	246	302
walking, 3.5 mph, uphill	354	422	518
walking, 4 mph, very brisk pace	236	281	345
walking, grass track	295	352	431
walking, upstairs	472	563	690
water aerobics, water calisthenics	236	281	345
weight lifting or body building, vigorous effort	354	422	518
weight lifting, light or moderate effort	177	211	259

NOTES